Investigative Computer Forensics

The Practical Guide for Lawyers, Accountants, Investigators, and Business Executives

ERIK LAYKIN, CHFI, CEDS

WILEY

Library of Congress Cataloging-in-Publication Data:

Laykin, Erik.
    Investigative computer forensics : the practical guide for lawyers, accountants, investigators, and
business executives / Erik Laykin, CHFI, CEDS.
        pages cm
    Includes index.
    ISBN 978-0-470-93240-7 (hbk.) — ISBN 978-1-118-22141-9 (ePDF) (print) —
ISBN 978-1-118-25988-7 (Mobi) (print) — ISBN 978-1-118-23522-5 (ePub) (print) —
ISBN 978-1-118-57211-5 (o-Book) (print)
    1. Computer crimes—Investigation.   2. Computer security.
3. Fraud investigation.   4. Corporations—Corrupt practices.   I. Title.
    HV8079.C65L395 2013
    363.25'968—dc23

10 9 8 7 6 5 4 3 2 1   2012038779

In memory of Melinda Laykin Brun Esq. (1942–2005),
senior trial counsel for the State of California Department of Corporations,
and known in the courtroom as "The Battleship." A fierce fighter for the
underdog, an advocate for victims, and an electronic data visionary
who gave me the gift of inspiration to enter the field of computer
forensics during its nascent days.

Contents

Foreword

Over the course of a 25-year career in corporate investigations that have required my expertise in places as diverse as San Diego to Shanghai and New York to New Delhi, I have witnessed a dramatic shift in the methodologies, technologies, and type of personnel deployed on fact-finding exercises. From traditional gumshoe-style investigations of larceny, fraud, and crime to sophisticated corporate electronic discovery boondoggles that require the analysis of mind-boggling volumes of electronic data, the world of investigations now requires a level of technical sophistication that was unimaginable a generation ago. The acronyms are daunting, the risks of taking missteps are found at every turn, and the ramifications of mismanaging data have been felt by plaintiffs, defendants, and corporations far and wide in recent years in the form of adverse inferences, sanctions, and default judgments.

One of my early major cases was the subject of a *New York Times* best-seller and film starring John Travolta and Robert Duvall titled *A Civil Action,* in which William H. Macy played my role, and he hit it out of the park. But what is interesting to me today these short 17 years later is that during that entire epic investigation and courtroom battle in which we were pitched against two of the nation's most fearsome litigation firms, the words *electronic discovery* were never uttered. Our world was of paper documents and the physical handling of evidence acquired the old-fashioned way.

A few years later I learned firsthand while working on the watershed *Zubulake v. UBS Warburg* matter under the watchful eye of Federal Judge Shira Scheindlin just how much things had changed, and scarier yet, just how out of touch so many of the players were with the complex terms, issues, and risks associated with this newly emerging world of managing electronic data in investigations and discovery.

Erik Laykin's book *Investigative Computer Forensics* zeros in on a real need felt by lawyers, jurists, accountants, administrators, management, and business executives around the globe. This need is to explain the investigative computer forensic process in layman's terms that the users of these services can understand so that they may be more well-informed while engaging the capabilities of a computer forensics professional. It is rare to meet a lawyer or business professional who has taken it on themselves to understand this landscape prior to their having an immediate and dire need for the services, so I believe there will be readers of this book who will find themselves far more empowered to make the tough decisions during an internal investigation or an electronic discovery exercise that they find themselves embroiled in involuntarily.

Having worked with Erik on some of the most challenging computer forensic investigations during the early years of this industry's formation as well as having competed with him earnestly in the marketplace, I am honored to provide this foreword. I can truly say that Erik is one of the unique pioneers of computer forensic investigations. He not only can distill complex technical information into easily understandable concepts, but he always retained a long-term global perspective on the relevancy of our work and on the impact of the information revolution on the social and business structures of tomorrow.

James Gordon
Managing Director
Navigant Consulting, Inc.

Preface

This book is different from other books on the topic of computer forensics insofar as the intended audience is not computer forensic professionals and technicians but instead the users of computer forensic services.

Much has been written on the topic of computer forensics from a highly technical perspective, but little exists to help guide an attorney, a judge, a regulator, an executive, or an accountant along important decision points and requirements for the deployment of computer forensic services for the purposes of investigation.

This volume seeks to demystify many of the computer forensic techniques and various technical terms and procedures used during the capture and analysis and presentation of electronic data within the context of investigation or litigation.

It also provides a viewpoint as to where the world of digital data is taking us. At times you may agree or disagree with some of the positions taken here and that is exactly the point. We are operating in a new world where the nuances of electronic data and its impact on our daily lives can no longer be adjudicated to one linear line of thought or reason. The reality is that the relationship that data has for each of us is often highly subjective and the investigative techniques that support fact-finding in this digital age are still developing their focus.

This book has nine chapters, each of which deals with various aspects of the world of investigative computer forensics. Many of the topics that are touched on could be the focus of an entire volume in their own right, and in fact there are excellent books written on each of the subjects covered, such as those that tackle broad-based topics ranging from *The Foundations of Digital Evidence* by George L. Paul to older classics like the *Road Ahead* by Bill Gates to highly specific volumes such as *Building and Managing the Meta Data Repository* by David Marco. This book provides the reader with a cross section of information gleaned from an expertise that covers vast and diverse realms of knowledge and experience. Computer forensic investigators are often confronted with diversity and challenge, which varies widely from case to case and forces the best of them to maintain an inquisitive and nimble mind.

In Chapter 1, I discuss some of the broader thematic issues that are felt throughout the "information ecosystem" and that are present-day drivers behind the converging worlds of business, technology, law, and fraud. This discussion on issues, such as privacy, trust, and the foundations of digital evidence, helps to provide a backdrop by which the significant changes in the investigative landscape being felt today can be better appreciated.

In Chapter 2, I discuss a broad range of topics that serve as a primer on computers and networks—how they work, what they are, and why certain things like metadata, databases, and IP addresses are relevant to an investigation.

In Chapter 3, I review some of the fundamentals of the computer forensic world, such as chain of custody, access controls, evidence handling, tools, technologies, and computer forensic certifications. In this section you get a taste of the many components that go into building and operating a successful computer forensic laboratory. Finally, I also provide an overview in this chapter of the various parties commonly found to play a role in a computer forensic investigation, from the bad guy to the judge and from the victim to the network engineer.

In Chapter 4, I detail a number of fundamental investigative issues from case management to trade secret theft. This section covers a variety of topics that a computer forensic investigator will be tasked with understanding and that a user of these services will need to have grasp of to better leverage the services of a forensic investigator.

In Chapter 5, I share some thoughts on the underpinnings of computer forensics— primary issues that are faced by investigators all over the world from deleted data to the proper seizure and examination of digital evidence. I cover topics as diverse as data classification and records management to ethics and social engineering.

In Chapter 6, I focus on some of the tactical objectives and challenges facing computer forensic investigations from early case assessment to the pacing, timing, and expectation setting within the investigative framework.

In Chapter 7, I deal with some of the real-time issues faced by what I term *cyber-firefighters*, those individuals who often find themselves on the frontline of digital defenses or investigations and who must perform highly challenging tasks in defending against cybercrime and other malicious online activity.

In Chapter 8, I outline the electronic discovery framework in which computer forensic investigation often finds itself. These emerging standards of care for the preservation, collection, processing, analysis, review, and presentation of electronic evidence can no longer be ignored and are no longer simply the province of the U.S. legal system as they are increasingly under the focus and scrutiny of participants in foreign jurisdictions.

In Chapter 9, I opine on some of the trends and issues that are affecting the future of the information revolution and society as a whole, particularly as it relates to the investigative process and the converging intersection of business, technology, law, and fraud.

Readers can also visit www.InvestigativeComputerForensics.com for more information and materials to use alongside this book.

Investigative computer forensics is playing an increasingly important role in the resolution of challenges, disputes, and conflicts of every stripe and in every corner of the world. Yet, for many, trepidation still prevails, like a veil of fear of the unknown, preventing those in need of these services from truly leveraging them to their best effect.

It is my hope that the technology-challenged and the expert alike, whether an attorney, a judge, a businessperson, an accountant, a teacher, or simply a citizen, will find some comfort in referencing this book to help guide the decisions that need to be made when considering deploying forensic teams to collect and analyze electronic data.

Acknowledgments

I would like to acknowledge the following individuals who have contributed to this book through their influence on my impressions of the converged world of business, law, technology, and fraud.

Jennifer Baker, Tom Gaeta, Peggy Daley, Greg Higgins, Bob Kirtley, Julie Howard, Julie Wilson Marshall, Charlie Balot, Dick Bernacchi, James Gordon, Manuel Beltran, Ron Lavender, Steve Wysong, Jana Cahn, Ben Leeds, Warren Reid, Sanjay Bavisi, David Stenhouse, Josh Buchbinder, Andrew Immerman, Marc Greenberg, Mud Baron, Eric Maurice, Mark Haas, Bobby Tomlin, Mary Mack, Richard Corgel, Richard Chew, Eiji Kosaka, Albert Allen, S. W. Laykin, Joel and Millie Laykin, Bill Gates, and most important, my ever-patient and encouraging wife, Lily Laykin.

In addition, I would like to thank Karen Hendry, my editorial assistant; J. Nino "Onin" G, my illustrator; Cerraeh Laykin, my photographer; Jennifer MacDonald, my most patient development editor; and John DeRemigis, my editor at John Wiley & Sons, who stood by this project through thick and thin.

Author's Note

Because of the evolving nature of technology, law, and business dynamics in the electronic discovery / computer forensic and investigative industry, it is important to bear in mind that many of the representations and issues outlined in this volume are in a state of development, and thus what may hold true in 2013 may be very different in only a few short years. In fact, there can be interpretations of some of the issues that are highlighted in this book where valid counterpoints or opposing opinions can be offered based on the context, geography, technology, legal principles, or other contextual facts that are being leveraged or contemplated at the time.

Consequently, I anticipate appending to this volume in forthcoming updates as the space develops, and it is important to note that the materials herein represent my opinions and observations in my individual capacity and are not to be interpreted as an endorsement by Duff & Phelps LLC or any other company or organization.

INTRODUCTION

Investigative Computer Forensics

The past 20 years have seen an explosion of investigations that involve computers and technology. This growth parallels the impact of the information revolution and has forced radical change in the skill set required to investigate everything from common crime to sophisticated corporate fraud.

One of the results of this change has been that investigators quickly found themselves lacking the primary skills required to manage even the most basic of investigations if there was a computer, a cell phone, or technology involved. Similarly, computer technicians who were called in to fill the vacuum were equally compromised by their lack of traditional investigative skills, which in many cases led to poorly managed investigations in which the human component of a crime was overlooked in favor of the technical "digital smoking gun."

Changes in Technology

Throughout the United States, Asia, Europe, and elsewhere massive backlogs of investigation work in which computers and technology played a role began to pile up and fill evidence cabinets, rooms, and storage houses. In many cases, particularly in the public law-enforcement realm, crimes against victims went unpunished for years while the accused languished in jail waiting for trials that relied on a technology analysis by experts that law enforcement simply did not have enough of.

I can remember one instance that I found particularly troublesome when I was provided a tour of a major U.S. policing agency's evidence vault and found that it was loaded from floor to ceiling with hundreds of hard drives and computers. When I made the comment to the presiding officer that I was impressed with how many computer fraud cases the agency was undertaking by virtue of the massive numbers of computers in the evidence vault I was met with the following response:

1

"Actually, Erik, these are the computers we have not been able to get to yet and that represent evidence in cases ranging from rape and murder to organized crime, theft, stalking, and Internet crime. We simply do not have the resources to work all of these cases."

Considering the impact on the judicial system, victim's rights, and even the morale of the policing agencies themselves, I could not help but leave that place with a deep sinking feeling.

The light at the end of the tunnel, however, was that while society as a whole was making what seemed to be a slow migration to the world of technology, there was in actuality an all-encompassing rapid transition to an information-based communications ecosystem, and with this the investigative needs of agencies and private enterprise alike would be met.

For hundreds of years, perhaps longer, traditional investigators have relied on a combination of process, intuition, deductive reasoning, the powers of observation, highly specific skill sets, and luck to find their way through the thicket of unanswered questions and murky half-truths. In more recent times, the investigator has been assisted by the application of forensic tools and recording devices, which allow for more complete quantitative analysis and capture of events, witness testimony, and other fleeting experiences that can lead to reasoned conclusions.

By example, investigators have learned to master the process of dusting for fingerprints. Criminal investigators learned to cross-reference those fingerprints against collected fingerprint images. Investigators have developed an understanding of the impact of motion and gravity on human blood when it is exiting a wound caused by gunshot. They learned how to interpret body gestures, hand signals, motions of one's eyes, and even the meaning behind the slant or posture of one's handwriting.

Over time, plaster casts of footprints and tire treads and other evidence hastily left behind by a criminal consumed by the activity of his crime became commonplace and part of the investigators' stock in trade.

But then something happened. Folks like Steve Jobs, Leonard Kleinrock, Vint Cerf, Tim Berners-Lee, Larry Ellison, and Bill Gates conspired to not only change the way investigators did things but quite literally the entire world as well.

It would have been interesting to have been a fly on the wall in the interview room or investigative conference room when the first old-school investigator to be confronted with an Apple II, which served as the machine that wrote the ransom note, asked the question: "And exactly what *is* this machine that we have here?"

Changes in the Role of the Investigator

From that moment and countless others like it, the role of the investigator has been both challenged and enhanced by the advent of modern technology.

Concurrent with the development of computers throughout the 1940s, 1950s, 1960s, and onward, there have been some number of frustrated computer users, technicians, software developers, and technology architects who have been forced to face the reality of their data being deleted at the most inopportune time.

Throughout this period data lived on a variety of media, including reel-to-reel magnetic tape and large-format hard drives. But the prospects of losing data due to machine error, accidental power surges, loss of power, operator error, software glitches, or just the plain old unexplainable became ever-more frustrating. A small number of technicians became intrigued by the necessity and possibility to recover electronic data that had been spoiled in some fashion. These issues were particularly acute in the military establishments of both the United States and the Soviet Union, where the great arms race was on and the loss of any significant chunk of data set a program back significantly.

During the 1970s, 1980s, and into the early 1990s, the techniques employed by the U.S. government recovering electronic data percolated from highly secretive military labs into more mainstream government agencies such as the FBI, and eventually the technique of examining or recovering deleted electronic data became known as *computer forensics*.

As computing technology proliferated in the 1980s and early 1990s, the consumer need for computer forensics expanded with it. It seems there has always been the busy executive who deleted the important file just before the presentation or the software developer who just lost a week's worth of work due to hard drive failure.

With this consumer need, innovation was driven and software products emerged that were designed specifically for the task of recovering and accessing deleted electronic data. By the mid-1990s, it was entirely feasible for a consumer to purchase software technology that had the ability to identify, preserve, and extract out deleted data from magnetic media for the purpose of reconstruction and it seemed as if the computing world had found its equilibrium in the space.

What few people saw coming, however, was the crest of the wave of what thus far had been a rising tide in what one could call the *information tsunami*. This massive and all-encompassing event was called the *Internet*. With its arrival, legions of change of every order imaginable, which would greatly expand the scope, purpose, and definition of computer forensics, were brought forward. The catalyst that was central to the evolution of computer forensics was the transition of the discovery process in the U.S. legal system to what is now termed as *electronic discovery* (e-discovery).

Electronic discovery required ordinary lawyers of every stripe and all of their support personnel to suddenly be conversant in the world of technology. For the early cases in this space there was a heavy emphasis on the investigative capabilities possessed by computer forensic technicians who had the ability to retroactively reconstruct electronic documents for inquisitive counsel to review.

Rapidly through the turn of the twenty-first century into the first few years of the new millennium, the electronic discovery industry—and with it the computer forensics field—mushroomed into an almost unbearable monster that has managed to consume and devour perfectly rational and healthy legal disputes by imposing on them technology burdens and costs that were insurmountable by either plaintiff or defendant.

Although this electronic discovery world was developing and computer forensic technicians were playing their necessary supporting role, traditional investigators also realized that it would be necessary to understand bits and bytes, TCP/IP, databases, and metadata just as they had once focused their attention on residual residue, interview techniques, and ink analysis. The result has been that the market met the need, and through a variety of training courses and certifications, and the wide availability of software and hardware in both the computer forensic and traditional information technology space, there has been a mini-boom in the world of law enforcement, traditional investigators, and the naturally inquisitive who have found a new home at the juncture of investigations and computer technology. This is the world of investigative computer forensics.

What Is Computer Forensics?

Some folks define computer forensics as an art, some consider it as a science (see Exhibit I.1), and certainly there are arguments that it could be both. Some folks consider computer forensics to be more of a specific task or procedure, whereas others consider it a profession; again there's an argument that both may be correct. Computer forensic practitioners come from a variety of backgrounds. Some may have found their roots in law enforcement and have developed either technology credentials or computer forensic credentials while in law enforcement or perhaps retired from law enforcement and moved into computer forensics. Some began in information technology and classic information security and were compelled by the interesting world of fact-finding in the digital age.

Other computer forensic professionals may simply have been investigators who understood that they needed to grow with the times and learn new skill sets to enhance their current investigative platform. The variety of other computer forensic professionals hail from different walks of life, whether they be students, lawyers, businesspeople, or otherwise. To be sure, computer forensics over the course of the past 15 years has evolved into an industry of its own that caters to both law enforcement and private enterprise as well as military needs for a variety of purposes, including internal investigations law enforcement response, corporate security and protection, electronic discovery, and finally fact-finding of the most common or complex nature, whether the fact-finder be a parent attempting to understand the behavior of his or her child on the family computer or a senior researcher in a government lab trying to reconstruct data found on a cell phone at the site of a terrorist bombing.

Most of the commentary and observations in this volume reflect a point of view developed over many years in the commercial computer forensic space providing these services to law firms, corporations, universities, government agencies, and individuals in the pursuit of fact-finding investigations or electronic discovery. By no means do these views reflect the entirety of the computer forensic world, but I do hope that they illustrate some of the primary concepts, challenges, and interests in the field.

EXHIBIT 1.1 Motherboard Circuitry Showing Two Receptacles to Accommodate RAM (Random Access Memory) Chips

RAM, which is volatile memory, assists a computer in processing calculations by allowing the motherboard quick and close access to space reserved for this function exclusively. The more RAM a computer has, the faster it can accomplish tasks. Modern forensics now allows for the safe capture of volatile memory, further enhancing the forensic analysis of a target computer.

There are a number of phases in the computer forensic life cycle:

1. The **collection** phase is when the forensic investigators take steps necessary to identify and collect media that contain digital data—floppy disks, flash memory cards, thumb drives, hard drives, external media servers, backup tapes, laptops, and any other device that can contain electronic data. The list of those devices is increasing yearly, and as of 2013 electronic data exists on or within printers, automobiles, airplanes, smartphones, buses, taxis, trains, shopping malls, alarm systems, gas stations, nightclubs, restaurants, security checkpoints, point-of-sale terminals, dog tags, red-light cameras, and every other conceivable location in the modern world. These repositories of electronic data will continue to proliferate until such time that the data itself is embedded in the human body.

2. The **preservation** phase focuses on ensuring that the electronic data contained on the devices that were collected is preserved in a manner as close as possible to its original form. This is achieved often by using read-only devices to connect to those devices so that the electronic data can be captured off those devices and sealed in some fashion. The most common method of sealing the data is to apply

a *hash algorithm* to each file, which gives it a unique number that one could rely on—a unique number for the identification of that file. During this preservation phase, it is vital to ensure that the methodology, policies, and procedures that are used in the actual capturing of the data are reliable, complete, accurate, and verifiable. This is so that, should a court of law question the authenticity of the evidence that has been collected and preserved, the computer forensic investigator will be able to provide these important assurances to the court.

3. During the **analysis** phase, computer forensic examiners will try to isolate the data of interest often by removing and filtering out extraneous and unnecessary data with such tools as key words, file extensions, date ranges, and other definable filtering constructs. The analysis of the data can continue for a few seconds to as long as months or years, depending on the complexity of the case, the tools that are available, the condition of the data that is being analyzed, and the goals of the investigation.

4. During the **presentation** phase, the forensic investigator needs to form conclusions and extract the required data from his or her analysis to support those conclusions and to provide that data in a format that can be observed, understood, appreciated, and verified by third parties.

Overall, this book reviews the realm of investigative computer forensics from the perspective of the practical and the technical and provides guidance for both those people entering the field as well as seasoned practitioners. More important, this book provides the decision makers behind most computer forensic investigations with the operational knowledge base to make informed decisions throughout the process.

There are a wealth of technical tomes on the topic of computer forensics that provide operational technicians with the ins and outs and minutiae of the bits and bytes. This book does not attempt to provide that type of guidance. Rather, the topics covered here deal with the broad landscape within which investigative computer forensics thrives, and provide the necessary, and thus far largely absent, perspective on why certain courses of action should or should not be taken during the investigative life cycle.

CHAPTER 1

The Glue

The global fabric that holds together social, political, and business structures is largely dependent on—or, at the very least, highly impacted by—the movement of electronic data at the speed of light. Routed through an endless array of devices, switches, cables, fibers, satellites, and the atmosphere itself, these systems have their own inherent vulnerabilities and strengths.

But aside from the obvious impact that is so widely reported that the global networks have had on society and the world as we know it, this information revolution has taken within its clutch the mechanics of such precious and unique human qualities as trust, privacy, and truth and in very meaningful ways has either enhanced or modified these constructs or in some cases threatens to obliterate them.

The converse, however, may also be true that these same precepts that provide the glue that society thrives on may over the long haul be strengthened and enhanced by these predictable, self-healing, and potentially transparent networks—networks that may allow the population of the planet to police itself in real time.

Is it possible that the global networks are not the instrument of an evil Big Brother but are in fact the technical incarnation of an earth-coating truth serum that will disallow and prevent antisocial behavior on the part of individuals, groups, and institutions? Could it be that the greater good of humankind finally transcends the individual negatives of petty criminals, Ponzi scheme fraudsters, banal corporations, and megalomaniac two-bit dictators? All on Facebook?

Until our descendants learn the answers to these altruistic questions, we will need to be satisfied knowing that we are all doing our part to keep the glue *sticky*—to use a cool, recent Internet term—by ensuring that we are pursuing the adoption and sanctity of the truth, privacy, and trust within the realm of the global networks.

The role of the computer forensic investigator is front and center in this epic challenge for humanity to find the right equation, structure, and balance in its new relationship with instantaneous and ubiquitous computing power, which theoretically will eventually allow for all of humanity to interact with all of humanity in real time.

Although any one computer forensic investigation may have inconsequential impact on these larger issues, collectively the framework that the field is creating provides part of the roadmap to the future mechanics of how society will function in the actual information age.

I say the *actual* information age, because I am of the belief that we are still very much in the information revolution and have many challenges ahead before the global information ecosystem has matured to adulthood.

If we allow our journey to adulthood to do away with the vital interests of truth, privacy, and trust, the glue that holds it all together, then the infant will be stillborn and our world may truly find itself in an Orwellian apocalypse.

This chapter, which I call "The Glue," deals with some of these issues in a practical sense and provides analysis from a number of points of view. These include truth, privacy, and trust as well as a discussion on the foundations of digital evidence and its historical context, an analysis of investigative objectives, and a discussion of the investigative process.

The Relevancy of Truth

The pursuit of truth requires objective observation. The fact-finder needs as much clarity as can be achieved through methodical analysis of the available data points. In some cases this is achieved through real-time observation of events that are unfolding in front of the observer's eyes, or for the benefit of the observer's ears. In other cases the observer must reconstruct the events that took place by using available evidence. This evidence can include a wide variety of things from electronic data to physical artifacts to eyewitness accounts.

The relevancy of truth is central to the human experience. This is because human relationships, from a simple relationship between two friends to the complex relationships of 100 million citizens of a country to its leadership, all seek the power of truth to strengthen the bonds of the relationship. Without the foundation of truth in a relationship, it will soon find itself on rocky ground, the results of which are found in divorce, hatred, and revolution.

Therefore, the relevancy of truth is in itself a universal truth that humans far and wide in ancient times, modern times, and the future have and will understand, value, and protect. Unfortunately, truth can often be easily obscured and as a result other human traits can come into play—lying, cheating, failing to perform. Lying through deception, for example, has as a matter of course been commonplace throughout the human experience. Whether it is for the personal benefit of a child who wants more food or of a global corporation that wants more market share, the act in itself is so pure that it is often difficult to distinguish, on the face of things, the family man from the fraud, the good corporate citizen from the predator. But because it is so vital to the structure and security of human relationships that truth prevail, we have also gone to great lengths to root out untruths and to identify falsehoods as expeditiously as possible. Countless checks and balances exist, from the reaction that you may have to a cheater's body language to the analysis that a U.S. Securities and Exchange Commission examiner may undertake when reviewing corporate filings related to complex derivatives.

The role of the investigator is as old as, if not older than, the earliest and perhaps first human relationship. This is because before a human is willing to enter into a relationship, he or she normally will investigate the other side and render a judgment. Is he a strong enough caveman to protect me and secure food? Is the architect educated enough to build the aqueduct? Is the money lender honest or is he giving me imitation silver or gold? Is the doctor competent? Is the general decisive? Will she be true to me? Can I believe my boss has my back? The list goes on forever, and for every one of these questions there is a truthful answer and quite possibly many untruthful answers of varying degrees. Why is this relevant? Because without the possibility of truth entering the equation in the human relationship trust can never be established. Without trust, human bonds cannot be formed and all relationships fail.

Think of it: Do you trust that FedEx will get the package to the sender tomorrow morning by 8 A.M.? Do you trust that the bailiff will draw his gun if the criminal defendant in the courtroom attacks the witness? Do you trust that your child's teacher will teach math and history as opposed to pornography and bestiality? Do you trust that the single malt whiskey in the bottle is in fact 18 years old? Do you trust that the truck will stop at the red light?

In each of these cases we have grown to expect these truths to exist, and as a result we have endowed the relationship with trust. When one of these relationships is violated, however, we are rocked by the consequences. The letter did not arrive on time to the client and you lost the bid. The witness was attacked and as a result refused to testify and you lost the trial. Your child has been traumatized by an errant teacher shattering his innocence. Your whiskey was a counterfeit and made you ill. The truck did not stop and you are now in the hospital fighting for your life.

Should your life be punctured by one of these terrible incidents, you or someone working on your behalf will undoubtedly be charged with establishing the facts of what happened, looking to preserve, protect, and analyze the evidence to establish the truth and to reassemble retroactively what should have been the trust that secured the relationship you had with the offending party.

Through this investigative process, culpability can be established and some measure of balance restored back into the relationship, often through such measures as apology, refund, judgment, restitution, fines, incarceration, execution, or even unconditional surrender. Ultimately the human relationship seeks balance and stability as well as a fair water level that can accommodate and sustain all.

Foundations of Digital Evidence

I have titled this section as a nod to the seminal work of the same name by George Paul as it rightfully contemplates in a deep and meaningful way the origins and provenance of digital evidence in a manner that had not been done before it. Through the ages, evidence has taken numerous forms, from the direct testimony of witnesses who have observed behavior and facts to circumstantial evidence that casts an inference on a set of assertions and finally to physical evidence, which is presented to support or refute the claim. Digital evidence is somewhat unique insofar as it is both physical evidence, and at the same time, because of its unique properties, can be a recordable and replayable record of the actual activity itself. For example, a murder weapon, such as a knife, that is used in an attack and that has been preserved as evidence is an inanimate object that can be understood to have had a role in the crime but that does not tell the story itself. After all, the knife, the blood that is on the knife, and its placement near the body can imply that this was, in fact, the knife that was used to kill an individual. However, the knife cannot give clues as to intent, methodology, timing, speed, defense culpability, or any of these other important aspects of the investigation.

On the other hand, a digital file that is found at the scene of crime—that scene being a computer—may be preserved at the time and in the fashion in which it was created by the criminal. If the crime that is being investigated is the fraudulent transfer of funds from the accounting department of the company for which the criminal works to an account that he controls, then the digital files that are captured as part of the evidence during the investigation of the crime may in fact provide the investigator with the ability to replay the actual chain of events just as the criminal saw them on his own computer screen.

For instance, the e-mail that was created by the criminal and sent to a colleague for the purpose of authentication can be shown on the screen and the path that that e-mail followed from the moment that it left the computer of the criminal and traversed the network to the computer of the individual to whom it was sent can also be captured and reviewed. The digital files and details may remain precisely as they did at the time of the actual events. Further, the individual who received the e-mail and who subsequently provided the authorization to the criminal to access a particular account can also be captured and reviewed. Continuing down the thread, the activity that occurred online as the criminal accessed the account and authorized the payment to a bogus third party can also be captured and reviewed. Finally, the electronic payment, which is made from account to account, can also be captured and reviewed in precisely the manner in which it took place at the time of the actual event.

Through this process of the analysis of digital data and its timeline, reconstruction of the crime scene and of the crime itself can take place. For this reason, digital evidence is both physical and dynamic and has properties that investigators have not had to contend with at any point in time during humanity's long run of perpetrating fraud and investigating its outcome. Whether we are speaking of clay tablets, cuneiform impressions, papyrus scrolls, or inscribed manuscripts of the Middle Ages, record keeping has essentially remained the same for millennia. As recently as just a few decades ago, most business records were still kept in written form, and at times would also be kept in duplicate or triplicate. The access to and examination of a business record and of communication between individuals during the eighteenth century more than likely rested on handwritten letters with a seal or signature of authenticity coupled with journal entries in ledgers that were kept under lock and key by the clerical manager charged with that task.

Other than this most basic physical evidence, investigators would have had to rely on the statements of individuals, which, as we know, are subject to interpretation, misinterpretation, and certainly biases. I hate to think of the grave number of individuals who have served time as a result of crimes or activities of which they were falsely accused but had little chance of disproving due to the dearth of physical evidence that could be reliably accessed to disprove the claim. However, in today's world, digital evidence is profligate and promiscuous and surrounds our every activity. It is nearly impossible to escape the intertwining vines of digital evidence that permeate our lives in every respect, and the positive aspect of this information age is the ability of both the afflicted and the wrongly accused to more effectively put forth their argument by trusting in physical evidence that can be relied on, and in many cases, can actually re-create the events that are the subject of the investigation.

Investigative Objectives

The purpose of an investigation is to gather factual information. Without gathering factual information, investigators would not have the ability to solve disputes, questions, or matters involving everything from missing persons to the recovery of stolen property to a dispute over a contract to a regulatory investigation. All of these types of investigations require fact-finding. Examples of the types of investigations that are likely to be managed by an investigative computer forensic professional would include employment investigations, trademark and patent infringement investigations, homicides, missing persons, and suicide investigations, slip-and-fall investigations, financial fraud, malpractice investigations, and undercover or internal investigations for private and public parties, to name a few.

Ultimately, regardless of the type of information one is seeking or the systems and applications that are to be queried using information technology as a tool, the goal is to establish facts and evidence. Once the facts and evidence have been firmly established by using proper process and protocol, a summary or report of those facts can be generated and provided to relevant parties. The investigative objectives in the traditional sense of investigations are no different from that of a computer forensic investigator, in terms of the pursuit of dispassionate observation of data and information, as well as related evidence. This is required to properly, reliably, and ethically encapsulate the observer's findings so that they can be provided to third parties for the purpose of disposing of a particular claim.

The Investigative Process

The investigative process, when applied to information technology, requires the same basic building blocks of traditional investigation, which include understanding the objective, compiling and preserving the available evidence, analyzing the evidence within the context of the original mandate, preserving the findings in a manner that they may be replicated and validated, developing a set of findings from the analysis of the evidence, and finally, providing those findings to third parties. The provision of the findings that the investigator may have developed could be in a variety of formats, including ad hoc conversational meetings; in person or over-the-telephone contact; formal investigative reports, as part of an analytical process that is feeding data into a third-party data analysis or document review platform; or even expert testimony before a judicial body. However, in all cases the goal of the investigator is the same—to provide honest, objective, and thorough analysis of the available evidence as it relates to the mandate provided to the investigator concerning the dispute or issue that must be assessed.

There are ethical and moral obligations to which an investigator must adhere in order to meet his or her mission, and it is vital for clear communication to take place between those parties who are managing the investigation and those parties with whom the investigator must interact so as to ensure that the investigation has met its mandate and that the investigator is provided with adequate information to form conclusions or report on his or her findings. Throughout this volume, I comment on the roles and responsibilities of investigators in the forensic space, from the perspective of interacting with managers, counsel, clients, victims, and others who are likely to come into contact with the investigative computer forensic examiner.

There are numerous treatises on the technology and mechanical processes that forensic examiners may undertake in the pursuit of fact-finding in the digital age. This volume touches on these lightly and instead focuses on the softer issues of technology investigations and how to most effectively balance the relationships between the numerous competing entities within a typical investigation. Whether the investigation is structured around the electronic discovery reference model and is part of an e-discovery exercise or whether the investigation is an internal matter operating in a clandestine form to quickly ferret out fraudulent behavior of executives, there are countless aspects of the process that should be considered and thought through when building an investigative plan, when exercising the investigative process, and when preparing findings to present to third parties.

Computer abuse is rampant and can impact companies large and small, from payroll issues, where fictitious employees are created for the purpose of defrauding the company, to inventory abuse, where falsified records can be leveraged to extract monies from vendors or companies. However, these are not all the areas of computer abuse, which can also include accounts receivable, disbursements, hardware and software thefts, physical theft of property, personal information theft, and intellectual property theft.

This is only the tip of the iceberg, due to the ubiquitous nature of computing technology, which nearly every individual in the modern world leverages. As a result of significant computing power being placed in the hands of billions of individuals around the world, there has been an explosion in the awareness of many of these people as to how to leverage that power for illegal pursuits. With the compounding effect of robust processing power and access to information, coupled with the anonymizing capabilities of the global networks, such as the Internet, it is hard to imagine that illicit behavior in the information age will ever fully be contained.

Trust

Successful human interaction relies on a number of primary building blocks and paramount among them is trust. As old as humanity itself is the pursuit and care for this notion of trust. Trust between individuals, trust between organizations, and trust between nations are all vital for the human experience and for the human condition to thrive. Without trust, the bonds that connect individuals to one another are broken and cooperation fails. Without cooperation between parties, achievement is impossible, and achievement is one thing that human society has been very good at. Whether it is planting and plowing a field, building a barn, or constructing an interplanetary rocket, the ability for humans to achieve is firmly rooted in humanity's ability to form the bonds of trust, which foster cooperation.

Fast forward to the Internet age, this information revolution of which we find ourselves in the opening acts and in which we have already established the primacy of trust, for our communication is now no longer face-to-face. Our commitments are no longer bonded by handshake or an audible acceptance of one's terms and conditions in the proximity of one's peers. Today, our communication takes place electronically over telephone wires, cellular networks, wireless networks, Ethernet networks, wide-area networks, local area networks, ATM networks, microwave networks, and satellite networks.

This results in humans forming the same commitments, while being physically removed from one another, often over great distances of dozens, hundreds, thousands, or tens of thousands of miles, and without the benefit of interpersonal human interaction. These commitments are based on trust. Acceptance with the word *yes* or declination with the word *no*, typed into an electronic communiqué known as an e-mail and sent around the world at the speed of light, across fiber-optic cables running under oceans, requires both parties, sending and receiving, to have trust that what was sent and what was received in fact conveys the intention of the party that sent it and is in fact a bona fide facsimile of that transmission, received by the intended party.

Electronic commerce relies on this notion of trust, for I must believe that my bank, as represented on my computer screen, truly is my bank. I must believe that the balance shown on the screen is truly the balance that is in the bank. I must believe that the transfer that I have made from the bank to the electrical utility company has in fact taken place and that the utility company has received the payment. The utility company, on the other hand, has to trust that I will make that payment electronically from my bank, which the utility company must trust exists.

In the realm of communications, I must trust that the individual who has sent me the e-mail is in fact the individual that he or she purports to be, even before I begin to trust the content of that person's words. But, oh, how trust has been shaken, for I often do not know the true identity of the individual who has sent me the e-mail, nor do I have the ability to validate the accuracy of the words that he or she has written. Do I send the $5,000 check to Nigeria to help the deported oil minister's wife who wishes to share $10 million of her family money with me, if it will simply allow them access to a U.S. bank account? Now, the Nigerian 419 scam is a well-known problem in the information age; while tens of thousands of individuals around the world have been and continue to be victimized by this scam, for the most part, possible victims are able to distinguish the scam using common sense when they read the e-mail from the purported widow of the Nigerian president or some other concocted story.

However, what does this do to trust when I have no way of validating the true author of the e-mail and I certainly cannot believe what it says? Should I use the same level of skepticism with every e-mail that I receive? Naturally, this would not work either, for I would spend my entire day questioning every e-mail that I receive. I would be paralyzed by inaction. This is how trust breaks down for the individuals who use the medium of communication used in this discussion—e-mail on the Internet. How, then, will cooperation be established and how can achievement take place?

Commerce and communication depend wholeheartedly on trust and it is vital to the continued development of the technologies that support the information revolution that they have mechanisms built in that allow for the cross-referencing, double-checking, and validation of entities, statements, and facts so that trust can be established, achievement can proceed, and this great new gift to humanity's future can be fully leveraged without enslaving people to Big Brother or to a world information anarchy.

The role of the investigative computer forensic examiner, while seeking out the facts of a given matter, is also, by association, one of establishing and protecting trust within the information age. Computer forensic examiners serve as the final stop on the information superhighway when it comes to ensuring that the data is what the data is, and they provide a vital service to defendants, plaintiffs, the accused, victims, individuals, corporations, government agencies, the judiciary, and society as a whole. Therefore, the imperative that investigative computer forensic analysts exercise good judgment, well-thought-out processes, and the highest ethical behavior is paramount within the discipline.

Privacy

Privacy is dead. Although trust still has a hope in this information age, for the time being, privacy is dying a relatively fast death and there well may be no hope to save the patient. It will be necessary for society to redefine privacy and to compartmentalize aspects of individuals' and organizations' existences in such a way that where there truly must be privacy, it can at least be private for most. However, this will come at a price, and I foresee that privacy, however tenuous it may be, will in the future be enjoyed only by those who have the resources to insulate themselves from the all-knowing electronic agents' grip on the metrics and statistics of each individual's behavior and movement around this fast-shrinking planet of ours.

Gone are the days when one can be born, live, and die in anonymity, for from the moment one enters this world to the moment one departs, there is now an indelible electronic data trail documenting and memorializing the activities of the individual down to a granular level that would have been inconceivable a mere century ago. Whether your life has been voluntarily added to the human encyclopedia of Facebook or whether you have tried to "get off the grid," there is little way for you to effectively interact with modern society without submitting yourself on a wholesale basis to the altar of the data barons, who are amassing the greatest fortune in history, payable in the currency of our time—electronic data. Richer than the spice traders of the age of Magellan, grander than the captains of industry who built the industrial revolution's factories and railroads, and with greater renewable resources than those of the oil nations of the Middle East, the data barons, whose stock in trade is you and your behavior, are only now beginning to blossom into the forces of nature that they will become.

Bill Gates and Microsoft, Steve Jobs and Apple, Sergey Brin and Google, Mark Zuckerberg and Facebook, Jeff Bezos and Amazon.com are merely the early entrants and the pioneering names of what is now the greatest commodity the world has ever traded. This unending resource of truly valuable data is the aggregate electronic manifestation of all human behavior and thought. So you see, privacy is dead because it must be dead in order for this engine to feed, and this engine is much greater than any the world has ever seen, for its catalyst is the desires and hopes and needs of the very people off which it feasts.

The investigative computer forensic professional will often find himself or herself at the crossroads of these issues of trust and privacy, commerce and freedom, truth and failure, and cast into a cauldron of human expectations, tensions, desires, needs, and forces. Therefore, the role of the investigative computer forensic examiner, while at times mundane and mechanical, is in fact a vital focal point of numerous sociological trends that are of the most extreme relevance and urgency in our society.

CHAPTER 2

A Primer on Computers and Networks

The average attorney or corporate executive spent his or her educational years focused on either the law or the mechanics and fundamentals of business procedure and process. It would be unreasonable to expect that these key decision makers have an in-depth understanding of information technology. There are the exceptions, and we have seen brilliant attorneys who are well steeped in the minutia of the technology world and business executives who make it their business not only to understand but to push forward the information technology landscape. For all of those attorneys who spent their time focused on how to write motions and business executives who spent theirs being able to dissect profit and loss (P&L) statements, this section hopes to alleviate some of the stresses felt when confronted with the topic of computers, software, and other information technology devices.

Although much time could be spent addressing issues of yesteryear's computers and technology, I focus instead on the contemporary landscape as it is faced in today's business world and will pay attention to technologies that I expect will continue to evolve. The notion of what a computer is today has changed dramatically from even 10 years ago. Today's computer (see Exhibit 2.1) can certainly be the obvious laptop or desktop, but it is now also found in a variety of new form factors such as tablets, automobiles, handheld devices, servers, embedded systems, cloud technology, and an ever-expanding collection of integrated systems.

Computers on their own are prisoners in isolation; they quickly lose their broader relevance. Computers have been able to exponentially expand their role in modern society through their interconnectedness in what we call the global information networks. These networks consist not only of the ubiquitous Internet but of numerous other networks, including the ATM network, government and defense networks, private networks, and other unique communication networks such as the global positioning system.

EXHIBIT 2.1 Computer Hard Drive with Its Protective and Hermetically Sealed Metal Casing Removed

This hard drive is an IDE drive with two platters and two actuator arms. Its capacity is 500 MB (megabytes). The hard drive is central to most contemporary computer forensic investigations as it is the primary storage medium used in the world today.

Twenty years ago, when the world had only a few tens of thousands of individuals who were connected by these global networks, information moved at an entirely different pace. Businesspeople and lawyers alike were still primarily relying on typewritten documents on paper, which would subsequently be mailed through traditional means or transmitted by facsimile (fax). Certainly there were those who were on the bleeding edge of technology and had adopted early electronic information systems such as bulletin boards and e-mail, but for the most part, the business world was as it had always been for most of the twentieth century—reliant on tangible hard-copy documents for the documentation of correspondence and business records. Clandestine communication would certainly find its way into the written word, but more often than not it was committed to conversations between individuals either in person or over a telephone.

The massive explosion of desktop and laptop computing then followed as interconnectedness on the network known as the Internet changed all the rules of the road. Within a short 10- to 20-year span the world witnessed a true information revolution in which businesses, governments, individuals, and all other human entities would find themselves at their own personal edge of a global information network that could be traversed at the speed of light.

Once the components of these networks, hardware, software, and devices are understood, much of the mystery surrounding how we all interact electronically can be done away with and investigators, lawyers, or business decision makers can focus on fact-finding and analysis. This chapter provides an overview of these mechanical issues.

The Mechanics of Electronically Stored Information

The purpose of maintaining computer hardware, software, and networks is for the creation, storage, monitoring, identification, transmission, and retrieval of information. Every device used on the global networks has been designed to facilitate one or many of these features. In order for these systems to interact with one another in a seamless fashion, great care has been taken by programming teams, data architects, and hardware developers to develop standards that each of these devices could adhere to for the whole ecosystem to function.

New applications and hardware devices are being developed every day by teams that are distributed around the world and that speak every known human language. However, the processes employed allow for a managed progression of technical development, which for the most part maintains interoperability with the devices, software, and networks that they are designed to interact with. It is for this reason that a programming team in China may respond to a vulnerability announced by a software company in the United States in what seems to be real time. The distribution of information across the global networks in a free and unfettered manner has removed all of the traditional barriers that allow for knowledge gaps and technological backwardness in various parts of the world. Today, a high school student in rural Alabama has access to fundamentally the same knowledge base and technical information as the graduate student at MIT, the industrial engineer at Motorola, or the newly connected villager outside of Nairobi, Kenya.

Magnetic Hard Drives

Central to most laptop and desktop computers, as well as server computers, is the existence of a hard drive that contains electronically stored information (ESI) on its magnetic platters. See Exhibit 2.2. Magnetic hard drives have been in widespread use in the computing industry for the past 40 years, and it is expected that they will continue to proliferate for many decades. The hard drive industry has on the whole

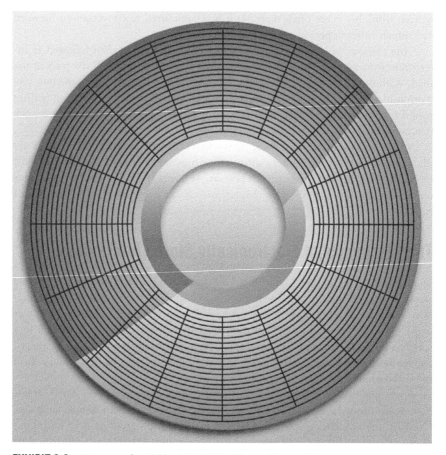

EXHIBIT 2.2   Cutaway of an Older Hard Drive Platter Showing Sectors

consolidated in recent years and where there were once dozens of manufacturers in the United States and overseas there are now only a handful.

The magnetic hard drive inside a laptop, desktop, or server computer for the most part serves as the repository of electronic data, which is managed, stored, accessed, and created on those given computers.

I started the discussion on the mechanics of electronic stored information with hard drives because this is often the first place that the investigator needs to go to preserve and search for data. Armed with the appropriate tools, a computer forensic investigator can learn a great deal about the manner in which the computer was used by conducting a granular examination of the contents of the hard drive.

Hard drives are terrific examples of sophisticated engineering designed in such a way that ultrasensitive equipment can be deployed in a rugged, day-to-day fashion and hold up to the rigors of travel, temperature and humidity fluctuations, continual use, and the unpredictable nature of human interaction.

Most hard drives found inside computers today have similar characteristics although they greatly vary in speed, capacity, and size. The two most fundamental components of today's hard drives are the platters and the heads. Most hard drives have numerous platters, which are fixed to a central shaft or spindle that turns at enormous speed. Most standard business hard drives turn at 7,200 revolutions per minute. In most cases, the hard drive is spinning at all times when the computer is plugged in and turned on. The platters are magnetically charged and have predefined divisions within them known as *sectors* and *clusters*. It is within these sectors and clusters that the magnetic medium manages the bits and bytes of its surface area by allowing the head device to electromagnetically change the orientation of any one bit from an on to an off position or vice versa.

The head is attached to an arm that travels across the surface of the spinning platters during their operation and reads or writes data in the form of ones and zeros to and from the discs themselves. Visually, the combination of a platter, the head, and the arm strongly resembles a record player (see Exhibit 2.1) with its spinning disc and a needle attached to an arm reading the grooves in the vinyl. See Exhibit 2.3, which illustrates the air flow between the arm and the spinning disc.

Ordinarily, a disc or platter contains 512 bytes in each sector. The number of sectors varies based on the manufacturing specifications. In addition to sectors and clusters discs also contain what are known as *tracks*. Tracks are the concentric circles that occupy the entirety of the disc from its center all the way out to its outer

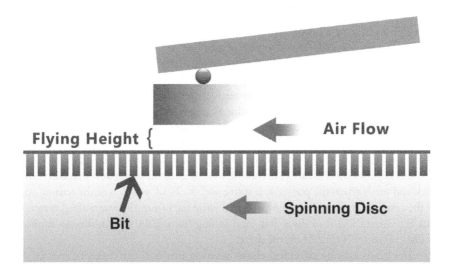

EXHIBIT 2.3 The "Flying Height" of a Read or Write Head on a Computer Hard Drive

The flying height allows for a small gap of air to exist between it and the magnetic properties of the spinning disc, which can be rotating at 7,200 revolutions per minute, a feat of beautiful and amazing engineering.

diameter. The closer these tracks can be to one another the denser the data storage is on the platter.

Hard drives were introduced in 1956 by IBM for a real-time transaction processing computer and were later developed to be used for mainframe minicomputers. The first IBM drive, known as the *350 RA and AC*, was the size of two refrigerators. In the 1980s, it was not uncommon to have a computer hard drive in your desktop computer with the capacity of 10 to 20 MB of data. Today, hard drives contained within a desktop or laptop computer can reach 4 TB of data. This is more than 1 million times larger than the early hard drives developed by IBM half a century ago. At the same time, the weight of hard drives has decreased from 2,000 pounds at their inception down to around 50 g for a small contemporary hard drive. Interestingly, the price per megabyte of data has decreased over the same time period from approximately $15,000 per megabyte to less than $100 per terabyte. This is a reduction of 150,000,000 to 1. Also of note is that the average access time has decreased from more than 100 milliseconds to a few milliseconds, a greater than 40-to-1 improvement.

Hard drives have stood the test of time due to their rugged durability and their increasing data capacity and are still the de facto standard for digital data, recording, and storage throughout the world. There are a variety of components that an investigative computer forensic examiner should be aware of on a typical hard drive. These include the connectors, which are for the most part these days either IDE or SATA, and which are used to connect the hard drive to the BUS or to the motherboard on the computer; a jumper block for modifying jumper settings on the hard drive, so it is compatible with the motherboard on the specific computer on which it is being installed; and the power connector, which is a standardized connection device for applying power from the computer to the hard drive.

A computer hard drive can range in size in today's business world, from that of a small paperback novel all the way down to the size of a pack of cigarettes or smaller. If you were to remove the protective cover from the top of the computer hard drive, there will be a number of primary components that one can see and with which the computer forensic examiner will be familiar, including the platters, which are the shiny gold or silver discs that spin in a clockwise fashion; the spindle, which is the metallic circular device that connects the platters to the drive mechanics; the actuator arm, which is an arm resembling that of a record player and that can move back and forth across the platter as it spins; and the head, which is at the narrow end of the actuator arm and is used to read and write data from the magnetized material that is coating the disc or discs that are spinning from 4,200 revolutions per minute (RPM) up to 15,000 RPM on the drive.

The heads operate extremely close, hovering just over the magnetic surface of the spinning platters, and when I say *close*, I am speaking of just tens of nanometers. The heads are able to detect and modify the magnetization of the platters as they are spinning underneath it, and the actuator arm, to which the heads are attached, is able to draw across the spinning platters to the precise location being searched for, depositing the data on those platters. As the computer sends commands through the motherboard and the hard drive, the actuator arm is able to modify the direction of magnetization on the platters, representing binary data, which is essentially a zero or one or on or off or positive or negative. The discs themselves are coded in a ferromagnetic material, which allows for the magnetization on the discs themselves to be modified by the heads.

In addition to these components, hard drives also contain two electric motors. One is used to spin the disc and one is used to power the actuator as it moves across the discs. Modern drives often contain multiple discs and multiple actuator arms and heads to achieve a greater density of data. It should be noted that due to the extreme closeness between the heads on the actuator arm and the surface of the disc itself, the drives are vulnerable to crashing, where failure of the disc takes place when the head actually touches the electromagnetic material on the spinning drive and creates scratches in the magnetic film covering the platter. This not only causes data loss but also, in most cases, renders the hard drive unusable and the data unrecoverable.

There are other types of hard drive failures besides crashes. Bad sector failures are where magnetic sectors on the drive are no longer usable because there has been some failure with that portion of the drive circuit or where some of the electronic components on the board attached to the drive have failed. Bearing failure is when the bearing in the center of the drive to which the spindle and motor are attached fails. Motor failure is where the electric motor that spins the platter or activates the actuator arm has failed. Data can sometimes be recovered from failed hard drives. However, this activity ordinarily needs to take place in a clean room, which is a room that is free of contaminants and is properly prepared for the opening of the drive and the replacement of failed parts, such as circuitry. See Exhibit 2.4.

Hard drives are used not only for laptops and desktops but also for servers, and within the context of servers hard drives may reside in a variety of configurations. A laptop or desktop in general will contain one hard drive within the computer, although certainly there are some desktop computers that contain multiple hard drives. However, server computers often contain multiple hard drives. In some cases, those hard drives operate as independent stand-alone storage, but in most cases, those drives are part of what is known as a *RAID*, which stands for redundant array of independent discs. The purpose of a RAID is to hold a large volume of data and to provide some level of redundancy. The primary concept behind a RAID is that it uses multiple discs to provide redundancy and performance improvements over the usage of one single disc.

For instance, if one single disc contains 1 TB of data, then you could use five discs in a RAID to achieve a single volume with 5 TB of data where the data is "striped" across all of the drives. In this configuration the computer sees the five discs as one hard drive. The purpose of this type of configuration is again for redundancy and safety, as one of the primary traits is that should one of the five discs fail, it can be replaced with a fresh drive and the RAID controller and its embedded software will "rebuild" the data set and the volume populating the new drive with data that was lost from the failed drive. These types of RAID configurations have caused many

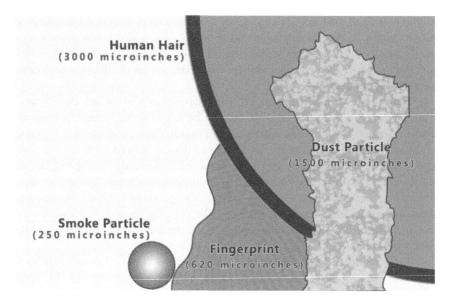

EXHIBIT 2.4   Relative Sizes of Microparticles That Must Be Prevented from Entering the Interior of a Hard Drive Enclosure

The head of the actuator arm on the drive rides in "flying height" position on a cushion of air just over the spinning hard drive platters. The required gap is smaller than a dust particle. Should the head ever touch the drive, it will crash and permanently damage the platters.

a computer forensic investigator sleepless nights as the imaging of these drives can in some cases require a specific protocol whereby exact duplicates of the actual hard drives are used for the imaging—in other words, drives made by the same manufacturer, with the same hardware and specifications and sizes. Once the imaging is completed, the drives may only be reconstructed by reestablishing them in the lab in the same exact order. These RAID images are fraught with technical challenges. As a result, newer server and RAID configuration capturing tools such as F-Response (www.f-response.com) have provided greater ease and predictability when imaging such a machine. In yet another RAID scenario, you could have two drives, one of which is a 1 TB and the second of which is also 1 TB, which are mirrored. This RAID configuration allows you to always maintain a current and up-to-date duplicate of the first drive so that, should there be a failure, you will not have to rely on backup tapes to restore your data. Yet another usage for hard drives is what is known as *network attached storage* (NAS). With greater regularity, organizations and individuals are now using NAS technology for the purpose of storing large volumes of data on their network, data that does not necessarily have to be regularly accessed by the CPU or by the computer. This often acts as long-term storage, but at the same time it is active data. This is an effective approach for individuals or organizations that have large volumes of data that require instantaneous access, but that do not need to reside on the individual hard drives of the users.

Optical Drives

The optical drive, otherwise known as an *optical disc drive* (ODD), is a type of drive that operates with the use of laser light or electromagnetic waves that exist in the part of the spectrum that is close to that of light. The laser or electromagnetic waves allow for the reading of data on an optical disc or the writing of data to such a disc. Examples of optical drives include those that can read and/or write to media such as CDs, DVDs, and Blu-ray discs.

Not only are optical drives used in CD and DVD players/recorders, they are also an integral component in computers. The once widely used floppy disc drive was made obsolete when optical drives came onto the scene. Optical drives on a computer are used to read discs that contain software and consumer media from optical discs and to write data to discs. In comparison to floppy discs, optical discs are inexpensive and have the capacity to store larger amounts of data. While laser disc technology was invented in the late 1950s and patented in 1961, it has had a very long gestation cycle. The commercial beginnings of what is now the optical drive can be traced back to 1972, to the Laserdisc, which was developed by a combined effort of MCA and Philips. These 12-inch video discs were costly to make and challenging to maintain. Later, Sony developed the first 5.25-inch optical drive, which was released in 1987 and allowed for broader adoption.

How It Works

The first thing that is required for an optical drive is an optical path. This is situated in something called the *pickup head* (PUH) and it has three components. One is a semiconductor laser, which then requires a lens that will guide the laser beam. Finally, it requires photodiodes, which detect the light reflecting from the surface of the disc. The wavelength of the laser beam has changed over the years. It initially began as a CD laser, with a wavelength of 780 nm, which is in the infrared part of the spectrum. Then came the DVD laser at 650 nm, which is in the red part of the spectrum. Most recently has come the Blu-ray with a wavelength of 405 nm, which is in the violet part of the spectrum.

Next there is a rotational mechanism, which is different for optical drives than it was for floppy drives. Floppy drives worked by keeping a constant angular velocity (CAV), which means that it spun at a constant number of RPM. This wouldn't work for an optical disc, for which there had to be constant throughput, so optical drives were designed to run at a constant linear velocity (CLV). This would allow the head to transfer data at a maximum linear rate without slowing down when it reached the outer rim of the disc. CLV was used until recently, when zoned CLV (Z-CLV) was introduced. This means that the disc is divided into zones and each zone has its own CLV, which is higher for the inner zone and becomes progressively lower in the outer zones.

Loading a disc into an optical drive is generally done one of three ways, either by placing it in a tray that can be either manually or mechanically operated or by placing it in a slot, in which the disc is pulled into the drive mechanically by rollers. A third method used with some optical drives, particularly those that are portable, is a top-loading model where a lid is raised and the disc is placed directly onto the spindle of the drive.

Early on it was difficult to include an optical drive in a computer. On most computers there was no space for the drive, and they generally had only one advanced technology attachment (ATA), which was already being used for two floppy drives. These problems have been overcome, and now nearly all computers, workstations, and servers are built with a 5.25-inch drive bay. Optical drives still connect to the computer using an ATA or using a serial advanced technology attachment (SATA). The information on the disc is extracted from it and then it can be converted into different formats or just played back.

Generally, an optical drive is compatible with all types of discs that came before it. There is a difference between the various types of discs and how the laser beam has to act on it. All discs have a polycarbonate coating on them, through which the laser beam must penetrate in order to read the disc. On a CD this coating is 1.2 mm thick, on a DVD it is 0.6 mm thick, and on a Blu-ray it is 0.1 mm thick. The thinner the polycarbonate coating, the smaller the area on which the beam is able to focus and this means it can read smaller pits in the disc thereby achieving greater data density and capacity.

Optical Recorder Drives

Many optical drives act as optical recorder drives, including optical drives on computers, allowing the user to record or write data to a disc. There are generally three different speed ratings on the drive, including one for write-once (R) operations, one for rewrite (RW or RE) operations, and one for read-only (ROM) operations.

When it comes to recording on CD/DVD, the recorder identification code (RID) was developed by Philips, thanks to concerns and pressure from the music industry. Now every CD/DVD has a RID, which includes a supplier code, a model number, and a unique ID from the optical recorder drive. It is mandatory that the RID be included on every disc that is written, no matter whether it is a data disc or a backup disc. Every CD-ROM also has a source identification code (SID) that identifies the manufacturer, the factory in which it was produced, and even the identity of the machine that made it.

The RID and the SID are very important when it comes to computer forensic investigations as they can tell investigators where the disc was made (SID) and what drive wrote the data on the disc (RID). This makes it easier for law-enforcement officers and investigators to track down the source of the data on the disc, which might be important evidence in a case. By example, on a recent case in which I provided both investigative computer forensic analysis and expert testimony, I was able to establish on behalf of the defendant in a copyright infringement case that the plaintiff's claims that they had written portions of a Grammy-winning pop song were untrue, partially as a result of what we learned from the forensic data and identifiers found on a compact disc provided by the plaintiff as evidence. It is extraordinary to contemplate that the disposition of a case valued in the tens of millions of dollars can hang in the balance on the interpretation of a few dot matrix alphanumeric numbers on the inside diameter of a seemingly obscure CD-ROM. But the reality is that these cases often turn on the most subtle, simple, or sensitive facts—facts that are often subject to obfuscation by a malevolent bad actor.

Computer Hardware

The reference to computer hardware in the context of a computer forensic lab refers to the physical, tactile components of computers. This can include the box within which a desktop computer is contained. It also refers to the sound card, the video card, or the Ethernet card that attaches to the motherboard inside the computer. The reference can also be to the motherboard itself, which is the large, integrated circuit board to which the various components of the computer, such as the RAM, hard drive, and the CPU or central processing unit, are attached. Hardware can also include modems, routers, and firewalls, as well as laptops and servers of every shape and size, including e-mail servers such as those running Microsoft Exchange or Lotus Notes. Hardware can refer to wireless routers, cell phones, flash memory, external hard drives, keyboards, monitors, and various cables and peripherals. Basically, hardware can refer to virtually any piece of physical equipment that allows computers and their associated peripheral devices to function.

The most prevalent piece of hardware in a computer forensic lab is a hard drive. The hard drive is a repository of data, and for the most part, in most commercial applications a hard drive is a metallic exterior case containing a circuit board within or attached to the unit, as well as spinning platters that are magnetically coated and can allow for data to be deposited on the discs in a predictable fashion. Whether you are using a database or a spreadsheet, an e-mail application or an instant messaging program, a graphics editor or iTunes, the data is stored, managed, and edited on the hard drive in the same fashion. This predicable standardized approach lends to the ubiquitous nature of computing regardless of the form factor, language, or geography.

The Server

The server functions as the nerve center for networks, large websites, and complicated programs. The server is the computer program that is designed to accommodate the requests of other computer programs, programs that reside on the same computer as the server or those that exist on other computers. See Exhibit 2.5. Many people also refer to the computer that houses the server program as a server. However, this computer might perform other tasks in addition to running the server program if the server requirements are small.

Although a server may look like a regular desktop computer on the outside, it is responsible for very different functions. The server has all the same hardware as

EXHIBIT 2.5   A "2U"-Size Rack-Mounted Computer File and E-mail Server, Typical of What May Be Found in a Corporate Server Environment

This server contained the e-mail accounts that had been hacked and co-opted by internal trusted employees and that were used to facilitate a fraudulent billing and payment scheme with false accounts and phantom vendors. A combination of forensic accounting and investigative computer forensic skill sets solved the crime.

a desktop PC, including a CPU, RAM, and hard drives. However, it is designed to run very different applications and to house more RAM, work more quickly, and have more power than the average PC. Desktop PCs are designed to run programs that require graphics and user-friendly interfaces. In contrast, the server is designed to hold databases and process the requests of the programs that run on the PC.

Physical Setup

Smaller servers look much like a desktop PC, with a tower that is only slightly larger. This is fine for a small operation. For larger operations and the needs of larger companies, a rack-mounted server is required, which is a series of boxes (1U, 2U, 3U, 4U, and so on) that are mounted onto a rack assembly for easy storage. A monitor, keyboard, and mouse can be hooked up to the server, although this is not necessary as the server can be accessed and managed through the network.

Network Capability

A contemporary server generally has a minimum of a 1-gigabit interface with the network. The interface is designed to operate on its own and perform certain network functions automatically, freeing up the CPU to handle tasks that are more complex. A high-end server that is designed to handle a large system can have more than one interface connected to each other to increase the bandwidth at which the server can function. This allows the server to process greater loads of data.

The Central Processing Unit

One major difference between a PC and a server can be found in the central processing unit (CPU). In a server, the CPU is designed to have different cache sizes. The cache is a portion of the RAM that acts as a temporary storage space. In the case of the server, it stores frequently accessed information, making data retrieval quick. A server tends to have a larger cache than the average PC, which allows for the storage of more data. This results in the quicker retrieval of data.

The CPU in a server is also designed to give the server more power by making good use of multiple cores. Although a PC can also have multiple cores, a server makes better use of them. The more cores it has, the more power it has. A computer forensic server should have a minimum of two cores to ensure that it has enough power to function at the required capacity. A quad core processor would give even more power.

RAM

When it comes to the RAM (random access memory) of the server, it is generally much faster than the RAM of a desktop PC. This is a requirement because the server is generally running many different tasks at the same time. It is common for a server to have fast RAM, a fast system bus, and for the RAM to be ECC (error-correcting) RAM. This is crucial as ECC RAM helps to protect the integrity of the data that is stored inside the system. A computer forensic system should have no less than 2 gigabytes of RAM but ideally should have 4 gigabytes although it is not uncommon for robust computer forensic labs to maintain workstations and processing machines with upward of 64 GB of RAM or more. The reality is that the more RAM there is on a machine, the faster it will be able to process and manage data. Because of the larger sizes of hard drives and data sets that forensic engineers are tasked with processing, it is important to have as much RAM as possible on at least a few machines in the lab so that the engineers will have the ability to scale their workflow and throughput.

Hard Drive Capability

Another major difference between a desktop PC and a server can been seen in the difference between the hard drives. A PC generally has one hard drive. When an additional hard drive is added, it is a separate device and functions as such. However, a server commonly has multiple hard drives and these hard drives are configured such that they show up as a single disc. This configuration is called redundant array of independent discs (RAID) and the function of RAID is to offer top-notch protection of the data on the system.

There are different levels of RAID, although the most commonly used are levels 1 and 5. However, regardless of the level, the RAID hard drive will house multiple drives that will each contain a complete set of the data. This means that when one drive crashes, the server will still function because all of the data still exists on the other drive(s). The higher the RAID level, the more disc space is available and the faster it operates. See Exhibit 2.6.

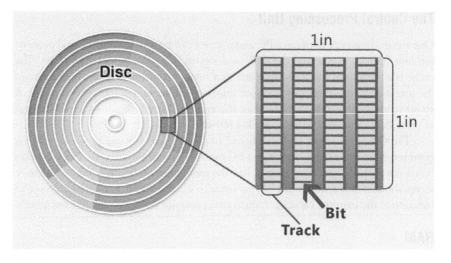

EXHIBIT 2.6   Tracks and Bits in a Sector on an Older Hard Drive Platter

When it comes to hard drives, a server will also make use of drives that run at a faster speed. The speed is measured in RPM and the average desktop PC runs at from 5,200 RPM to 7,200 RPM, whereas a server hard drive runs at a minimum of 7,200 RPM (generally for an entry-level server). Servers for computer forensics store large databases and run heavier applications and therefore would work better with faster hard drives that run between 10,000 and 15,000 RPM.

Power Requirements

When it comes to power requirements, it is common and even necessary for a server to have a minimum of two sources of power, known as a *redundant power supply*. The system will draw power from both sources during normal operation and each source of power is completely independent of the other so that if one fails, the server can continue to operate. The server should also be protected from a power surge with the use of an uninterruptible power supply (UPS).

The Router

The function of a router is to connect two or more networks together, to connect together the computers within a network, and to send data from one network (or computer in the same network) to another. This is useful and even necessary for those who are using home computers right through to very large companies. For those who have home access to the Internet, the router can allow more than one computer to connect to the Internet without having to pay for the connection for each individual computer. For a company, the router links all networked computers with each other and with the Internet. In fact, consider the Internet. It is just one giant network connecting together individual computers and small networks.

How It Works

Routers are set up at the gateways between networks, such as LAN (local area network) and WAN (wide area network), and they allow data to be sent from one network to another. When data is sent between networks, or even between two computers on the same network, the router sees this data and sends it to the proper destination. The data is in the form of packets and is sent to the proper destination, which is based on the IP address of the destination computer.

First the router uses a routing table to locate the destination IP address. This table is made up of information that each router has accumulated on each of its neighbors. The information that is stored in the router includes the IP address and networking considerations, such as time and delay, which themselves are considered by the host. Each data packet has a header, in which is stored information that helps the router determine the destination. Based on this information and the IP address from which the data packet was sent, the router chooses the best neighbor to which to forward the data packet, ensuring that it sends it along the fastest possible route.

Physical Setup

A router can be an inconspicuous piece of hardware. In fact, in its simplest form a computer can act as a router for another computer if they are attached via Internet connection sharing (ICS). Even a modem that connects a PC to the Internet service provider (ISP) acts as a router. When it comes to more complicated networks, such as that of a big company or a computer forensic lab, something more sophisticated than a PC or a modem is required to act as a router.

The next step up from an ICS connection is to use a piece of hardware that acts as a dedicated router. This router is known as a *broadband router* and it is what allows multiple computers to share one Internet connection. This type of router generally requires an Ethernet hub and has ports in the back of it into which a number of computers can be plugged in order to gain Internet access. Some routers might even have ports into which fax machines and phones can be plugged.

There are also wireless routers, otherwise known as a *wireless access point*, designed to give multiple devices a wireless connection to the Internet. They may look the same as regular routers, except for a small antenna protruding from them and the fact that there are no wires running from the router to the computers. A wireless router will require additional security measures to be put into place as security is an important issue over a wireless connection. Wireless offers more mobility, which is important in some situations. Where wireless isn't required, it is better to have a wired router as it is less expensive and generally has fewer security issues.

Applications and Functions

Aside from the basic home setup in which a router connects the home PC to the Internet, there are a number of other applications for which routers can be used. More than one router can be used for interconnected networks and routers can be equipped with various interfaces for different types of physical network connections, such as fiber optics, wireless, or copper cables.

Some businesses, research institutions, academic institutions, and ISPs have the need for the most powerful routers. When a series of routers is used, there are routers that can accomplish different tasks. The access router is the most basic router, used in small businesses and in the home. A distribution router connects multiple access routers and collects data from multiple streams in order to store it in one place. A core router might also be used to connect multiple distribution routers from separate buildings or locations. These larger, more industrial-strength routers require significant bandwidth.

Routers perform several functions aside from the basic connections and sending of information. They manage congestion as it arises, ensuring that the queue of data packets does not exceed a certain limit. When that limit is exceeded, the most common and simplest thing for the router to do is to perform a "tail drop," dropping data packets that exceed the limit. In addition, routers determine the order in which data packets should be processed when there is more than one queue. A router can also implement something called *policy-based routing*, which occurs when special circumstances arise that require the router to apply special rules that override the rules from the routing table.

Application Data

Applications are designed to handle data and that data can come in many forms. Application data includes any data that is handled by the application, whether it is displayed, protected, transmitted, received, deleted, modified, or put into storage, and any data that is required by the application to run, such as the application settings. Essentially, applications and their data are run by the operating system (OS), transferred and shared over networks, and stored in files. Application data is generally stored in the computer's memory or in files on the computer's hard drive. The data that is stored in the memory is stored as temporary files and the data that is stored in files can be either temporary or permanent.

Application Architecture and Types

There are three main categories of application architecture. The first of these is local. In this case the application resides within a single computer system and all of its application data is stored on the computer's hard drive. The second of these is client/server, and in this case the application is stored on the server and may be divided among multiple computer systems. Client/server application data can be accessed from the server via any of the connected computers assuming that you have the appropriate credentials. The third type is peer-to-peer, in which individual client hosts communicate directly with each other rather than over a server-based network. The application data in this situation would be accessible via any of the peer-to-peer systems. These different styles of application architecture are generally flexible so that local applications can be divided among various systems or client/server applications can be installed in tiers on a single system. For the most part, the applications make it clear as to where data is to be stored.

From an investigative viewpoint there are a number of different types of application uses to be considered. They include e-mail, web usage, interactive communications, file sharing, document usage, security, and data concealment.

- **E-mail applications:** The data included in these applications are a header and a body. The header includes a great deal of information that may be relevant to a computer forensic investigation, such as message ID, routing information, creation dates, message importance, and the type of e-mail client used to send it.
- **Web usage:** The best source of information in this case is often the host that is running the web browser, which will contain cookies, a history of the websites visited, and cached data. The data for each request may include a time stamp, IP address, web browser version, the operating system (OS) of the host making the request, the status code, the type of request, and the resources requested.
- **Interactive communications:** These include group chats, instant messaging, and audio and video applications.
- **File sharing:** This group is based on an architecture that includes peer-to-peer and client/server. Peer-to-peer file sharing is generally done for the purpose of sharing software, graphics, music, or images over the Internet. In this case, data can be distributed among a number of hosts. Client/server file sharing is done via a central server and can involve FTP or another file-sharing service such as cloud-based services.
- **Document usage**: Much work is done with the use of documents. These documents include word processors, spreadsheets, presentation software, and database software, each of which will have unique data points, time stamps, and other relevant metadata.
- **Security:** Applications related to security include antivirus software, spyware detection and removal software, content filtering for antispam purposes, and software for the detection of host-based intrusion. These often have unique data points that can be relevant in an investigation.
- **Data concealment**: Tools to conceal data might be used to protect the integrity of data and they can also be used to conceal malicious activity. These tools include data encryption, system cleanup, and steganographic tools, all of which leave unique footprints and various nuanced clues that a trained specialist may be able to reveal.

Application Data Storage

When it comes to OS data, there are two types of data: volatile data and nonvolatile data. Volatile data is data that is generated or used when the computer is turned on. Once the computer is turned off, this data is lost. Nonvolatile data is the data that still exists after the computer is turned off, such as data that is associated with the file system.

Taking nonvolatile data first, this is often the data that is associated with the file system of the OS. It includes configuration files, logs, application files, data files, swap files, dump files, hibernation files, temporary files, and more. In addition, the BIOS (basic input–output system) is also part of the nonvolatile data. The BIOS is the source of hardware-related data, such as components of the motherboard and devices that are attached to the computer. The volatile data exists within the random access memory (RAM) of the system. The RAM is constantly changing when the computer is on. Volatile data includes data from the slack space, free space, network configuration, network connections, running processes, open files, login sessions, and operating system time.

Application data is often part of the volatile data of the OS. When it comes to file systems, the application data is generally stored in the form of executable scripts and files, supporting files, data files, configuration files, and logs. Network application data is related to the connections and communications between the different application components of the network system. In addition, network application data can include network connections used for remote printing and DNS lookups.

Collecting Application Data

The method of application data collection depends on whether the data is volatile or nonvolatile. If required, volatile data should be collected first as it is the most sensitive in terms of time and the state of the computer; however, it is a more difficult and uncertain process. In addition, volatile data is not always required to meet the mandate of the investigation or the discovery project. This data can be collected only if the computer has not been turned off or rebooted. If either of these conditions occurs, the data will be lost. Collecting this data also comes with many risks. Data could be compromised during data collection and, if there is a malicious party involved, then rootkits (software programs that may be surreptitiously installed on a computer for the purpose of gaining control of the "root" or core of the operating system) may have been installed that could delete files, give false data, or perform other malicious functions.

Once the volatile data is collected the computer can be powered down and taken for the collection of nonvolatile data. Powering down the computer must be done properly to best preserve the application data. This can be done by simply unplugging it, or removing the battery if it is a laptop, or by shutting it down via the shutdown option available through the OS. Removing the power source of the computer is often the better option as it can result in preserving temporary files, swap files, and other data that might be lost during an OS shutdown.

When it comes to computer forensics, the key is not only to determine the best way to access application data but also to determine which data is required. This involves determining which applications are of interest in the investigation and then how to access the required data from those particular applications. When it comes to the user's computer, all data can be collected and analyzed later, but data related to the user's activity could also be stored on web servers, the firewall, software logs, web browser caches and cookies, and more. In these cases, each computer or machine that may have pertinent application data must be located and the data retrieved from each one.

Metadata

Metadata is a term that means different things in different environments. A library will refer to metadata as something slightly different than will an organization that keeps records. A common definition of metadata is "data about data." Metadata can be likened to the cataloging system of a library, archives, and museums. In a metadata record there will be information about various aspects of the data. These might include how the data was created and by whom, the time and date it was created, the purpose of the data, where the data was created on the network, what standards were used when creating the data, and other basic pieces of information. Computers can capture basic information or *metadata* about a file, including when it was created, who created it, how big the file is, and when it was last updated.

Metadata of any particular file will vary depending on what the metadata is describing. If it is a digital image, then aside from the information related to who created it, when and where it was created, how it was created, and perhaps clues as to why it was created, there might also be information on the dimensions, resolution, and color depth of the image. Metadata is often stored in a database that is referred to as *a metadata repository* or a *metadata registry*. Most metadata, however, that is the focus of a computer forensic investigator is that which is embedded within a file type such as an e-mail, a word processing document, a web page, or other specific file type. These files all contain metadata fields that are relevant in an investigation, such as "File type," file "Creation Date," "Last Modified Date," "Last Accessed Date," and other file characteristics.

Types of Metadata

Metadata can describe publications and textual works, photographs, video, web pages, and an unlimited number of other data types. One of the earliest forms of metadata was the Dewey decimal system of the libraries, which is still in use today. Before the days of computers, libraries had all their "metadata" on small cards that were kept in a card catalog. With the digital era upon us, metadata can be included or written into a number of digital media, including photographs, videos, and even web pages, on which metadata is referred to as *metatags*.

There are three types of metadata that are currently in use. The first of these is descriptive metadata, which is created for the purpose of identification. This type of metadata includes information such as author, title, abstract, and keywords. The next type of metadata is structural metadata, which refers to information about how compound objects are organized. An example of this is information on how pages are organized to create chapters. The third type of metadata is administrative metadata, which refers to information about how resources are managed. This includes information about the resource, such as who created it, when it was created, the file type, who is allowed to access the resource, and any technical information about the resource.

Administrative metadata can be divided into two subsets known as rights management metadata and preservation metadata. Rights management metadata is information pertaining to intellectual property rights and preservation metadata refers to information regarding the archiving and preservation of a resource.

Metadata Schemes

Metadata schemes are an important part of the data management ecosystem and are sets of metadata elements that are designed to serve a specific purpose. The definition of the elements is called *semantics* and the values of the metadata are referred to as the *content*. Metadata schemes generally either give the names of the elements and their semantics or they might give the content rules, specifying how the content is to be organized. Syntax rules may also be applied.

There is a wide variety of metadata schemes and element sets that are in use or being designed. This is because there are so many different disciplines and user environments. Some of the more common schemes and element sets include the Dublin Core Metadata Element Set, the Text Encoding Initiative (TEI), the Metadata Encoding and Transmission Standard (METS), Metadata Object Description (MODS), the Encoded Archival Description (EAD), Learning Object Media (LOM), E-Commerce and ONIX, Visual Objects–CDWA and VRA, MPEG Multimedia Data, and Metadata for Datasets.

How Metadata Is Created

Metadata can be created manually or via an automated process, and it is generally a cooperative effort. In large part a technical team spearheads the effort and creates the initial digitization of the metadata, particularly when it comes to structural and administrative metadata. For descriptive metadata, the creator of the resource generally provides the metadata information, especially when the topic is very specialized, such as scientific metadata.

The creation of metadata generally begins with creation tools that have been designed by those who have undertaken metadata project initiatives. These tools include templates, markup tools (to structure the metadata values and attributes), extraction tools (to analyze and automatically create metadata from a digital resource), and conversion tools (to translate one form of metadata to another).

When creating metadata, there must be quality control, especially when the metadata has been created in an automated fashion or the manual entry of the information is done by those who are unfamiliar with the data. To accommodate the need for quality control there is a resource entitled the *Framework of Guidance for Building Good Digital Collections*, which can be found on the National Information Standards Organization (NISO) website (see www/niso.org). NISO lists six basic principles that must be followed to create good metadata and has a wealth of additional information about governance standards and development.

Common Metadata Types in Standard Computer Files

Common files used by all computer users are filled with various metadata fields, which include everything from the file date and time stamps of Microsoft Office and Adobe documents to the plethora of data points contained within a sent or received e-mail. These can include time and data stamps as well as IP addresses of the various computers that the e-mail traversed across in its journey to your inbox, from the names and identities of the authors and contributors of the e-mail to the applications used to generate them. With graphics files it is even possible to have metadata related to the latitude and longitude of where the photo was taken. Microsoft Word documents contain special metadata fields that account for "track changes" and other embedded data.

Metadata is often dynamically updated by some particular event that the specific field is programmed to record, such as the file "last accessed" date and time. This metadata field is particularly important in investigative work as it will tell the fact-finder when the file in question was last accessed or touched by the computer that held that file during the time of forensic capture. This field, however, may be updated by innocuous activity such as an antivirus scan on the computer, or some other event. As a result the quick and decisive forensic capture of electronic data is often warranted even if the data capture is perceived at the time as overinclusive or costly. Given the fact that metadata fields are often the pivotal evidence in a matter and that they are often so easily impacted by unintentional user activity on the host computer, there is normally a strong argument to be made for capturing this data and preserving it so that the metadata fields are left intact for the eventual review by a fact-finder, investigator, or lawyer.

Databases

A database is a collection of data that has been organized in a specific manner to serve a number of purposes. The database allows users to easily collect, access, and update the information when required. In the strictest of interpretations, the term applies to the data itself and the systems that house the data, but not to the database management system, which is the system designed to manage and process the data. The database and the database management system go hand in hand as the latter provides the tools that allow for the querying and management of the data itself. The term *database* and the use of such a method to organize information began in the 1960s when it became clear that there had to be a way to organize mass quantities of information for a wide variety of end-users in a large, complex organization.

Database Classifications

Databases can be classified in different ways depending on the way they are organized. The first database classification was the navigational database. In this type of database, an application would search for information by moving from one record to another, following pointers along the way.

One of the most common classifications, and the one that followed the navigational database, is the relational database. In this type of database, the information is accessed by an application based on the content of the data itself. The data is organized in tables that allow users to quickly access information in various ways. For instance, a database of rock samples might allow a user to access information based on rock size, color, type, or place of origin. This type of database could not be widely used until the mid-1980s, when computer hardware had enough power to run it. It quickly became popular and is still widely used today.

The entity-relationship database is another popular model for a database, one that is less rigid than the relational model. This type of database is object-oriented, meaning that it is one in which the information is organized in object classes and subclasses.

Physical Appearance

Databases are generally not integrated with their hardware. Although this approach was tried, it ultimately failed because the technology could not keep pace with developments in general-purpose hardware. For this reason, databases are run on general-purpose computers and stored on general-purpose hard drives and other general-purpose mass storage units.

Why a Database Management System?

The simplest form a database can take is a list in a word processor or spreadsheet. This is fine if the amount of information contained within the database is limited. However, once there is sufficient information stored within the database, redundancies begin to show up and accessing the desired data becomes difficult. This is when the need for a database management system (DBMS) arises. The data can be transferred to a DBMS where the data is organized into objects, such as tables and entities, that are based on real life. Common objects included in databases could include any number of data fields such as customers, invoices, meetings, and inventory lists. There are a wide variety of DBMSs available, including Oracle, FoxPro, Microsoft Access and SQL Server, IBM DB2, Linter, MySQL, and Paradox.

Types of Databases

There are many different types of databases that serve different functions based on the needs of the user. One such database is the access database, which operates on an event-driven architecture. This means that the database can respond to requests and events that happen both outside and inside the system.

Another type of database is the cloud database, a database that is designed to function in a cloud computing environment. The database and the DBMS both exist remotely, in the cloud. It is developed by programmers and then maintained by the end-user.

An operational database is used to store all information regarding the operation of an organization or entity. These databases are generally organized according to subject matter, and they use transactions to update the high volumes of information that enter into the system. There are also databases that are designed for knowledge management, graph structures, documents, and many more types. Essentially, if there is a need, then there is probably a database to fill that need.

Requirements of a Database

There are a number of functional requirements and operational requirements that a database must meet to provide the necessary service for which it is intended. In terms of functional requirements, requirements include defining the structure of the data and manipulating and protecting the data. Database security is of particular importance in computer forensics, where the integrity of the evidence is at stake.

The operational requirements for a database are those requirements that ensure that the database can supply support for an application using the database. In a quick overview, these requirements include availability, performance, isolation between users, data recovery, backup and restore, and data independence. These operational requirements ensure that the requests of the user will be fulfilled within a specific time frame, that the data will be backed up and restored when system failure occurs, and that when there are multiple users each of them will have uninterrupted access to the database.

Ultimately, a database is designed to meet the needs of the end-user, using the appropriate model, language, architecture, and security. The design usually incorporates a database architecture that includes the external level, the conceptual level, and the internal level. The external level defines the different views or needs of each end-user and how those end-users understand the organization of the data. The conceptual level brings together the various external views to form a unified whole. It is made up of all the data that any end-user might request. The internal level operates within the DBMS and is designed to deal with the practical aspects of operating the database, including cost, scalability, and performance.

Database Storage

Database storage is the "container" in which the internal level of the architecture is stored and where all information required for the external and conceptual levels is also stored. During data storage, data can be compressed so that it takes up less space or encrypted so that it is safe from a security point of view. Encrypted data prevents the possibility of the data being reconstructed by someone with unauthorized access to the data. The data can be stored on magnetic media, dynamic random access memory (DRAM), nonvolatile storage, and volatile storage.

Internet Data

Internet data that is collected in the course of a computer forensic investigation runs the full gamut of style and type. To begin with, Internet data can simply be screenshots of computer usage by individual, laptop, or desktop or Internet data may be represented by temporary files that are located within the Windows operating system, another operating system, or within the unallocated space of a hard drive, representing imagery of what the users of the computer saw when they were browsing a particular website. For instance, if I were to go to Yahoo.com and then to www.myyahoo.com to review my e-mail and browse a travel website to book an airline ticket to Japan, there probably will be residual data in the unallocated space and in the temporary files that will allow a computer forensic examiner to reconstruct those pages as I saw them on my hard drive and those pages can be offered as evidence.

The pages could be complete with text or images, links, URLs, and other relevant information. The types of Internet data that is subject to a forensic investigation include data that is pulled from Internet servers. An Internet server is a computer server that processes requests from Internet users. These could be requests for web pages that are received by the Internet server. These web pages are displayed by applications that are running on the server or are dynamically created from database-driven applications that are feeding the web server. In many cases, particularly in complex database-driven websites, pages that are created in any one web session are highly customized for the user who has made the request. For instance, a web page displayed by www.orbitz.com while I am logged in and requesting flight information for a particular route will be unlike any other webpage ever created on Orbitz as it will have embedded metadata related to my account, the time and date of the request, and the particular flight information that I asked for. In fact, the page may also have unique advertisements that are targeted to me and my account based on my user habits and demographics.

The computer forensic examiner, if he or she gains access to the web server that served up those pages, will have the ability to capture certain data on the server, such as records of requests to the server, user information of registered users, and metrics indicating the type of usage of the website, web page, or server itself from a wide variety of perspectives, including IP addresses, geographies, and length of time. Depending on what applications and tools the web server was hosting, the forensic examiner may have the ability to capture additional data such as e-mail data from an e-mail server that is being hosted in conjunction with the web server, particularly where a website allows users to create e-mail from their own environment.

When it comes to Internet chat data, if the server is hosting a chat platform or transactional data for e-commerce websites, then log data may be available for servers and just about any other type of data you can possibly imagine, including application data for online or web-based applications that are supporting the internal mechanics of the particular business. In addition to data that can be gleaned from a web server, it is also possible to capture data from router logs and other Internet devices that use log-in information from user traffic and other activity. These types of devices include routers, firewalls, intrusion detection systems, content filtering systems, spam filters, load-balancing applications, statistical management applications, and a variety of other tools, each of which in some capacity have the ability to capture data that has been transmitted over the Internet.

However, not all devices are storing this information. Therefore, a forensic examiner, during the interview phase with the custodians of these devices, needs to gain an understanding of how they are being leveraged. If one is conducting an investigation in which the technicians and investigators have the ability to leverage preexisting infrastructure for the monitoring of existing behavior, then the investigator may have great flexibility in the type of electronic data that can be captured. During a forensic investigation of an ongoing issue, this can allow your IT department to enable logging or filtering/nonfiltering of particular types of data during the investigative process so as to ensure that you are capturing that for which you are looking.

Other types of Internet data that may be available include that which can be captured by conducting packet-level capture and review. Packet analysis can take place if one has the ability to install a packet sniffer for examination of a network and to monitor the traffic that is taking place on the network at the packet level. This is particularly useful in malware investigations and other investigations in which there is a suspected external breach or the risk of Trojan horse monitoring and filtering of data to a third party. Packet-level analysis is highly granular and often costly as technicians must review the actual network communications as they are taking place for anomalous or malicious data or behavior. Sophisticated antimalware tools often have this capability, although they generally rely on a predefined set of malware definitions by which they are able to flag malicious software. That being said, isolated data from a network can be reviewed at the packet level by technologists with the required skills and tools and in some investigations this will illustrate patterns of deception or theft.

With the advent and proliferation of wireless activity, it is also possible to capture wireless connections, wireless data, and in certain cases, the actual activity that is taking place across the wireless field. These wireless interceptors are available to forensic technicians as easily as they are to the bad guys and can provide great insight into the behavior that is taking place at any given facility over the wireless medium. One does need to use caution when using wireless interception devices to ensure that you are not running afoul of privacy or trespassing laws that govern the jurisdiction in which you are working.

E-mail Mechanics

E-mail is short for *electronic mail*, and it is the method used to send various forms of communication, primarily text, from one computer to another over the Internet or another type of network. With over 3 billion e-mail accounts in existence as of 2012, hundreds of millions if not billions of e-mails are sent around the world every day. This form of communication has begun to replace other forms, including telephone, faxing, and regular mail (otherwise known as "snail mail"). In fact, e-mail sent anywhere in the world will arrive almost instantaneously and can carry text, images, and facsimiles as well as include video and sound.

How It Works

The first requirement for sending an e-mail is to have e-mail software, also known as a *client*. This is software that allows the sender to compose a text message and to attach various forms of files, including text documents, spreadsheets, images, and video and voice recordings. Once the sender hits Send on the e-mail, another piece of system software called *Transmission Control Protocol* (TCP) is actuated. This software takes the e-mail message and all its contents and splits them up into smaller packets of information. The TCP also adds information within the packets to ensure that the packets are handled properly. An example of this is to include information about the order in which the packets were sent.

Once the e-mails are passed through the TCP, they make their way to a mail submission server, which is a computer that is often either with the Internet service provider (ISP) or resides within the company network. To understand what the mail submission server does, it is important to take note that each e-mail has at least two Internet mail addresses attached to it, that of the sender and that of the recipient. There are more than two e-mail addresses if there are multiple recipients. Each e-mail address looks something like this: webmaster@example.com. The .com represents the top-level domain, the word *example* represents the second-level domain, and "webmaster" represents the mailbox name of the recipient(s).

The job of the mail submission server is to query the domain name servers in order to determine the Internet Protocol (IP) address for the recipient. The IP address is a numerical address, and the mail submission server will convert the recipient's e-mail address into the IP address once it has been located. Then the e-mail is sent along the Internet via routers, which examine the IP address and determine the best and fastest route for the e-mail to take. Once the e-mail has arrived, it is housed in the mail server at the destination, where the packets are put back together in the proper order, based on the instructions left in the packets. Then the e-mail is placed on the recipient's computer to be read via the client software installed on that machine.

SMTP

SMTP deserves mention here. It stands for *Simple Mail Transfer Protocol*, and it is the standard for Internet e-mail transfer over IP networks. All mail servers and mail transfer agents use SMTP for both incoming and outgoing mail, but when it comes to the client software, generally SMTP is used strictly for outgoing mail. When it comes to receiving mail, the client software may use a different protocol, known as *Post Office Protocol* (POP), *Internet Message Access Protocol* (IMAP), or another proprietary system.

When an e-mail is sent, it is the SMTP of the client that communicates with the server. It is connection-oriented and text-based and communicates by issuing commands and sending the data through the TCP. An SMTP transaction has three parts or sequences when it comes to command/reply. The first of these is the MAIL command, which tells the server who the sender is in case there is a need to return the e-mail. Next comes the RCPT command, which is the command in which the recipient(s) are established. Both the MAIL and RCPT commands can be considered as the envelope in which the message is stored. The final sequence is the DATA command (really a group of commands), which sends the actual message. It contains both the message header and the message body, which are separated by an empty space.

Access Restrictions

There needs to be control over who accesses the e-mail server and this control is in the hands of the server administrators. These are the people who determine who can access the server, from where, and when. The older and less-used method was to restrict access based on IP address. Only those accessing the server from certain IP addresses were allowed to proceed. More commonly used now is the requirement for clients to go through an authentication process to prove they are allowed to access the server. Access can also be determined based on which port is being used. SMTP uses TCP port 25 on the server and submission uses TCP port 587. Server administrators can determine who can and cannot access these ports. These ports, which are associated with each IP address, are available for ingress and egress into a computer, and there are many of them as each IP address has 65,535 available ports for TCP. A favorite early vulnerability that hackers would often exploit through the use of port scanners would be open and unprotected ports that would allow for one-way or two-way communication to take place between the attacker and the target. Many of these ports have standardized uses, such as port 25 for SMTP and port 21 for FTP. While FTP is generally bound to port 21, administrators have the flexibility to change the port to 2121, 30,500, or any other number that is not in use for another function.

The requirement for authentication prior to accessing the system, particularly from a remote location, is important in terms of security. It cuts down on the instances of spam, but cannot eradicate it entirely as there are other issues, such as broken or unintelligent message transfer agents and security weaknesses within the operating system. The Anti-Spam Research Group (ASRG), part of the Internet Research Task Force (IRTF), is examining ways to improve e-mail authentication.

The IP Address

The Internet Protocol address, otherwise known as the *IP address*, is essentially a number that is assigned to each device that is connected to a network. Not only are computers assigned an IP address but also printers, modems, routers, and any other device that uses the IP standard for communication over the network. There are two functions served by having an IP address. One is that it allows for the identification of the computer on the network. The other function is to identify the location of the device in use. Without the IP address, the computer or other such device would not be able to communicate over the Internet to either send or receive data.

There are two IP address numbering systems currently in use: the Internet Protocol version 4 (IPv4) and the Internet Protocol version 6 (IPv6). IPv4 is a 32-bit system and was the original IP address system to be used. It is still being used today. However, due to the dramatic increase in the number of network users across the globe, another system was needed. In 1995, IPv6 was created and since the middle of the 2000s it has been in use on a global scale. The IPv6 is a 128-bit system.

IPv4

The IPv4 is actually a string of binary numbers. However, these binary numbers are translated and stored as strings of numbers that make a little more sense to people. An example of an IPv4 is 183.14.255.1. The address is denoted by four numbers separated by decimals and each of which is a number between 0 and 255. Each of the four numbers represents a group of eight bits and the bits are a binary code sequence.

IPv6

Since the IPv4 addresses are being used up at an alarming rate, the Internet Engineering Task Force (IETF) developed a new form of IP address, the IPv6. IPv6 has a larger address size, with 128 bits, that is also in binary code. The layout or structure of the address is different from that of IPv4 and can take on a few different forms, all of which are the same, but some of which are a shortened form of the full version. Essentially, they look similar to this: 1995:0000:0000:0000:0001:4521:DF33:0000. This can also be written without the zeros as: 1995::0001:4521:DF33::. There are still concerns that in the future IPv6 will not be able to accommodate all the computers that will inevitably be used, but there is still some time before that happens.

The Assignment of IP Addresses

An IP address is much like the address of a house. When new houses are built, an address must be created for it in order for the occupants to receive mail. When a new computer or other device accesses the Internet, an IP address must be assigned to it for the owner of the computer to receive and send e-mail and access data on the Internet. There are both permanent and temporary IP addresses. Permanent IP addresses might be assigned to business or e-mail servers. Temporary IP addresses are usually assigned by the Internet service provider (ISP) and are more likely to be used with a LAN connection.

An IP address that does not change is known as a static IP address. This is the type that is generally assigned by the ISP. In contrast to this is the dynamic IP address, which is an IP address that changes frequently. This type of IP address can be assigned by either the ISP or the Dynamic Host Configuration Protocol (DHCP) server. It is a good option for those users who do not require a static IP address and a new IP address will be assigned each time they log on to the network. This makes things easy as there is no need to remember any details regarding the IP address.

The dynamic IP address also helps with the overwhelming number of computers on the Internet. As IP addresses are limited and would eventually run out, using dynamic IP addresses allows a larger number of users to make use of a smaller number of IP addresses as not all users will be online at the same time. This removes the need for each of them to be assigned an IP address of their own.

There is also a sticky dynamic IP address that is used in situations in which an IP address is assigned as a dynamic IP address, yet, despite this, it doesn't change often. They are generally assigned by DHCP to devices such as modems, for which the power is turned on for long periods of time. In cases like this, the IP address is usually left with the device for a long time and is often renewed. If the device is turned off and then on, it might even keep the same IP address it had previously.

The domain name is familiar to just about everyone and that is the reason it is used. The domain name is essentially a translation of the IP address into words that are easy for people to remember. It is far easier to remember www.example.com than to remember 183.14.255.1. The same goes for e-mail. Remembering an e-mail address with someone's name or a business name in it is far easier than remembering one that contains a long number.

Computer Time Artifacts

One of the most important areas of digital analysis and reconstruction is the establishment of time and date stamps as they relate to particular data elements or files that are recovered for analysis. Every file in the computer will have some element of a file time and date stamp associated with it. However, different operating systems manage file, time, and date stamps differently, whether they be Windows 98, Windows XP, Windows 8, or Macintosh files, in which time and date stamps are commonly called *MAC times (Modified, Accessed, Created)*. These time and date stamps allow investigators to see who had access to and created the modified time stamp, indicates when a file has been changed in some manner, and records the date and time that the change took place, and when it was saved to the device that you have captured, such as a hard drive or thumb drive.

The last-accessed time stamp is, in most cases, the last time that the file was accessed, such as when a file is deleted. When a file is deleted, it is accessed through the file system to perform the actual deletion, and at that time the last-accessed time stamp is updated. However, last-accessed time stamps need to be viewed with a great deal of caution as there are a variety of other activities that may modify the last-accessed time stamp, including antivirus programs and backup programs, which may access those files and modify the time stamp.

The file creation time stamp is the date on which the file was first created locally on the file system, but this date should also be viewed with caution as you may have a date for file creation that is more contemporary than the last-modified or last-accessed time stamp. Why? Because if the file was created on a device such as a third-party computer and accessed on that computer, but then subsequently copied to another computer, then the creation date that will be recorded is the date on which the file was first copied to the more contemporary computer. Therefore, you may have a creation date that is more contemporary than the last-modified date.

Social Media

Social media is a web-based and mobile-based method of communication. It has been defined by Michael Heinlein and Andreas Kaplan in a 2010 issue of *Business Horizons* as "a group of Internet-based applications that build on the ideological and technological foundations of Web 2.0, and that allow the creation and exchange of user-generated content." In essence, social media is any web-based service that allows users to create profiles that are public or semi-public and that allows those users to post information and connect with others on the same platform, accessing other users' information as well as their own. Social media has changed the way people communicate on both a private and a professional level.

Social media comes in many forms, including blogs, online magazines, podcasts, Internet forums, videos, photographs, wikis, and social bookmarking. These various forms of social media can be divided into six main groups: virtual gaming worlds, social networking sites, microblogs and blogs, collaborative projects, content communities, and virtual social worlds. Into these six groups fall the familiar sites, such as YouTube, Facebook, Twitter, MySpace, and Wikipedia.

Social media stands apart from industrial media, such as print and electronic forms of media, as it offers user-generated content that is easily accessible by just about anyone at little or no cost. Users can publish information and access information quickly and easily no matter where they are in the world. Social media is accessible, reaches millions of people in a decentralized fashion, does not require the user to have training or specialized skills, is instantaneous, and can be altered and edited at any given moment.

Security Issues

Social media depends on having large numbers of users sign up for the services. This creates an environment in which anything goes. When it comes to social media, it depends on the form of the social media as to the level of privacy and protection a user has. Since social media are based on Web 2.0, it is important to consider Web 2.0 dynamics. Web 2.0 is ever changing, different services have different privacy policies and different backup procedures, users can have many identities, not all services are stable, and there are traffic limitations when it comes to extracting data.

Some social media sites encourage users to share personal information while others encourage high levels of anonymity. However, overall there is a low level of security on most of these platforms, and this lack of adequate security can allow many online crimes to be perpetrated, including phishing, identity theft, corporate espionage, viruses and worms, spam, and stalking.

Any employer faces the risk of liability and exposure due to the activities of their employees on social media sites. Whether they are sending e-mails, posting on Facebook, or tweeting on Twitter, these employees can pass along confidential or sensitive information and photographs or images, either intentionally or unintentionally. These days, social media is closely linked with business and even government agencies. Businesses advertise and reach out to potential customers via Facebook, Twitter, and other popular social media platforms. They also search for new employees via these platforms. However, there is more than this to the reach of social media. Not only can companies create their own profiles on these platforms but also individuals, both employees and customers, can create profiles and pages for a company without the knowledge or permission of the company in question.

Data Storage

Data storage has been a big issue for social media sites. Consider Facebook. It has more than 1,000 million (1 billion) users and more than 600,000 of these users are online at any given time. These 600,000 users are all accessing information at the same time. Now consider the size of database that would be required to manage that much information, information that is largely user-generated. The task would be monumental and too much for a traditional relational database management system (RDBMS). There would be too much information to be stored on one database, and the use of multiple databases would pose a problem when trying to link databases together. Facebook and other forms of social media would slow to a crawl if a standard RDBMS were used.

RDBMSs use SQL (Structured Query Language), which is a programming language that was designed for managing databases. The solution to the social media data storage problem has been to use NoSQL (Not Only Structured Query Language) systems, meaning that the storage of data does not require the use of SQL. Social networking sites (SNSs) use a combination MySQL (which is a basic database) and NoSQL. There are a number of NoSQL databases that are used by different SNSs. Cassandra is used by Facebook and has a high data-access speed. Hadoop/HBase is used by Facebook and Yahoo and is a large storage system that stores copies of the SQL system. LinkedIn uses a system called Voldemort, which is a distributed key-value data storage system. With these NoSQL data storage systems large amounts of data can be stored and accessed by multiple users at the same time.

Social media data storage and the NoSQL database solution is linked with cloud computing. Cloud computing allows data to be stored on a server (or servers) that is off-site and that hosts numerous platforms and has data that is simultaneously available to numerous websites. Most web-based applications, such as Gmail, Google documents, and Facebook, use cloud computing. In fact, cloud computing is becoming so popular that not only are social media platforms using it to store their data, but companies and corporations are also shifting to cloud computing for data storage and the use of software and applications designed for day-to-day business activities.

Computer Forensics and NoSQL

Essentially, NoSQL allows for the following to happen:

- A shift away from traditional databases that cannot manage super-large amounts of data, such as what is being generated by social media.
- The ability to build infinitely scalable systems.
- The ability to avoid distributed data transactions.
- The ability to choose the right database for the needs of the website.

However, there are problems when it comes to computer forensic investigations. The first of these is that these NoSQL databases are designed to allow real-time access to data and information and this data can be changed at a moment's notice. This can make it harder to track down evidence in a case.

In addition, because the NoSQL databases exist in the cloud, computer forensic investigators do not have direct access to the hard drives that store the data. Legally admissible evidence in a court of law must be collected, protected, analyzed, and reported in an appropriate manner. Due to the fact that hard drives are not directly accessible and there is low security when it comes to social media, the result can be difficulty in obtaining the information as well as the risk of contamination of the evidence, which means that there are challenging issues with the legal handling of cloud-based evidence originating on NoSQL-based systems. These challenges are beginning to be addressed by more sophisticated cloud-based data collection systems, such as X1 Rapid Discovery where the collection of the data takes place locally on cloud-based systems and allows for the collection of active and dynamic data across the wire.

Tablets

A tablet is a mobile computerized device that operates via a flat touch screen. The tablet looks similar to an iPhone or smartphone but is larger. Because it has a touch screen, it often has no keyboard attached and instead users will have access to a virtual keyboard, a digital pen, or a stylus pen. The concept of the information tablet came about as early as the nineteenth century, with concept ideas and prototypes being introduced throughout the twentieth century. However, it wasn't until the end of the twentieth century that the idea of the tablet was put into a digital framework.

One of the earliest digital tablets was the Microsoft Tablet PC, which was primarily picked up by hospitals and outdoor businesses as it was designed to be used by professionals who had to leave their desks and go out in the field. The Tablet PC was not used widely because it was too expensive and offered problems with regard to usability. It wasn't until 2010, with the release of the Apple iPad, that the tablet became a highly successful product with widespread use. The iPad was based on the same technology used in the iPhone, and since then other companies have successfully released their own versions of the tablet. Among these is Microsoft's 2012 release of the Surface Tablet that has presented consumers with an entirely new interface and operating system in the form of Windows RT, which focuses on the capabilities and strengths of this new form factor while also providing significant new interoperability among the desktop, laptop, smartphone, and tablet through SkyDrive, a cloud-based data storage and collaboration platform that allows for real-time synchronicity between each of the consumers' Microsoft-based devices.

Features and Functions

Tablets offer a number of features and functions that make them incredibly useful devices. Besides the fact that they are fully mobile, these devices have touch screen capability, which allows for easy navigation when in use. The tablet also has a virtual keyboard. The touch screen function makes hand–eye operation easier and more natural than that of clicking a mouse. Newer models use what is known as a *finger-driven multitouch* interface and many of them better emulate the behavior of real-life objects. Tablets often also have a handwriting-recognition function.

There are two primary forms of touch screen hardware: resistive touch screens and capacitive touch screens. Resistive touch screens respond to any amount of pressure exerted on the screen and allow for a high amount of precision. In fact, resistive screens have such a high resolution for the detection of touch that some people use a stylus or even a fingernail. Capacitive touch screens have evolved to accommodate multitouch capability and are more responsive than resistive touch screens. Capacitive touch screens require a conductive material for use, which means that a stylus is normally used. In addition to these two main types of touch screens, there is also the less-often-used palm recognition.

Other features of the tablet include the ability to be wireless, ambient light and proximity sensors, and an accelerometer, which can detect the physical movements of the tablet. In addition, the larger tablets come equipped with a storage drives like those found in laptops and smaller ones have storage drives similar to those found in MP3 players. They also generally have ports for removable storage devices. There are 3D slate tablets that come with 3D glasses and some newer tablets come with docking stations that have a full qwerty keyboard and USB ports.

Operating System

A tablet will run an operating system (OS) in the same way a computer does. There are two types of operating systems that are used on tablets: the PC (computer) operating system and the post-PC operating system. The PC operating system is the same kind of OS that is used by a desktop computer. The post-PC operating system is more like the mobile phone OS. Among the widely used PC operating systems are Microsoft's Windows RT and Windows 8, as well as QNX, which is a Linux-based operating system that also powers the BlackBerry tablet. When it comes to post-PC operating systems, the most popular are the Apple iOS and Google Android, which have collectively secured the present lead in the global fight for tablet dominance.

Computer Forensic Challenges with Tablets and Other Mobile Devices

When it comes to computer forensics and retrieving deleted data from a tablet or other mobile device, things become tricky. These generally do not have a hard drive that can be removed like that of a PC. Furthermore, tablets have solid-state memory devices and often manage data via the use of SQL database files. This makes it very difficult for forensic investigators to access deleted data without first accessing the raw data in the system, and it is only recently that there has been software available that can accomplish this task.

Another major issue with tablets and other mobile devices is the use of *apps* (short for *applications*). Although these have made life easier in so many ways, they also pose a challenge when it comes to corporate security and the use of computer forensics in an investigation. Apps such as Dropbox and those that are similar make it possible for users to transfer data, including confidential data, to anyone, anywhere, at any time. When an investigation is in process, it can be easy to overlook the possibility of these apps being used. There are other apps, such as TigerText, that allow users to set their text messages to self-destruct after they are sent, which means that these messages will be wiped from the device and the device of the recipient.

With this information and these issues faced by computer forensic investigators in mind, it is obviously crucial that any tablet that is seized in an investigation must be isolated from its network immediately or the potential exists for data to be lost or transmitted. When it comes to recovering the data on such a device, there is often no way to boot the device from a CD or connect it to a network or another device. This means that in order to access and acquire the data, investigators must use system commands, AT commands, flasher tools, JTAG, or, as a worst-case scenario, forensic desoldering of the solid state media from the motherboard itself. This final option has numerous risks and should only be attempted as a last resort as this process will damage the evidence and alter its physical characteristics.

System commands are the least expensive route to take, but they also carry the risk of losing data. AT commands can be used only on devices that have modems, as they are older modem-based commands. Flasher tools are available from the manufacturer and are a combination of hardware and software that will program the memory of the device and then make a copy of it. JTAG involves a scan called a *boundary scan* that can produce a forensic image of the memory. Finally, forensic desoldering is the process of physically removing the memory chip and placing it in a chip reader. It is the most invasive and potentially the most destructive of the methods. My expectation is that as tablets and similar devices continue to proliferate, computer forensic engineers will develop reliable tools for the predictable collection and analysis of data contained on these new form factors. Until then, it will be vital for examiners to use available work-arounds with an emphasis on capturing data that the tablet stores or access on the cloud through embedded apps and other third-party software.

Cellular Telephones and Smartphones

Cellular telephones and smartphones have proliferated in the business world. What was once an adjunct to a typical user's communication platform, smartphones are now the primary medium for many. The processing power and capabilities of smartphones have expanded exponentially in just the past few years. Users now have the ability to maintain tens of thousands of business files and e-mails on the smartphone. Not only does the device retain onboard memory, but it can now be expanded to include removable flash memory the size of your pinkie nail but that has the capacity to hold data surpassing that of the most robust personal computers built 10 years ago.

The net result is that investigations are increasingly requiring access to smartphones. Imaging a smartphone presents a number of challenges as most computer forensic providers are not equipped to properly image the onboard memory devices. Investigators should use care in reviewing their computer forensic provider's capabilities and experience in this area. From an investigator's point of view, one should always pay close attention to the various possible sources of electronic data; particular attention should be paid when collecting data from custodians in Asia, Europe, and other regions outside of the United States as there is an even greater propensity to maintain electronic data on smartphones in those regions.

If you were to take the subway in Tokyo, Shanghai, or Seoul during rush hour, you would see a great number of individuals feverishly typing away on their smartphones. These individuals are not only browsing the Internet, they are also chatting with colleagues and friends on various systems from Facebook to localized social media platforms for business and pleasure. Many of my investigations over the years have found that key documents live not on an individual's hard drive but instead on the smartphone. As one can expect, smartphones are easily disposed of, and they should be part of any reasonable protocol for the collection of electronic evidence to at minimum identify the entire inventory of potential sources that may be required to secure an image. Interestingly, while my observations regarding Tokyo, Shanghai, and Seoul have been true for a number of years, U.S. cities have followed the trend since the release of the iPhone. Today, one can see entire tables of diners engaged in online communications while fully ignoring their fellow dinner guests. Children, adults, professionals—everyone seems to be guilty of allowing their electronic communication device to take the place of traditional human-to-human communication. The results of this are found not only in the digital record but also from the perspective of the decline in interpersonal skills within the workforce and society as a whole.

Although there are many technologies employed by cell phone makers and telecommunication infrastructure providers such as CDMA and 3G, phones still retain data in the same basic fashion. This retention is not dissimilar to the manner in which flash drives save data; therefore, a proficient computer forensic examiner will ordinarily have the ability to preserve and review data stored on cell phones. Once data has been captured from a cell phone, the investigator will normally have to manually poke and prod around in the data set to identify the applications and data stores that it was using. Cell phones have had until recently rather simplistic data storage structures. This is changing somewhat with the advent of more sophisticated cell phone operating systems such as Android Ice Cream Sandwich and BlackBerry OS version 10. The systems have the ability to store data in a more traditional hierarchical fashion using directories and subdirectories that can be searched during an examination.

During investigations in which cell phones, BlackBerries, and Apple iPhones have been preserved, there is often debate as to whether it is worthwhile to undergo the effort of examining the data on these devices. Although it is true that one may learn more from examining a laptop or desktop computer of a given custodian, there is much to learn about day-to-day habits, peculiarities, and even intimate thoughts of an individual by examining the activity maintained on his or her cell phone. Never before has an individual object maintained such a comprehensive record of the owner's life. Whether one is examining the inbound and outbound phone logs or the geographical recordings of when and where a particular photograph was taken by the camera on the telephone, there is much to be learned during this examination.

On a recent case, where two executives from two competing companies were barred from speaking or communicating with each other in any fashion by a TRO (temporary restraining order), we learned that their respective wives were suddenly communicating with each other over their cell phones after the TRO had been entered. What was unusual is that we had prior testimony from both parties that the wives did not know each other. So why were they communicating? Were in fact their husbands using their respective phones in order to circumvent the court order? This fact pattern assisted in bringing a swift win for our client, but it is easy to speculate that had we not undertaken a broad-based approach to the data analysis, this important fact pattern would have gone undetected.

Audio and Video

Data can come in both audio and video formats and these file formats are becoming increasingly important in forensic investigations. In today's technological world, audio and video data can be captured by cameras, mobile phones, and other mobile devices and then stored on computers, servers, MP3 players, mobile phones, tablets, digital cameras and camcorders, video cameras, and more. In addition to the many types of devices that can record and store audio and video data, audio and video data can also be tied into social media, such as YouTube. This means that not only can the data be stored on the computer hard drive or other device, but it can also exist in the realm of Internet servers.

Audio Files

Audio file formats come in three different types. The first of these are the uncompressed audio file formats, which include PCM, WAV, AIFF, or BWF. PCM, or pulse-code modulation, files are often stored as WAV (.wav) files on the Windows operating system and as AIFF files on the Mac operating system. The AIFF is based on the Interchange File Format (IFF) and the WAV format is based on the Resource Interchange File Format (RIFF), which is similar to the IFF. In addition, the WAV and AIFF formats are flexible and ideal for creating and storing an original recording. The BWF (Broadcast Wave Format) was created as a successor to WAV and the benefit of this format is that it allows metadata to be stored within the file. Metadata can contain identifying information, such as when, where, by whom, and on what device the recording was made. BWF is generally used in the television and film industry.

The second type of audio file format is the lossless compressed audio file format. This format stores data in a manner that does away with unnecessary data that is stored in the uncompressed files. Uncompressed files store silence and sound with the same number of bits per unit of time, meaning that a minute of recorded silence would take up the same amount of space as would a minute of recorded sound.

Lossless compressed files would make the silence take up almost no space while the sound would take up less space than in an uncompressed file. Lossless compressed files include file types such as WavPack, FLAK, ALAC, and Monkey's Audio and they allow the uncompressed data to be recreated exactly as it was recorded.

The third and final type of audio file format is the lossy compressed audio file format. Lossy compressed files typically take up even less space than lossless files, but they do so by removing some of the data and in turn risking the quality of the data. However, while the quality may be compromised, in general this is imperceptible when it comes to everyday use of the data. The most commonly known forms of lossy audio data are the MP3 file format and the ACC file format found in the iTunes Music Store. There are varying degrees of compression with lossy files that are measured by bit rate. The smaller the bit rate, the smaller the file and the higher the risk of loss of quality.

Video Files

As with audio file formats, there are a number of video file formats. The reason for the large variety of video file formats is because there are many methods of compression. In general, video files are very large, and the better the resolution, the larger they are. In order to play videos on a computer, the file must be compressed, and there are a number of ways to do this. However, compression of the video file can result in a loss of quality and resolution. What follows is a description of the primary video file formats.

The first file format is known as AVCHD, which is a high-definition format that is becoming popular these days. Although this format is not good for sharing on the Internet, many video cameras these days shoot in AVCHD format, something that is not readily accepted by most software programs and, thus, is not easily edited. Another file format is AVI, which is a container or wrapper format. AVI will act as a container and hold all the other parts of the video, including both the audio and video signals. It is one of the oldest file formats and is generally compatible with most players and software programs. Next comes WMV, or Windows Media Video. WMV files are highly compressed, which means that they are very small files that have poor resolution. Since they are Windows-compatible files, they can be played on almost any player. MOV are Quicktime Movie files, which are an Apple product. These files are not as highly compressed as WMV files, which means that they are larger and have better resolution.

FLV is flash video format, which is very common because it strikes a good balance between file size and quality of resolution. It is currently the most commonly shared file format on the web. Most videos available for viewing on the Internet will be in FLV format and it is compatible with most web browsers and computers. MPEG2 is the type of file format used to store movies on DVDs and as such they are too big for the web. MPEG4 is a file format that is designed for the web and creates very small files that have decent resolution.

Storage of Audio and Video Files

Audio and video files will generally be stored on the hard drive of a computer in its compressed state. They can also be stored on a server, memory or flash drive, optical drive, external hard drive, or thumb drive, on a mobile phone, a tablet, or other mobile device, on a video recorder, and on devices such as an Apple iPod or an MP3 player. If the device itself is in the possession of forensic investigators, then the extraction of the audio and video data can be accomplished relatively easily, provided the right software is used to access and edit the file. However, if the data has been erased from the device or is strictly on the Internet, then access to the data becomes more difficult and the integrity of the data can become compromised.

When it comes to audio and video data, part of the issue with the recovery of this data is the quality of it. The quality of audio and video data depends on the device by which it was recorded and on the file format that is used to store the data. As discussed earlier, these types of files are often compressed as they are very large and would otherwise take up a lot of disc space. Compressed files, depending on the type, may result in compromised quality, something that can hinder a computer forensic investigation. Not only that, but there are so many methods of compression that it may be difficult to access and edit the data. To have audio or video evidence that is admissible in court, the file must be generally obtainable, readable, and of acceptable quality.

Because the compressed audio and visual files may be a challenge to access, it is important to use software that is compatible with as many formats as possible. The very basic requirements of a software program that can read compressed audio or video files are that it can play a file, can play a file beginning at any point within the file, can play the file at faster than normal speed and still have clear audio, and can allow certain segments to be cropped in order to isolate small portions of the recording. In addition, it is beneficial if the software can also convert the file to a standard audio or video file format, reduce the amount of background noise in audio files, add subtitles to the video, and change the brightness of a video, making it either darker or lighter. The ultimate goal of the software used is to edit the data down to a small clip that is clear, concise, and has subtitles (for video) so that it is admissible in court and will have the greatest possible impact.

The Global Nervous System: Worldwide Data

The investigative objective or purpose of an investigation is to gather factual information. Without gathering factual information, investigations would not have the ability to solve disputes, questions, or matters involving anything from missing persons to the recovery of stolen property to a dispute over a contract to a regulatory investigation. All of these types of investigations require fact-finding. Examples of the types of investigations that are likely to be managed by an investigative computer forensic professional would include employment investigations; trademark and patent infringement investigations; homicides, missing persons, and suicide investigations; slip-and-fall investigations; financial fraud; malpractice investigations; and undercover or internal investigations for private and public parties (see Exhibit 2.7).

Ultimately, regardless of the type of information one is seeking or the systems and applications that are to be queried using information technology as a tool, the

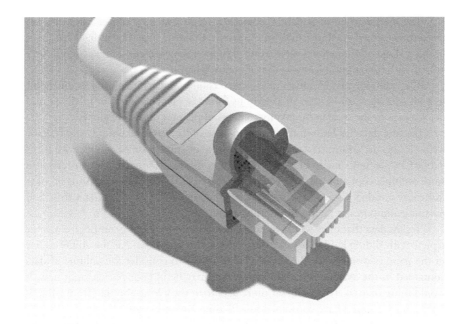

EXHIBIT 2.7   RJ-45 Ethernet Plug and Cable

The connection point of your desktop computer to a network or the Internet and the entry and egress point for much of the world's electronic communications.

ultimate goal is to establish facts and evidence. Once the facts or evidence have been firmly established by using proper process and protocol, a summary or report of those facts can be generated and provided to relevant parties. Investigative objectives in the traditional sense of investigations is no different from that of a computer forensic investigator insofar as the dispassionate observation of data and information, as well as related evidence, is required to properly encapsulate the observer's findings so that they can be provided to third parties for the purpose of disposing of a particular claim.

Where Does Data Live?: The Cybersystem

When I was born a mere five decades ago the overwhelming majority of the world's data was stored on paper (that had been written on by human beings or imprinted on by machines). Printing presses, mimeograph machines, offset printers, and photocopy machines were the norm. Data was bound. It was filed. It was annotated with handwritten notes. Data was kept in bank vaults, data warehouses, and filing cabinets. Data was to be found in my spiral notebook in my drawer and permeated the emulsion of the exposed but undeveloped Kodak film in my camera. My understanding of data was that you could touch it. You could hold and protect it. You could rip it up and throw it away.

The metamorphosis of data as something represented by objects of a tangible three-dimensional medium into an electronic pulse or a magnetic field has been nothing short of miraculous—a treasure of human achievement that has significance on par with humankind learning to walk on two legs.

The explosive manifestation of the conversion of data from an object one holds to a bit or a byte can be seen all around us from the great advances in medicine and the sciences to the sudden interconnectedness of peoples across the globe.

Because data has been unleashed from most of its terrestrial bounds and because we no longer are committed to inscribing images of animals on cave walls with rocks dabbed in pigments made of water, animal fat, dirt and charcoal, and, instead, can store multiple copies of the same data in dozens of locations each thousands of miles from one another all at the same time, the consequences of where data lives find meaning and purpose in any fact-finding exercise.

Today, data that once would require a paneled library room in an English manor replete with sliding ladders and a card catalog index of its own has the ability to live in the palm of your hand. Realistically, if you were to consider the volume of data contained in the average Apple iPhone, which may be in your pocket right now, it would more than likely contain far more data than the average human from a developed country would have consumed in a lifetime 100 years ago.

Our voracious appetite for the creation, distribution, and consumption of data as a species is on the ascendant but it is hardly satiated. On the contrary, as new data delivery and dissemination vehicles are invented, they are shortly followed by even more consuming systems. We moved from Internet bulletin boards of the early 1990s to Facebook in 2004 (where it hit its first 1 million users) and its initial public offering in 2012, carrying with it a snapshot of the cumulative data of nearly one in every eight human beings on the planet.

As the data carried by the systems that we rely on is accessed with relative ease by end-users the question that is central to an investigation is: "How do I preserve the data?" The preservation process must, however, begin with the question of: "Where is the data?"

Data on the global networks is often both transient and dynamic but it can also be relatively stable and accessible should appropriate protocols be put into place. Today, much of the world's data lives on what we refer to as *spinning discs* or in other words, *hard drives*. These hard drives are found on both personal computers as well as servers and data warehouses. It is currently estimated that global data storage has reached nearly 600 exabytes. This is equivalent to 600 billion gigabytes. To provide an illustration of how that volume of data would translate into the old-fashioned format of my childhood—books—one could blanket the entire landmass of the People's Republic of China and all of the United States in books, 13 times over. If one were to move all of that data onto CDs, a relatively recent technology, one could stack them all the way to the Earth's moon, circle it, and return to Earth.

Global storage capacity has roughly doubled every three years. Presently the world's data should fit on approximately 1.2 billion average-size hard drives. By 2018, make that 4.8 billion hard drives. But not all data lives on hard drives. In fact, there are numerous data storage technologies, which are used as primary storage media. It is estimated that although hard drives, or spinning discs, contain approximately 52 percent of all stored data, digital tape accounts for 11 percent, optical storage devices hold 28 percent, and other forms of stored data hold 9 percent. Billions of individuals around the globe contribute to this volume with their personal computers, smartphones, video cameras, tape recorders, CDs, DVDs, thumb drives, and so on, but there are also large concentrations of data in what are known as *data centers*. These centers provide massive data storage and processing capabilities to every conceivable type of service from Google.com to United Airlines Reservation system, from the clearinghouses for commodities trading to the centralized medical records that your insurance company relies on.

These data centers can be found throughout the world and serve as supernodes on the global interconnected networks such as the Internet. Among the largest data centers is 350 East Cermak in Chicago, Illinois, which maintains 1.1 million square feet of data storage capacity. This facility leases space to companies to store their servers that store their data, and in most cases those servers are connected via the Internet to the outside world. These facilities are commonly referred to as *colocation facilities*, or *colos*, and can house tens or hundreds of thousands of servers. Other significant colos include QTS Data Center in Atlanta, Georgia, with 990,000 square feet, NAP of the Americas in Florida with 750,000 square feet, Next Generation Data in Wales with 750,000 square feet, and the Microsoft Data Center in Dublin, Ireland, with 550,000 square feet. In all, there are hundreds of these facilities of various sizes and capabilities all over the planet.

At present most of these colocation facilities are storing data on magnetic hard drives, which contain spinning discs. Present technologies commonly will allow for 2-terabyte drives to populate the servers that are hosted on many of these servers. Due to the constant and unflinching demand for more storage in smaller and faster environments it is expected that the density of these discs will continue to evolve until such a time that the physical properties of magnetism are leveraged to their maximum capacity. Scientists estimate that we are in fact closing in on this point of maximum capacity with current technology and thus we should expect the advent of new mechanisms for storing greater volumes of data in even smaller spaces.

One promising new technology was announced by IBM in 2012 where the magnetic bits on the surface of the hard drive have been reduced to their atomic level and it is now possible to create a bit of data out of only 12 atoms. As a result it is expected that we will see in the not-too-distant future hard drives that can have as much as 400 terabytes of data on a single drive. For comparison's sake, as of April 2011, the United States Library of Congress maintains 235 terabytes of data and adds approximately 5 terabytes of new data every month. I would also expect that as a result of these higher densities you will see further advances in the miniaturization of flash storage technology and you will see 1-terabyte flash drives, which are small enough to be embedded into your bifocals, thereby allowing for an entirely new data-viewing experience.

So while data can live on hard drives of increasing density it can also live in multiple places at once. Due to the manner in which Internet storage and communications is managed it is entirely possible and actually expected that data created on your laptop in the form of an e-mail that is subsequently sent to another individual will not only live on both machines but also may live on backup tapes, archives, the storage of your mail server and the recipient's mail server, and possibly in the unallocated space of the physical hard drives of each of these systems as the e-mail is being processed.

As a result of the data living in so many places, there are a number of opportunities for fact-finders to discover the location, purpose, properties, and content of data either partially or in total given the right tools, capabilities, and access to preserve the data prior to its destruction.

In the context of an investigation, the question, "Where is the data?" permeates all activities. Because of the dynamic and at times fragile nature of digital data one can never truly be free of the risks of data destruction, spoliation, or alteration. Efforts to counter these issues go hand in hand with the efforts to simply identify where data may live. Developing an understanding of the data habitat is only the beginning of what can be an arduous trek through the cybersystem to actually locate and preserve the data in a pristine state.

Computer forensics provides the platform by which investigators are able to identify and to preserve data throughout the cybersystem; however, it is often the case that computer forensic professionals cannot complete their work without the direct assistance of other information technology professionals with specific domain expertise or access rights.

Fundamentals of Network Traffic

Nearly all investigations today deal with computers or devices that are communicating with the one another over networks. There are a number of different types of networks with which computer forensic investigators will need to be familiar, including a wide area network also known as a *WAN*. This is a term that refers to networks that are able to connect disparate networks or geographically dissimilar networks. Another common network term is a *LAN*, which is a local area network and is generally an enclosed network within one confined geographic area, such as an office or home. Another type of network that is often dealt with is a wireless local area network known as a *WLAN*. This is a network made up of devices that are connected to wireless technologies, such as 802.11 G and N.

In addition to these types of networks, examiners are also confronted with peer-to-peer networks, which are networks in which each user and system configures its own resources and connects to other components of the network. Another type of network is known as an intranet, which is essentially a corporate local area network that leverages Internet protocols and applications, such as web servers, for communication. Finally, the most ubiquitous network of them all is the Internet, which is yet another network that one will come across during investigations.

The Internet essentially is the largest WAN and it uses its own set of transmission control protocols, known as TCP/IP. This allows communications to take place across disparate systems and platforms, software, and computers because of the standardized communication protocol. The TCP/IP address, also known as an IP address or

Internet protocol address, is a 32-bit phrase, which means that it holds four bytes of data and the address will normally appear in a dotted decimal format, such as 23.52.98.189. Each decimal number can range from 0 to 255.

An important tool during the investigation of activities or events that have taken place on a network, whether large or small, is the ability to diagram and map that network. Network maps will illustrate the physical and logical location of the various devices, along with your IP addresses, Mac addresses, and other unique identifiers. These network maps help provide a visual and graphical illustration for the attorneys, investigators, and other interested parties so that they can better understand the relationship between devices in people's environments and activities or actions that took place on the network.

These network maps can also be integrated with timelines, which would run from left to right and provide time and dates for activities that are taking place on the network or within the environment that is being investigated. Because so many of the activities that take place in an investigation involve either the Internet or network activity, as well as simply activity on a single computer, visualizing those events using network diagrams or maps and graphical timelines will go a long way to establishing clarity for the audience so that they may understand with greater certainty the events you have uncovered.

The Firewall

The firewall gets its name from what was considered the original definition of the word: a wall that was designed to contain a fire in a specific part of a building. In the computing world, the technology behind the firewall was put into use in the late 1980s, a time when the Internet was fairly new. Since the introduction of the firewall, when there were attacks on Internet security that no one was prepared to deal with, firewall technology has undergone a transformation that has led to the technology in use today.

Before describing the various stages of firewall development, it is important to understand that the goal of the firewall is to filter incoming communications, data transmissions, and access in order to allow legitimate communications and access to pass through and block those that do not have the authorization to do so. The firewall is set up between the Internet and the computer network and can come in the form of software or hardware. Most PCs have operating systems that have a built-in firewall. Routers can also act as a firewall. In fact, the very first firewall protection was offered by the routers used in the late 1980s. A brief history of their development is helpful when trying to understand how they function.

Firewall History

The first type of firewall to be used was referred to as a *packet filter*. It was developed in 1988 and eventually led to a sophisticated system of computer security. The information sent between computers via the Internet was formed into "packets" and each packet was passed through a packet filter. If it did not pass a defined set of rules, this packet of information was rejected.

The next step up from packet filters was known as *stateful filters*. Unlike the packet filters, which looked at each packet of information as an isolated piece of data rather than part of a whole, the stateful filter of a circuit-level firewall was able to include filter criteria based on the position of the information packet within the stream of data being sent. The filter was able to detect whether the packet was connected with a stream. Unfortunately, a firewall with a stateful filter could be overwhelmed if it was sent many nonconnected packets. This could ultimately cause a breach in the security of the system.

The third and final type of firewall is the application layer firewall. This firewall detects applications and protocols and filters incoming information based on what is allowable and what is not. An application layer firewall can be customized by adding and/or removing filters that are based on a number of factors. These include, but are not limited to, IP address, domain names, ports, and defined words and phrases. For example, a firewall can be set to filter out any data or information coming from a certain IP address or a certain domain name. Another example is a filter that is set such that all computers except one will be blocked from accessing the FTP port.

The Need for a Firewall

There are many different threats to the security of a computer, whether those threats are personal attacks against one person, against a company, or against all computers connected to the Internet. The most commonly known threat to a computer or a group of computers is what is known as a *virus*, which is a program that can copy itself over and over again and spread itself to many computers. These viruses can be relatively harmless, or they can be designed to wipe a hard drive clean. However, there are a number of other threats that a firewall stops, including spam, e-mail bombs, denial of service (which causes a server to slow down or crash), remote login to a computer or network, macros, redirect bombs, and source routing.

Many of the threats listed earlier are difficult to stop with a firewall alone, but the most common practice is to begin by blocking everything and then select what you will allow through the firewall. In addition, one of the very best things about a firewall is that no one outside the organization can log into a computer from a remote location. This is incredibly important when it comes to the operation of computer forensic investigations as it protects the integrity of the evidence that is stored on the computer forensic server.

The Proxy Server

A proxy server is something that is usually teamed up with a firewall for added protection. This is a server that acts as a buffer between a computer and the Internet. When a computer has requested access to a web page, the proxy is what actually retrieves the web page and then sends it on to the computer. The proxy server can also store web pages in its cache, and this will ensure that it can be recalled faster in the future because it doesn't have to be reloaded.

Demilitarized Zone

What if remote access should be allowed only for some things, such as FTP or for managing the company website? This is easy to do by setting up a demilitarized zone (DMZ). The purpose of a DMZ is to ensure that those areas for which remote access should be granted are actually located outside of the firewall. This might be one computer that is set up between the Internet and the firewall. Firewall software generally allows the user to create a directory that is outside the firewall.

Data- and Traffic-Gathering Applications

Data- and traffic-gathering applications, or computer monitoring applications, include Internet bots, botnets, spyware, and sniffers. These are software applications that are designed specifically for the purpose of crawling around a computer, network, or even the Internet to extract information and to work at a rate that is faster than a human can perform. There are many different uses for computer monitoring applications. Some of these uses are designed for utilitarian and administrative needs, and others are designed for malicious data capture and can be remotely monitored and sometimes remotely installed without the user's knowledge.

Internet Bots

Internet bots, also known as *web bots* or simply *bots*, are software applications that are designed to run simple automated tasks that are repetitive and are required to run at a rate that is faster than a human can handle. These tasks vary greatly in their uses. However, one of the most popular uses for bots is what is known as *web spiders* or *web crawlers*. These crawlers are scripts that obtain information from web servers in a methodical manner and then analyze and file away this information.

A good example of the use of this technology is when search engines use it for the purpose of indexing all the pages that exist on the World Wide Web. These crawlers go through and make a copy of each website they visit. This copy will then be analyzed by the search engine and the downloaded pages will be indexed. Once these web pages are indexed, they will show up on the search engines and any keyword or key phrase typed into a search engine will bring up the results faster when sites are properly indexed. These web crawlers can also be used to check HTML code or to gather information from web pages, such as e-mail addresses, which can then be used for sending spam.

Bots can also be used in situations where a faster-than-human response is required, such as with gaming or auction sites. A more recent application of bots is search advertising, such as with Google AdSense. Bots can also be used maliciously in a number of ways. As mentioned earlier, they can be used to gather e-mail addresses from websites for the purpose of sending spam. They can also be used to collect content from websites so that this content can be reused without permission, to download entire websites, to automate the process of entering a sweepstakes to gain an advantage, and for various other purposes.

Botnets

Botnets are a specific use of bots. *Bot* is shorthand for *robot* while *net* is shorthand for *network*, hence, a robotic network. Software is installed on a computer and it turns that computer into a bot that joins a network of other bots. This network of bots is then controlled by what is known as the *botmaster* or *botherder*. This botmaster accumulates a lot of power by controlling hundreds, thousands, or even millions of computers behind the scenes. These bots under his or her control can be used to perform a number of malicious attacks in concert with one another and in a variety of configurations. For instance, the botnet can be programmed to attack a single IP address with requests at once or programmed to make requests to a series of databases that feed an online system, such as the Internal Revenue Service's online filing system. One of the most common uses for botnets is what is referred to as distributed denial-of-service (DDoS) attacks. DDoS occurs when numerous computers are used to send information or requests to a specific website with the result of effectively overloading the bandwidth or using up the computational resources of that site so that legitimate traffic cannot access the site. In addition to DDoS there are a large number of other uses to which botnets are put, including spamming, click fraud, and even the more serious crimes of theft of login IDs, application serial numbers, and financial information, such as credit card numbers and bank account numbers. These botnets can install spyware or adware on a computer or be used for phishing or the storage of criminal material and information.

Spyware

Spyware is a form of malware (malicious software) that is installed on a computer and then collects information from that computer without the owner having any knowledge of what is happening. Spyware is designed to remain hidden on the computer and can be very difficult to detect. In its simplest form, spyware that has been installed on a PC will allow remote access to a network through that computer and it can collect information from said computer. This information can include a list of websites that were visited, personal information, and Internet surfing habits. However, spyware can do so much more. It can interfere with or redirect a browser and can install software on the computer, both of which can interfere with the user's control of the computer. One example of spyware is called a *keylogger*. A keylogger records every keystroke made by a user, and this information is reported back to the source of the spyware. Often in cases of spyware use, the information gathered via spyware is sold to third parties who have need of the information.

Sniffers

Sniffers are a type of spyware, but they are generally designed to monitor networks, rather than a single computer. As with spyware, they can be designed to gather information, such as login IDs, passwords, credit card information, and bank account numbers. Information of this nature can then be used to access the bank accounts of others, create fraudulent bank accounts, gain remote access to a network, and gather sensitive information.

Detection of Computer Monitoring Software

The unauthorized presence of any bot, spyware, or other type of data-gathering software on a computer or system is in most cases illegal, but in many instances these amount to not much more than a nuisance. However, there are cases in which the use of these software applications is intended for larger crimes against individuals, corporations, or government agencies. The very first step in the fight against computer monitoring software is prevention. Having a properly configured firewall, disabling unused ports and services, ensuring that passwords are up-to-date and complex, ensuring that systems are up-to-date and tested on a regular basis, and ensuring that users are made aware of the existence of things such as bots and spyware will help prevent malicious software from being installed on your computers or systems.

If any computer monitoring software has been successfully installed on a computer or network, it can remain undetected for a long time. However, there are some indicators that will alert a user to a possible infection. Computers should be scanned regularly to test for the presence of malware. Logs should be monitored for anomalies on a consistent basis. Watching for anomalous traffic or high levels of traffic is also important. Organizations can use their own form of sniffer, a network sniffer, to determine what server and channels are being used by the malicious software. If malicious software is suspected, as long as it is created on a fixed server, the channels and shell account can be closed. If software is using a dynamic address, then the address can be null routed, which means it goes nowhere.

When it comes to a computer forensic investigation involving bots, botnets, or spyware, data collection and analysis can be done offline or live. If done offline, the data should first be transferred to a clean, new hard drive. If performed online, then a log should be kept of all changes in the network and host system. A technique referred to as a *honeynet* is popular and effective. A honeynet is a series of computers that act as bait for the malicious software that can detect and log the activity of malicious software. The honeynets and their communication with the host server can be monitored by a honeywall, which is a combination of a firewall and an intrusion detection system (IDS). This will allow investigators to learn more about the specific intrusion software.

Dynamic Data Capture

As the cybersystem continues its march toward ubiquitous cloud computing environments investigators will be faced with new data identification and preservation challenges due to the transitory and migratory nature of the data of interest. Traditional computer forensics allows for the physical capture and preservation of an actual hard drive or device. But what happens when the data of interest is fleeting, momentary, or available for capture only during transmission? These issues have been addressed by using a variety of technologies from packet sniffers to intrusion detection systems and firewalls or even keylogging software. The challenge for the investigator is to capture data while it is being transmitted in real time. This is normally due to the inability of the investigator to gain access to the machine that the data is being created on or the machine that the data may be sent to.

Examples include matters where an internal investigation must be brought to bear against employees suspected of the theft of trade secrets. If a suspected employee is using his Internet access within the corporation to move files off of corporate servers and onto off-site storage facilities such as DropBox or an FTP site, it may be challenging to capture direct evidence of this behavior. The usage of keylogging software is one simple method for monitoring behavior and capturing evidence for analysis. Keyloggers can be purchased as either a piece of software that would be loaded on a target machine or a hardware device that would be inserted on the physical machine itself, ordinarily through a USB port.

Once a keylogger is activated it will record each and every keystroke undertaken on the keyboard of the machine by any user. Some keyloggers will record the activity and allow you to review it once you have physical access to the machine or to the keylogger itself. Others will send real-time or batch reports to a designated location by e-mail, FTP, or other network protocol so that activity can be monitored as it is happening. The obvious investigative advantages of using keyloggers cannot be overstated as the investigator will learn of passwords, usernames, and a host of other activity that would ordinarily be unobtainable. It is important to note, however, that there are serious privacy and legality issues associated with the use of keyloggers, and it is vital that investigators review and detail their obligations under local and federal statutes as well as other possible civil agreements that would prevent their use prior to using such a device. Often corporations have obtained agreement from their employees that there is no expectation of privacy while that employee is using company equipment and networks. However, investigators should not only rely on these commercial agreements in determining whether they should move forward with devices such as keyloggers; rather they should also work with counsel to clearly establish what if any legal guidelines have been set within that jurisdiction governing this type of monitoring.

Although keyloggers are effective, easy to obtain, and easy to deploy there are a number of other methods for real-time dynamic capture of data on systems and networks, including a number of industrial-strength software and hardware utilities that have been designed and manufactured by some of the largest names in the computer industry. Tools such as Access Data's "SilentRunner Sentinel," which was originally developed by Raytheon in the 1990s for the purpose of monitoring network traffic in real time in stealth mode, invisible to all users, is now available as a commercial product. Its investigative application is far reaching as it promiscuously monitors and records network traffic in all seven layers of the Open Systems Interconnection stack. This includes the application, presentation, session, transport, network, data link, and physical layers.

SilentRunner's capabilities allow investigators to visualize, capture, and replay the movement of electronic data across and throughout networks much in the same fashion as one would visualize a traffic map of a highway system. The system once implemented can capture any traffic on a network and remain entirely invisible and undetectable to the end-users. Activity is recorded in centralized databases, which will allow for the reconstruction of events. Systems such as SilentRunner have the ability to capture electronic data in unique situations such as when the investigation calls for the real-time monitoring of VoIP telephonic traffic (Voice over IP) and other types of data carried over the Internet in real time where there would be no memorialization of the data on the transmission or receiving end.

Because of the complexity of systems such as SilentRunner, it is normally necessary for computer forensic investigators to work with the local information technology staff of a target company to most effectively implement this tool and others like it. This wide disparity of ease of use between a simple keylogger and SilentRunner should not, however, negate the effectiveness of the former. In proper hands each of these tools has specific investigative benefits that can help identify bad acts and foul play in real time.

Cloud computing environments add a layer of complexity to the task of the investigator of dynamic data because of the technical and legal limitations of monitoring these remote third-party systems. However, in many cases these cloud providers will have baked-in tools for data and systems monitoring from a data management perspective that can be co-opted for effective investigative use. These include various systems activity logs, firewalls, intrusion detection systems (IDSs), archival systems, and application monitoring software, which may by default or by modification capture relevant data that can be subsequently analyzed by a computer forensic technician for particular activity or evidence.

The Cloud

The cloud, or cloud computing, refers to a new way of using computer and IT technology and programming in the business environment and it is all the rage in the computing world. In essence, cloud computing is simply relegating computing and information technology to a service, rather than a product. Up until recently, companies and businesses buy products. They purchase the IT infrastructure, the hardware, software, platforms, networking, and anything else required to meet their computing needs.

Cloud computing can be likened to a utility service, such as "water and power." In fact, in the 1960s, John McCarthy said, "Computation may someday be organized as a public utility." The person or company who buys the service from the provider does not need any knowledge regarding the location or source of the service.

The idea behind the service is that it is pay-per-use and, therefore, is more economically feasible in light of today's economy. The cloud does away with the need for the company to put out money for hardware and software as the applications are stored on central servers and managed, updated, upgraded, and maintained by the provider. It also means that companies can often provide their customers with services that they may not otherwise be able to afford.

Cloud Layers

The cloud has five layers and once a connection is established between multiple computers via an Internet protocol connection (IPC) services can be shared between them over any one of these layers. The first layer is the client, which is the hardware and/or software that relies on the cloud. Without the cloud the client is virtually useless.

With SaaS (software as a service), the user will have access to the provider's applications over a network. This means that instead of installing software on his or her own system, the user simply pays for the use of the software over the Internet. The software is flexible and can be scaled according to the needs of the user.

With PaaS (platform as a service), the user will be able to pay for the use of a platform and/or solution stack, which will eliminate the need for the required hardware and software to be purchased, installed, and managed/maintained at their end. The PaaS allows users to create and deploy applications to the cloud and they can use services delivered by the cloud.

With IaaS (infrastructure as a service), the user will lease a number of resources, including network capacity, storage, processing, and anything else that is required. This eliminates the need for the user to purchase, install, and manage and maintain servers, network equipment, data center space, and software. The user is billed in the manner of a utility and the cost will depend on the frequency and level of use.

The server is the layer that consists of all the hardware and/or software that is designed to ensure the cloud services can be delivered to the user. This might include multicore processors, operating systems designed for cloud operation, and any other products that are required.

Cloud Delivery and Deployment

In addition to the layers, there are four models for deployment:

1. **Private cloud.** This internal cloud is secure and set up behind a firewall and is owned or leased by a single entity.
2. **Public cloud.** This external cloud is sold to the public, not necessarily secure, and ordinarily rolled out on a large scale.
3. **Hybrid cloud.** This is a virtual private cloud that is the combination of two or more clouds.
4. **Community cloud.** This is a cloud that is used for a shared infrastructure by a specific community, such as the academic community or a nonprofit organization.

Cloud Architecture

In simple terms, cloud computing can be divided into two broad sections: the front end and the back end. The front end is the client—the individual or company—that is paying for use of applications and other elements in the cloud. This leaves the back end, which is the cloud itself, comprised of all the hardware and software required by the user.

There are multiple and differing components of the cloud that communicate with each other. This communication is accommodated via messaging queues or other such loose coupling mechanisms. There is also the possibility of having a cloud within a cloud, which exists on a global scale.

Potential Challenges with Cloud Computing

There are a number of challenges relating to cloud computing that have been identified by the computing community. These include issues with privacy, security, legality, and compliance. When it comes to computer forensics, there are a number of issues that are unique to this discipline. First and foremost of these is the fact that investigators do not have direct access to the hard drives and this means that when it comes to accessing and handling data and potential evidence, there are potential issues regarding the risk of contamination and the legal handling of data that is to be submitted as evidence of a crime or in litigation. The cloud, however, is here to stay and represents an important step toward leveraging concentrated centers of technology for the purpose of reducing the requirement that every company and individual have a significant investment in software and hardware as well as the education that goes along with managing it. As the cloud continues to develop, so too will the tools needed to preserve data housed on it.

International Data Security and Privacy Issues

The application of security and privacy standards around the world has failed to keep pace with the stunning advances in data proliferation. Numerous initiatives have taken shape that address various aspects of privacy and security; however, they have for the most part been developed based on the specific requirements of the country or jurisdiction crafting them as opposed to omnibus protocols that are universal and applicable across all states.

Countries such as Japan and Taiwan have adopted national data privacy policies, which are different from those found in Malaysia, South Korea, and Thailand. Similarly each of the European countries have adopted data privacy regimens, each slightly different. Overlaying those European nations that are part of the European Union is the European Data Privacy Directive, which attempts to bring harmony across the board.

Computer forensic investigators need to be particularly aware of the data privacy issues within the jurisdiction in which they are working and within the context of data that they may be collecting, which is either outside of their jurisdiction or subject to the privacy regulations of another country or state, as significant civil or criminal liability may be at stake.

Vulnerabilities and Threats

One of the reasons computer forensic examiners have so much work on their plates is because the world at large relies on computing devices for communications, commerce, and every other conceivable human interaction. In the not-too-distant past, a decade or so ago, most conversations were still conducted either in person or by telephone. Banking took place within the four walls of the branch, in front of a teller or perhaps at an ATM. Commerce took place in retail stores or a cashier took your money, which by the way, was often cash or perhaps a handwritten check, in addition to the now-ubiquitous credit cards. The social barriers, structures, and rules that have fallen and been reshaped over the past decade were still well in place, but as humankind has relied more and more on the capabilities of electronic devices and networks, so too, have the inherent vulnerabilities in these systems made themselves evident to those who wish to exploit them, and clearly to the victims as well.

The role of the computer forensic examiner is not only to combat corporate fraud or to assist in the investigation of criminal activity, but in a more altruistic perspective, the computer forensic examiner provides the last line of reality and observation by the human race into events and activities that are more compounded by the opaque and intangible world of electrons and their combined computing manifestations. Vulnerabilities are found throughout the computing world, whether it be within the laptop on your desk, the software it runs, the integrated circuits and chips that allow your desk speakerphone to function, the GPS wireless function on your handheld camera, the downloaded application on your iPhone, the Bluetooth component of the speaker headphones in your car's backseat entertainment system and onboard vehicle computer, or the pacemaker embedded in your chest and the wireless device on the desk of the doctor who regulates it.

Vulnerabilities within a system are the result of the confluence of three primary concepts: a system's susceptibility to the vulnerability of an institutional flaw, the hacker's access to that vulnerability or susceptibility, and, finally, the hacker's capability or willingness to exploit that vulnerability. These three elements combine to define the essence of many of the technical challenges that are faced by hardware and software manufacturers and providers today, but more importantly, this is the inflection point that gives meaning to the fears that so many of us have in this brave new world of technology and is the ground on which computer forensic investigators find themselves.

CHAPTER 3

Computer Forensic Fundamentals

The practice of computer forensics requires a great deal of structure to support the process, which must be predictable, repeatable, and documentable. But on the other hand, there needs to be enough flexibility within the structure that an investigator can still apply intuition, creativity, and the occasional professional hunch.

This section presents an overview of three primary computer forensic fundamentals issues:

1. This first issue is called the *safe zone*, and it deals with the establishment of a computer forensic laboratory and the necessary structure, tools, and personnel required for its efficient operation.
2. Second, I review what I call the *human quotients*, which are the various players in a computer forensic investigation such as the network engineer, the plaintiff, the attorney, the researcher, the judge, and the client. Each of these parties plays a distinctive, important role in the process from the perspective of the computer forensic investigator and in this section I attempt to provide a cursory overview of where they fit.
3. The final section deals with miscellaneous issues (see "The Devil Is in the Details") where I highlight a number of challenges and pitfalls that are often overlooked at the start of an engagement, but which can doom it to failure if not addressed in a sensible way.

The Establishment of the Computer Forensic Laboratory

The computer forensic lab is a safe zone. It is a location where electronic data can be managed, preserved, and accessed in a controlled environment, where there is a reduced risk of damage or modification to the evidence, and where computer forensic examiners will have the tools close at hand that are necessary for them to elicit meaningful data from the devices that they are examining. See Exhibit 3.1.

There are many elements to the forensic lab, including the technicians, management, the policies and procedures, the forms and checklists, the evidence inventory control, the technology, the hardware, the software, the physical location, the access rules, the supplies, and all the other elements. Each of these is designed to provide the forensic technician with the required tools and environment to meet the needs of an investigation or requests from litigation, regulators, or management of organizations that are seeking to ferret out the meaning behind activity that is documented in the usage of computers and attached systems and to preserve electronic evidence that can be presented to validate or challenge a given position.

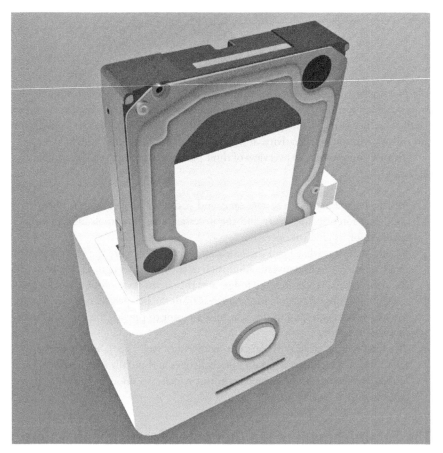

EXHIBIT 3.1 A "Toaster" Box That Can Allow a Computer Forensic Investigator to Quickly Access a Hard Drive

These devices can be attached to a computer forensic workstation by USB or FireWire and can also be mounted in front of a write blocker, allowing for easy access to multiple drives during an investigation.

The Physical Requirements of the Computer Forensic Lab

The establishment of a computer forensic laboratory is one of the first steps in building out an environment that will support the proper preservation, collection, and analysis of electronic data. The computer forensic laboratory does not need to be a 10,000-square-foot high-tech facility but can be as small as a one-room facility that has the appropriate controls in place to serve its function. In fact, a computer forensic lab could even reside in a mobile unit, such as within the cargo area of a truck or an airplane; but for the most part computer forensic laboratories will exist in a building and will be comprised of one or several rooms that will allow for secure work that needs to take place during the course of the examination of electronic data.

Establishing this safe zone prior to conducting computer forensic work is important from a number of perspectives, including ensuring that you have put the requisite forethought into the layout and design of the workspace and through the various aspects of the workflow, and how electronic evidence as well as physical evidence will be handled and managed.

One of the fundamental aspects of the computer forensic laboratory is its distinguished and separate security protocol. A computer forensic laboratory should have highly restricted physical and network access, and there should be appropriate controls in place preventing individuals who are unauthorized from accessing the facility through a door or any other physical entry as well as by electronic means such as wireless networks, wired networks, or any other telecommunications method with the exception of telephone. Having the ability to show that forethought was placed into the process of the design of the lab to an inquiring party may be instrumental in ensuring that you can establish the sanctity of the electronic data, which is entrusted within the computer forensic lab.

When designing your lab it may be necessary to have Internet connectivity to certain workstations; however, it's important that these workstations are not connected to the workstations that are managing or analyzing electronic data or evidence. Maintaining a clear and distinct separation between systems that are analyzing data versus systems that are used for correspondence, e-mail, research, and the general management of a practice is important.

There have been occasions where persons working on the opposing side have tried to access computer forensic analysts' systems and either corrupt, tamper with, or delete data that they are working on. Although this may be a remote possibility and an extreme condition, removing the capability of an outsider to access your systems is important in establishing the validity of data and evidence that you are managing. It is quite easy for a computer forensic lab to quickly grow beyond its initial anticipated size and capabilities. Managing one large case or even several small cases can rapidly tax the available resources of a small to moderately sized computer forensic lab. Therefore, giving consideration and thought to the expandability and interoperability of the technology at the beginning of the design phase will pay dividends down the road.

Often a small forensic lab will start with two forensic workstations and will also have a network-attached storage (NAS). This NAS is essentially a repository for maintaining large volumes of data and images from machines that are collected in the field. It is recommended when designing a computer forensic lab at the beginning to give thought to how the forensic workstations may need to be expanded and whether your network capacity and attached storage or external servers can handle the volume of data that you expect to manage.

I also recommend when designing a computer forensic lab that you think about how you will manage the administrative aspects of the lab. For instance, when investigators are required to write reports outlining their findings, should that function take place on the administrative computers or on the forensic computers themselves? In my experience, separating the forensic computers from the administration computers can remove potential errors and mismanagement of forensic data. Maintaining a separation between these two functions also removes an area of attack that your forensic experts may sustain while testifying on their findings.

Some of the primary areas that should be considered when designing a forensic lab include the following concepts:

- **Availability.** Consider whether your network and your systems can sustain failures or disruptions and what your path is for restoration, backup, and failover should you sustain hardware failures or software corruption. It is important that a forensic lab can maintain operations even in the event of a critical failure of one of the components of the system. It's understood that there may be downtime and contemporary analysis or that processing may need to be rerun, but if the availability question has been addressed in advance of operating your forensic lab, you'll reduce the risks associated with technology failures.
- **Performance.** One of the bottlenecks that is quickly identified in computer forensic lab operations is associated with the processing of large volumes of data. Often events on the ground or in the investigation require that the computer forensic professionals process and analyze the data as quickly as possible. When hardware bottlenecks exist the process can be unnecessarily slowed, thereby diminishing the effectiveness of the overall investigation. Early investment in robust processing power and capabilities on your computer forensic workstations and servers that are assisting with the work load is an important step that will pay off quickly. It is also recommended that the physical network installed in the forensic lab have the bandwidth and capacity to manage significant volumes of data moving across the network at all times.
- **Security.** Every computer forensic lab requires a security protocol that accounts for both internal controls and protections from external threats. These threats may be environmental or human. Depending on the location, mandate, and environment of the forensic lab, there may be a different set of security-related issues to contend with. Physical security-related issues such as doors, access points, windows, and all other points of possible ingress/egress, including ceilings,

should be considered and sufficiently secured to meet the mandate of the lab. The sanctity of the evidence, the security of the professionals working in the lab, and the confidentiality of the work product and work environment are all issues that must be considered. It is not uncommon to have labs that have keypad-driven electronic doors, biometric or two-factor authentication systems, or even separate fire-retardant systems and bulletproof doors and glass. The lab must be functional, and it is important to not let the security protocol become so onerous that it will impede the ability of the team to work effectively.

Operational Requirements of the Forensic Lab

As discussed earlier, the forensic lab must have a number of controls in place to ensure that the integrity of the data that is contained within the lab is maintained and so that the processes that are undertaken by the technicians, managers, or investigators within the lab are defensible, repeatable, and clear. The operational requirements of the lab also need to be integrated into the organization or environment within which the lab finds itself.

For example, a forensic lab that is operating within a police facility will have one set of operational requirements, and a lab that is operating within a corporate environment will have another. The forensic lab that is part of a private investigator's office will have yet another set of operational requirements that need to be factored into its design, construction, and operation.

Questions that could be asked when setting up the lab include: Is it required for the forensic lab to have 24/7 access? Is it required to have Internet access? Is it required to have an inventory of hard drives on hand, and if so, how many should be anticipated for contemporary work or future investigations? Is it okay to have five hard drives that are two gigabytes each in size or is it necessary to have 150 hard drives of a terabyte each? These are the types of questions that should be asked during the process of setting up a forensic lab so that it will be effective and useful in its mandate.

Evidence and Access Controls

Control over evidence and access is the responsibility of any individual working in the lab as a technician, assistant manager, or investigator, and maintaining these controls requires constant diligence. Among the first sets of controls that should be instituted within a lab is the physical security of the lab itself. If the lab has a door, then it must have a lock, and anyone who has access to the lab must be known to the lab manager. If a lab has a door with a simple key lock, then there should be a limited number of keys for that lock and those keys should be marked with a "Do Not Duplicate" stamp. The keys should be assigned to registered users and associated with a number so that the lab manager will know to whom each one of the keys is assigned. See Exhibit 3.2.

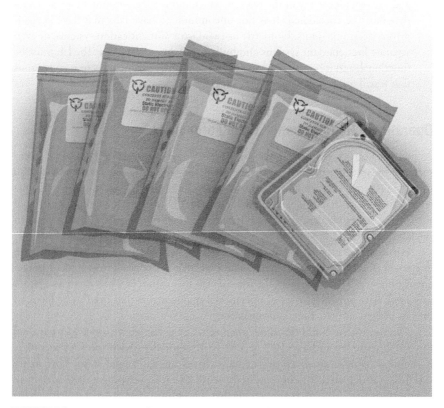

EXHIBIT 3.2   A Collection of Evidentiary Forensic Hard Drive Masters Collected While On-Site at a Factory

Each of the drives is properly packaged in an antistatic tamperproof evidence bag for transportation and is attached to a chain-of-custody form and a data acquisition form.

It's possible for a lab door to have an electronic lock, which will register each time the door is opened or closed. Preferably, that registration will correspond to the user by the use of a key card or other device. Some labs go so far as to have biometric locks, which require an individual to place a thumb on a thumbprint reader, or a forefinger on a finger reader, or even more complicated devices, such as an iris scanner that scans the eye of an individual or the full hand print of an individual's hand. If a lab has a door, then it should be locked. If a lab has a window, there should be a lock on it as well. Entry and exit points need to be controlled.

If the lab has a drop ceiling, then it should be secured so that an individual cannot climb into the lab from an adjoining office by removing tiles from the ceiling and then climbing into the lab. The building code should ensure that the walls between adjoining offices and labs be constructed so that they continue all the way up to the ceiling. Regardless, methods must be taken or some device installed to ensure that individuals cannot access the lab via the ceiling or even through the floor, on the rare occasion that there is floor access.

Once the physical perimeter of the lab has been secured, attention needs to be given to the electronic network that is accessed by the lab. Although it is often important for forensic lab technicians to access the Internet for a wide variety of reasons, such as conducting investigative research, downloading software, and more, it is vital that the forensic workstations that contain evidence are not connected to the Internet and that they are prevented from accessing the Internet, except under specific circumstances that can be controlled and documented.

In most cases, a good forensic lab will have an internal stand-alone network that connects the forensic workstations to each other, as well as to other specific devices, such as printers, mass storage servers, and other computing equipment that will allow the forensic examiner to do the required job. However, to the extent that is possible, the forensic network within the lab should not be connected to the network of the corporation, the building in which the lab is located, or to broader global networks, such as the Internet.

Fundamental to the control of evidence within the lab is a proper evidence numbering system, a chain-of-custody system, and a process by which physical evidence can be locked into an evidence safe, locker, or vault. Evidence numbering in a basic computer forensic lab can be a very simple system, such as starting with the number 0001; but as computer forensic labs take on more evidence and have relationships with other computer forensic labs, or other individuals supporting that lab over broad geographies, the numbering system may become more complex. For example, an evidence numbering system may include a letter representing the city, a letter or number to identify the lab, or a number representing the case or matter. It might also include a date or year, representative of when the matter was opened, and it may include a client name or number.

An example of a numbering scheme that we've used in the past is as follows: L for Los Angeles, 2013 for the year, and 006 for the client (the sixth client on our list of clients for that year), 001 for the case number for that client in that year and for that lab, followed by a sequential number such as 001, indicating the item number for that case, and then by a hyphen and MC for master copy or WC for working copy. As I've covered elsewhere, master copy refers to the original evidence that has been captured through forensic collection. It is not the original evidence itself, but a copy of the original evidence. The evidence number can also have an "o," representing original evidence, if you have assigned an evidence number to a computer or to a piece of evidence that is been provided to you by the client.

A working copy refers to the copy of the master copy that the computer forensic examiner will use for the examination. All evidence needs to be tracked either by hand on a worksheet, on a Microsoft Excel spreadsheet, in a database such as SQL, or within the context of a specially designed evidence-tracking application, of which there are several. I should note that many labs choose to create their own database, using some simple programming in SQL or Microsoft Access. With a decent interface one can create their own evidence-tracking database with relative ease, one that will address the specific needs of their own lab, or finally, one can opt to purchase a prebuilt evidence tracking system such as Evidence Tracker (www.evidencetracker.com), ASAP Evidence Tracker (www.asapsystems.com), or JusticeTrax (www.justicetrax.com) to name a few.

The second area I mentioned is chain of custody. Chain of custody needs to apply to all original evidence, all master copy evidence, and depending on the needs of the case, all working copy evidence. A chain of custody is a document that is attached to the evidence and stays with that evidence for as long as the lab has custody and control of the evidence. Its primary components should be the date of the creation of the document, the name of the client or individual you are serving, a description of the evidence that is being held, a description of the reason for its transfer from Point A to Point B, and a listing of each person who had physical control over that evidence.

A chain of custody will also contain appropriate space for individuals to sign when they receive evidence and a space to sign when they release evidence. This means that each time the evidence is moved from one person to another, you will have two signatures for each transfer that is made, one signature representing the individual who released the evidence, and one signature representing the individual who received the evidence.

The use of a chain-of-custody form makes it easy to document who had access to and control over the evidence during its lifetime within the computer forensic lab or even in the field. It is important to establish who had access to and control over the evidence at all times so as to ensure that no tampering of the evidence took place and that there was no lapse in the control over the evidence that might have allowed for foul play to take place.

New evidence is managed on an as-needed basis. For instance, on day one the forensic examiner may be required to examine electronic data on a hard drive, but on day two the examiner no longer needs access to that hard drive, in which case the hard drive needs to be placed into what is known as the *evidence lockup*, or in some cases, the *evidence vault*. In the smallest of computer forensic laboratories, a simple drawer with a lock on it may suffice. In fact, I've had to build and operate computer forensic laboratories of less than 100 square feet, in which case space was at an extreme premium, but more often than not, in most labs the evidence lockup will be a storage locker that has a key-operated lock and shelves inside. Evidence is generally placed on the shelves, sometimes in plastic, wooden, or metal bins that have the case name affixed to them. These contain the hard drives or evidence related to that case.

In some labs, particularly larger ones, actual walk-in evidence vaults may be present, where you will have either shelving or large high-density storage bin racks that serve as the repository for evidence during its life cycle and while it is not being used by forensic examiner. Often, evidence will sit in a computer forensic vault or locker for years and years, awaiting the disposition of a trial or investigation to be completed. It is vital that there is a clear chain of custody and documented procedures governing how evidence is handled while it is in the custody of the forensic lab, particularly due to employee turnover and all the uncertainties that take place over time. One thing must remain certain—that the evidence is secure, has been documented, and can be retrieved.

Managing evidence in the field requires an extra level of care and caution, being that there are an unlimited number of variables that can and cannot be contemplated, from simple distractions, such as telephones ringing, to physical and logistical challenges, like not having an appropriate workspace within which to conduct a computer forensic examination in the field. These and other challenges in the field require a forensic examiner to maintain diligence and control over the electronic evidence at all times.

Often in the field, particularly on larger data collections, the computer forensic examiner is required to leverage a space within a corporation as a temporary forensic lab, specifically for the purpose of data collection. This often means that an individual or individuals will be assigned an office, where they will maintain their computer forensic equipment and where they will maintain the evidence until such time that they leave the site. When this takes place, it is important for computer forensic examiners to treat that space as their own computer forensic lab, even if it is a simple locked office or conference room or even a storage closet, and look to maintain the sanctity of the evidence under their control.

Often, when I've been in the field and have required the use of an office at a client's location, I have demanded that I have the only key, and if it is necessary, I change the lock on the office door to ensure that I have the only key. When I leave the office, I try to seal the door using tape and secure the ceiling and the various gaps and cracks in the doorjamb itself, simply as an extra measure of caution and to ensure that anyone who happens along that door during the night will think twice about trying to open it.

The scenarios and instances in which evidence control needs to be addressed in the field are innumerable and include traveling in your own vehicle or on public transportation, such as airplanes, trains, or boats. When transporting electronic evidence in your own car, it is a hard-and-fast rule not to leave the evidence in the vehicle unattended. You must think of it as you would think of your own child—you wouldn't leave him or her unattended in the car. There have been numerous occasions in which cars have been stolen or broken into or even left unlocked, and evidence has been stolen out of those cars. This often results in further litigation, as well as the potential exposure and dissemination of confidential information and what we call personally identifiable information, which requires, in most states, disclosure and which not only can be damaging to your client or to your company but is personally embarrassing as well.

Maintaining commonsense approaches to the handling of evidence while in transit is vital, and being that your evidence will be under a chain of custody, it is common sense that you do not leave it unattended when you are driving along the highway and stop at a restaurant. You must take the evidence with you into the restaurant and then take it back to the car with you. If you are flying, then you must carry the evidence with you on the airplane and check it as carry-on luggage. Do not check the evidence as a box or bag because then you will no longer have custody or control over it. In each one of these cases, I've seen the repercussions of failing to heed this simple advice. I've seen evidence stolen from the cargo hold of airplanes, as well as the trunks of cars parked in well-lighted parking lots in front of five-star restaurants.

Chain-of-Custody and Data Acquisition Forms

Investigative computer forensics relies on the acquisition of electronic data, often in the form of hard drives, and physical evidence, so it is also necessary to document the process that is used to preserve those systems and to have the ability to validate and authenticate the manner in which those systems are held, preserved, or used by the forensic examiners. To this end, the chain-of-custody form and the data acquisition form are used.

The chain-of-custody form, quite simply, is a document that should be prepared at the time that the investigative computer forensic analyst takes possession of a piece of evidence, whether that is an electronic file on a thumb drive, a physical computer, a hard drive, or even a mainframe computer. The chain-of-custody form has some primary elements, one of which is an area reserved to describe the evidence that is being held. For example, the chain of custody may have a line that is filled out by the technician on hand that states, "One Seagate hard drive, serial number 13608HL4524–7H A 300 GB, SATA Drive." In this example, the forensic examiner is identifying the physical hard drive to which the chain of custody relates, complete with the serial number.

The next section of the chain-of-custody form should allow for an individual to sign his or her name, with the date and time, and perhaps even an identification number, as being the individual who first took receipt of that evidence. When individuals release the evidence to a new party, such as an attorney, the opposing side, or other forensic examiners within their own lab, they will then sign the document releasing the evidence to the receiving party and the receiving party will also sign the same document, indicating that he or she has received the evidence. A chain-of-custody form will generally have multiple lines like this, which will allow for the evidence to be exchanged between various parties multiple times. It is not uncommon to receive a piece of evidence with a chain-of-custody form attached to it that has 8, 9, 10, or more transactions, which are identified by the signatures on the document of all those individuals who at one point in the investigation had custody and control of the evidence. This chain-of-custody form is a critical piece of evidence in its own right as it can establish who had control of the evidence and at what time, thereby removing yet another potential objection by an opposing side as to how that evidence was handled, who had control over it, or who could have modified it.

The second form that is ordinarily attached to computer evidence in the course of a forensic investigation is the data acquisition form. This form will identify the computer evidence that is being acquired and will also provide information on the methodology of that data collection. For instance, if the computer that is collected is a laptop computer made by Sony, then the data acquisition form will state this information and will include its serial number and any other unique identifiers. The data acquisition form will also include information related to the methodology employed in acquiring the data, such as forensic software version number and serial number. It will also include the date and time of the beginning of the acquisition and the completion of the acquisition and will include the value provided at the conclusion of the forensic capture.

The data acquisition form will also include information related to the individual who collected the data, the name of the technician, the date and time of the acquisition, the location of the acquisition, and other reasonable information so that at some point in the future, when those computers are being examined yet again during the course of further investigation or litigation, it will be abundantly clear as to how and by whom the data was collected, preserved, and managed. It is important for forensic examiners who are filling out these forms to be diligent and use legible, clear written language that is understandable by all as these forms often serve as the best evidence during a dispute regarding the processes and procedures used during the forensic capture. These disputes are more common than one would think, and I have seen many a forensic examiner get shredded to pieces on the witness stand by competent trial counsel who will use the omissions or inaccuracies in the data acquisition form to call into question the competency of the entire investigation, its findings, and the investigator himself.

The Forensic Workstation

The computer forensic lab needs to have at least one computer forensic workstation. The more active the lab and the more data you will be processing through the lab, the more workstations you will need. It is quite possible to run a computer forensic lab with one workstation, if you anticipate that you will have a light volume of work and only the occasional computer forensic analysis. As you begin increasing the volume of both analysis and data that needs to be managed by the lab, it will quickly become evident that you need to have multiple computer forensic workstations in order to achieve your goals in a reasonable period of time.

Computer forensic analysis requires robust processing speeds and power on the part of the computer forensic hardware and it also requires specific computer forensic software to achieve the goal of analyzing the data in both the active and unallocated space of a hard drive. When selecting a computer forensic workstation, it is important that the highest-grade computer components are used in the building of the machine. A computer forensic workstation can be built with components that are available at most computer hardware and software stores. There are also companies that specialize in building computer forensic workstations that have been tested and validated and are optimized for certain types of computing work that is specific to the computer forensic tasks a technician would be running.

Although it is important to either build or purchase high-grade systems to populate a computer forensic lab with workstations, it is also possible, in a pinch, to use off-the-shelf computers that are ordered directly from the manufacturer, such as Dell or HP. However, those systems may not be ideal for use in all cases. Many labs opt to purchase prebuilt lab workstations to remove the possibility of error during the construction of the machine and also to save time and resources when working to set up a computer forensic lab.

Aside from the aforementioned, there are other benefits to building your own workstations, which includes the knowledge that is gained during the process of assembling and configuring those workstations.

Some computer forensic workstation manufacturing companies are:

- Forensic Computers, available at www.forensic-computers.com
- Silicon Forensics, available at www.siliconforensics.com
- Digital Intelligence, available at www.digitalintelligence.com

Each of these companies focuses on building high-quality computer forensic workstations that are ready to go right out of the box. Although they may be more expensive than sourcing parts yourself and building your own computer forensic workstations, it will take a lot of the guesswork out of the process and can help you have your computer forensic lab up and running in days rather than weeks.

A good computer forensic workstation will have an abundance of convertibility and flexibility. In other words, that workstation should be supremely customizable and configurable by the computer forensic examiner, who is often required to do so on-the-fly during the collection and analysis of evidence. Examination processing systems will fail, techniques will hit roadblocks, and it will be necessary for the examiner to customize or configure the desktop to allow for a new approach to be taken when necessary. Examples of the types of systems that should be highly configurable on a computer forensic workstation include all of the input, output, or paired ports, which should be easily accessible by the technician, located on the front of the machine, and should include every known or reasonably expected type of input/output port, such as USB, USB 2 and 3, SATA, and FireWire.

Often when you walk into a computer forensic lab, you will notice that the computer forensic workstations do not have all of the covers on them. In other words, you may have a computer forensic workstation that has its side panel removed. This is so that the forensic examiner can have easy access to the components within the computer itself, such as the motherboard, the connectors for hard drives, and other peripherals that might be used during the examination. Because the computer is often open and exposed and the examiner is holding electronic components, such as hard drives, without a protective shell around them, it is important that the hardware and equipment, as well as the examiner, are well grounded.

When it comes to the equipment, one of the techniques I have taken advantage of in various labs that we've built is the use of antistatic carpet or antistatic tiles, which are laid on the floor and which help reduce the possibility of damaging electronic components through static electricity. In addition, common sense should be used, such as disallowing drinks, food, and other items not relevant to the case at hand to be placed on the computer forensic workstation or surrounding area. I've seen Coca-Cola and coffee spilled on computer components in forensic labs, and it is not a pretty sight.

A few other miscellaneous items that should be considered when building a computer forensic workstation include giving the examiner or manager of the lab administrative rights and privileges to the software and operating system that are in the lab machines or to the network itself. In a crunch or late at night when a configuration change needs to take place on the network or on any one of the workstations, the individuals who are performing the work will have the physical ability to make these changes without relying on corporate IT or others higher up in the decision-making chain. It is also recommended that when purchasing the computer forensic workstations, one leverages multithreaded processing and the most powerful chipsets available, quad-core or dual-core processors, and the bus architecture to support these processors. This will pay dividends when trying to push significant volumes of data through the environment and on short notice.

Even if a computer forensic lab purchases all of its computer forensic work-stations from a supplier or vendor and they come preconfigured, I deem it highly relevant and necessary that at least one of the computer forensic examiners, and preferably all of them, have the technical capacity and ability to assemble, disassemble, or troubleshoot any of those machines from the ground up and have had the experience of building machines from scratch using sourced components. This hands-on experience is vital so that the forensic examiner has a full appreciation of the manner in which components interact with one another, the time that is required to assemble and disassemble computers, and the interaction between components.

The computer forensic workstations will also be populated by computer forensic software. This is the software or programs that allow the computer forensic workstation to process and analyze electronic data contained on evidence media. The two most prevalent computer forensic software programs are EnCase and FTK. These two programs allow a computer forensic examiner to securely capture electronic data from a hard drive in a read-only manner, thereby preserving the integrity of the original evidence and disallowing it from being modified in any manner. It also gives the examiner the ability to collect what is known as the unallocated space of a hard drive, which is the portion of the hard drive that is used for the management of data and memory, but is not visible to the user through the vantage point of an operating system such as Microsoft Windows. This area often contains fragments of data, temporary files, and previously deleted files, which have not been overwritten and can often serve as an important repository of best evidence. These two computer forensic programs also allow for the analysis of the electronic data that is captured and the very granular examination of all the properties of each file, fragment, or data point that is captured during the collection phase.

There are a variety of computer forensic tools in the software world covered in other sections of this book and this software assists the examiner in performing certain specific tasks. In many cases, labs will maintain different versions of the computer forensic software, as well as different configurations of that software to achieve different goals. However, in more cases than not, labs will standardize across each of the computer forensic workstations that have a specific build and that contain a primary and a secondary computer forensic tool, such as EnCase or FTK, and further supported by certain specific utilities for searching, parsing, and managing data.

The purpose of maintaining a standardized image or build across each of the workstations is so that a manager of a computer forensic lab can have standard practices and processes, which each of his or her examiners will need to follow. In addition, should a machine fail and need to be rebuilt in rapid order, the preapproved image containing the standardized tool set can be quickly laid down on the new drive when building the new environment.

Equipment Applications and Processes

In the context of the building and operation of a computer forensic lab, care must be given to the type, quantity, use, and deployment of the equipment that will be used within the lab. Applications that support the activity of systems engineers, whether it be for forensic acquisition, preservation, analysis, or even management of technicians, time and billing, project management, and report writing should be considered. Processes need to be thought out in advance of the development of the lab and followed and improved on throughout the lab's life cycle. These processes should define responsibilities, challenges, and activities for each member of the team and should ensure that every task undertaken within the lab has a responsible party associated with it who has visibility into the manner in which that task is being executed. See Exhibit 3.3.

Primary components within the lab include the perimeter security system; the entry and exit control; a local network; computer forensic workstations; some form of storage devices, preferably network-attached storage with redundancy; additional and expandable equipment that will allow for sand-boxing of drives, applications, and large data sets for analysis on-the-fly; a wide variety of tools and hardware components for laptops, desktops, servers, cell phones, and other computing devices that may be required on the fly; an inventory of available internal and external hard drives; and a system for managing tasks, hours, and evidence control, such as an inventory database. These, among other essentials, form the fundamental components of a computer forensic lab.

I would say that proper care and attention should also be given to the ergonomic and physical characteristics of the workspace itself. This is important, because the task of reviewing massive volumes of data day in and day out can be very trying on the human body and eyes. Appropriate steps must be taken to ensure workbenches are set at the correct height; chairs are flexible, comfortable, and modifiable; and sufficient space exists within the lab to allow technicians to converse both formally and in an ad hoc manner without stumbling over one another, impacting evidence from different cases, or confusing equipment, artifacts, and paperwork between different cases due to poor office design.

EXHIBIT 3.3 The Logicube Talon

A computer forensic hardware capture device that allows for an investigator to quickly and predictably capture and preserve electronic data in the field at speeds in excess of 4 GB per minute. A number of peripherals exist that allow for the capture of different types of devices in unusual circumstances. A well-prepared computer forensic investigator will have a collection of these and other devices for the preservation of data so that the failure of one device or methodology will not deter him or her from success.

Digital Evidence Storage and Transportation

The storage and transportation of electronic data is an often-overlooked risk area in the field of computer forensics and electronic discovery. Electronic data that is generally contained on hard drives requires special care in handling when transporting from point A to point B. Not only is the chain of custody critical to maintain, but the physical conditions in which the drive(s) is handled is also an area to which proper attention must be given. In most cases, when a computer forensic examination has taken place in the field, the hard drives that are created as a result of that examination or collection will be one of two types. The first type is self-contained USB-enabled hard drives, which are hard drives that are preconfigured within a hard drive container that usually has its own electrical power source and USB connection. The other type is what we call internal hard drives, which are hard drives that are not enclosed in an exterior container. In some cases, particularly with older evidence, you may find that the hard drives are what are known as IDE hard drives. The difference between a SATA hard drive and our IDE hard drive is the connectors that allow for a cable to be connected to the hard drive and from the hard drive to the motherboard or a peripheral board on the computer itself. These connectors are known as either SATA cables, IDE cables, or IDE ribbons.

Once a forensic examiner has completed the forensic collection of the hard drive and is now in possession of either an internal or external SATA or IDE hard drive, steps need to be taken to package that drive for transportation in such a way as to ensure that it will not become damaged. Some of the practices that I follow include placing the hard drive into an antistatic pink bubble wrap container, which ordinarily will have a ziplock fastener on one end and will also have a pouch on one side of the container or envelope that will allow you to insert paperwork. The paperwork included is commonly the chain-of-custody form and a data acquisition form. In this manner you are able to keep all of the relevant documents together with the hard drive that you are going to transport and the hard drive is then protected by the bubble wrap, while also being protected from static electricity by the antistatic properties of the bubble wrap package.

In addition to the above, I also recommend labeling the hard drives themselves with at least an evidence number. The labeling can be done with a black marker pen, such as a Sharpie, or with a PTouch machine, with which you can affix a label. However, my real preference is to place a large label on the drive itself, with the evidence number, the custodian name, the date, and any other relevant information that needs to be conveyed to the person or persons who will be unpacking and receiving this data in the lab. Remember that it is quite possible that evidence collected in the field may not actually be reviewed for days, weeks, or months after the collection takes place, depending on facts that are governing the case. Therefore, one wants to be as obvious and deliberate as possible with one's markings, notes, and labeling on these devices.

Transporting evidence poses all sorts of logistical issues and questions, depending on the *who*, *what*, *where*, and *when* of the logistics on the ground:

- Who will be transporting the evidence?
- To whom will the evidence be delivered?
- What mode of transport is to be used?
- Where will the evidence be going?
- What is the purpose of moving the evidence?
- When will the evidence depart?
- When must the evidence arrive?
- Should the evidence be encrypted?

Paramount among these questions is the issue of the security and sanctity of the evidence. It is vital that the custody of the evidence is always clear and documented and that it cannot be challenged. For instance, when flying, it is highly recommended that you carry the drives themselves as your personal carry-on baggage, as opposed to checking the evidence as luggage in the cargo hold. If this is not an option, then the risk/reward ratio of shipping the evidence via a courier or transport company, such as UPS or FedEx, should be considered. Should the evidence be shipped, then I would recommend that the packages be split up into master copies and working copies. Then each package should be sent separately. Optimally, one would wait for the first package to arrive before sending the second package.

Another choice is to simply send them on two separate days. If you must send them on the same day, then I would recommend sending them with two different carriers. The goal is to ensure that if something happens to one of the packages or the delivery mechanism being used (car, truck, boat, train, airplane), then the other package will make it.

When traveling in a car with evidence, it is important to keep it as out of sight as possible, perhaps by placing the drives in a suitcase or a box and placing the suitcase or box in the trunk of the car. If the car does not have a trunk, then you can lay the evidence on the floorboard in front of one of the seats and then place a jacket or some newspapers over it so that it does not attract attention.

Never leave the evidence in a vehicle unattended. There have been many well-documented cases of persons leaving drives, backup tapes, and other evidence in a car, a trunk, or some other transport vehicle, only for it to go missing and later show up for sale on eBay . . . or worse.

Staffing and Skill Sets

When staffing a computer forensic lab, there are a number of things to consider. Fundamentally and initially, an individual must be appointed who has operational responsibility for the integrity of the evidence. This is the primary and most important role within the lab. Presuming that a manager for the lab has been identified, whose responsibility includes managing the resources of the lab, both human resources and the physical elements of the lab, the next step, depending on the size of lab, is to identify individuals to carry out specific tasks.

For a large lab it is not unusual to identify a sole resource with the responsibility of managing evidence. This evidence manager has the final word on the disposition of all inbound and outbound physical data and electronic data and has the responsibility of signing off on data, systems, and evidence that the lab controls. Most labs, however, do not have this luxury, and this role is often delegated to the entire team. In this situation, it is required that each individual forensic examiner manage the evidence for his or her specific case. Some labs that have moderate-size matters can afford to have a single individual working on every single case, whereas other labs that take on more complex work may need to work in teams with multiple technicians working on any given case.

I have found that in the staffing of computer forensic labs, it is optimal to assign a senior forensic technician to the lab, someone who has primary responsibility for the systems, controls, hardware, and software in the lab, as well as investigative and analytical protocol. This individual sets the tone for the entire lab's work product and will work with outside counsel, investigators, and other interested parties to ensure that the lab is meeting the mandate or standards of the organization that it serves.

Under the tutelage and direction of the senior lab manager or senior lab technician, one can assign additional technicians at different levels, each with different mandates. For instance, a lab may have a senior technician, who is relying on junior technicians, each one of those junior technicians having slightly different responsibilities. One technician may be responsible for managing the lab network and its resources and connectivity with the outside world, while at the same time conducting computer forensic analysis and acquisitions on an as-needed basis. A second technician may be responsible for database-related work and manage either the SQL server or some other database that is employed in the lab for data analytics and the review of structured data. A third analyst may be responsible for and have the subject matter expertise to focus on cloud-based and network-based data and serve as the subject matter expert for network investigations and activity. A final lab technician may be the subject matter expert on handheld devices, smartphones, tablets, and other miscellaneous technologies that the organization may be required to deal with.

In some other labs there are individuals who may be responsible for report-writing, filing affidavits, expert testimony, or even managing data collection teams in the field for specific applications such as EnCase, Enterprise, or distributed data collections within the network using a tool that allows for over-the-wire collection of electronic data and images from computers.

Current Tools and Services

There are a multitude of forensic software tools and services available to the forensic examiner. The following pages offer details on some of the more common.

EnCase

EnCase was developed by guidance software in the 1990s and has proven itself to be the gold standard in both law-enforcement and private investigations. The tool allows you to complete data acquisitions of suspect media; these acquisitions are stored in a proprietary and case evidentiary file format and are passed with an MD5 or Sha-1 hash algorithm value for every 60K of data. In addition the entire drive that is imaged also receives an MD5 hash value so as to ensure the integrity of the data. EnCase software can be found in the United States and elsewhere for expert inquiries into both criminal matters and civil investigations and is useful for network investigations into compliance issues and certainly for electronic discovery.

The software is available to be purchased by law-enforcement agencies, corporations, and private individuals. EnCase offers training modules on its software and will also certify those trainees who pass a certification test and are then able to use the EnCE designation, which is an EnCase Certified Examiner appended to the end of their name in professional use. The acquisition capabilities of EnCase are robust and allow for examiners to collect laptops, desktops, and all forms of hard drives both for standard computing as well as even servers. In addition, the EnCase platform maintains a robust analysis environment that will allow the reviewer or analyst to review every document resident on a hard drive both in its original document format as well as in a text format or as its hex value. EnCase is also able to examine the file system of the computer, its applications, temporary files, deleted files, and other areas of what is known as the unallocated space of the hard drive. At the completion of the analysis that a computer forensic examiner undertakes by using the EnCase platform one also has the ability to produce reports in electronic or paper format illustrating the findings of the examiner.

As of this writing EnCase can be used on both a computer forensic workstation as well as on a standard laptop or desktop. It is activated by the use of a USB dongle, which is sold by Guidance software to the end-user. The software can be downloaded or loaded onto a computer by DVD and then activated by using the supplied dongle. Prices range from just under $3,000 for a stand-alone copy of EnCase to many tens of thousands of dollars for more sophisticated EnCase variants, which are designed for tasks such as electronic discovery processing, early case assessment, or cybercrime remediation.

FTK

Like EnCase, the makers of FTK or Forensic Tool Kit provide for a software platform that allows a forensic examiner to quickly acquire electronic data from hard drives or other digital media in a secure and sound manner, which is both verifiable and defensible in its process. The FTK system is made by AccessData, a component of the Summation brand, is effective for reviewing, locating, and producing both active and deleted e-mail, and has many if not all of the same features as EnCase. While FTK and EnCase are the two primary competitors in the computer forensic acquisition and analysis software space there are distinct differences between the two. Among FTK's advantages as of this writing is its user interface, which allows for intuitive navigation and ease of understanding. But that graphical simplicity should not obscure the relevancy or quality of the product that EnCase provides the forensic examiner. Most forensic labs and most forensic analysts will in fact leverage both EnCase and FTK as well as additional applications and tools. This is because each of the tools handles data and processes data and allows the analysis of data in slightly different ways.

One may find that FTK will process a specific data file format faster than EnCase, whereas in another matter EnCase may process the data faster than FTK or may provide results that are easier to interpret. I've had a number of cases where the ultimate client wishes the examination to take place on both platforms so as to ensure that no stone is left unturned; however, for the most part FTK and EnCase will provide equivalent analysis capabilities and certainly acquisition capabilities. AccessData also offers a certification program based on its FTK product, which will allow a computer forensic examiner to distinguish himself or herself as being certified on this product. Both FTK and EnCase have been accepted by courts in the United States and abroad.

Write Blockers

Write blockers are an indispensable tool for the computer forensic examiner. Their purpose is to allow for the collection of electronic data from a device without writing to that device. In most cases, a write blocker is a physical device that is attached to the device that is to be captured and is then commanded to pass information through the write blocker to the device that is going to capture that information. The capture device may be a specific tool designed for data capture or it may be a laptop that is running EnCase or FTK and has an external hard drive attached to it to serve as the repository for the data to be captured. Write blockers that are specifically designed for forensic acquisition of data make every effort to remove the possibility of damaging the contents of the drive. One of the methods used to minimize damage is to ensure operability by allowing the write blocker to write at slower speeds than the hard drive that it is acquiring is ordinarily used for writing. Many of the high-speed hard drives that are running in UDMA mode are spinning at high speed and as a result the head moves back and forth more frequently across the platters. See Exhibit 3.4.

Many write blockers allow the data acquisition to take place in slower modes such as PIO. Although acquiring the data at a slower rate may increase the time it takes to acquire the hard drive, the likelihood that an error will take place is reduced. Write blockers specifically block all commands that could be sent to the target drive letter of a write nature while letting everything else through. Therefore, with a write blocker and appropriate forensic software, a forensic analyst can attach the blocker to a computer commanded to send an image of its drive across the interface into a repository drive, thereby allowing the forensic examiner to capture a pristine image of the exact drive bit by bit, not only its operating system and the active files within created by the user but also the unallocated space on the drive, which contains fragments of files, slack space, deleted files, and other such remnants of electronic data.

Write blockers come in both hardware and software variants and are referred to in two forms: tailgate and native. A tailgate device is one that uses an interface other than the interface of the original target drive, such as FireWire to SATA. A native device is one in which the interface on the write blocker is the same as the interface on the target drive, such as SATA to SATA or FireWire to FireWire or IDE to IDE. Some write blockers are integrated with forensic data capture hardware such as the

EXHIBIT 3.4   A Tableau Device That Serves as a "Write Blocker" during the Capture of Electronic Evidence

This crucial piece of hardware, or one like it, should reside in duplicate in every computer forensic investigator's tool kit.

Logicube and the SoloMaster, which we discuss shortly. Commercial write blockers come in both hardware and software varieties:

Hardware Write Blockers

- ICS Drive Lock: www.ics-iq.com
- MyKey Technology, Inc., NoWrite FPU, and FlashBlock II: www.mykeytech .com
- Tableau write blockers: www.tableau.com
- WiebeTech write-blockers: http://wiebetech.com

Software Write Blockers

■ SAFE Block XP: www.forensicsoft.com
■ MacForensicsLab Write Controller: www.macforensicslab.com

Imaging Hardware

Among the tools that a computer forensic examiner or lab will maintain are hard-ware-based imaging devices. These devices are appliances that have been built specifically for the purpose of collecting electronic evidence in a predictable and safe manner in the field or in the lab. Two of the most popular forensic imaging hardware devices are the Logicube and the SoloMaster. See Exhibit 3.5.

Logicube started in the late 1990s building a device known as the *MD5*. Later it released a product that has gained popular acceptance, known as the *Talon*. This device allows for the collection of electronic data in such a simplistic fashion that even junior-level forensic staff can master the technique quickly and with ease. The Talon has the ability to capture hard drives, while at the same time it is rugged and will take a beating in the field. These devices have been used by military and law enforcement in combat arenas as well as by corporations in the boardroom. Year by year the data transfer rate of these hardware devices increases, which is important because the hard drives themselves are growing larger and larger by the year. In the late 1990s, it was rare to see hard drives over a few gigabytes in the field, and today it is not unusual to be confronted with 2-TB drives—the growth is exponential. The present Talon by Logicube can transfer data at more than 7 GB per minute (depending on a variety of factors such as the speed of the target media) and can capture those drives in a variety of formats, including DVD images, and E01 evidence file formats (this is the EnCase format), and have the ability to hash the files or the entire drive with an MD5 or a Sha-256 hash algorithm. Interestingly, the new Talon even supports Spanish and Chinese on its operational menu, which is quite telling in its own right. These hardware devices also have the ability to capture USB drives, flash drives, thumb drives, and are shipped with a variety of cables enabling access to ESATA, MicroSATA, and other interfaces. During the process of capture, standard best practices would require the forensic examiner to also conduct what is known as a *verification* of the drive that has been captured. This is a process whereby the forensic hardware tool verifies the integrity of the data that was captured and provides a verification code at the completion of this task. The verification process usually will take an equal amount of time as the acquisition process.

SoloMaster and the Logicube can be useful in the field; by example, the Logicube allows for a data capture using USB cloning software, which can allow for the capture of Macintosh computers. The Talon also has an integrated keyboard on the top surface of the device, which allows the field examiner to input evidence names and to run in the field quick searches for keywords without having to retreat back to the lab. Logicube builds a number of other devices related to the Talon, including a device known as the Quest, which is specifically designed for the requirements of

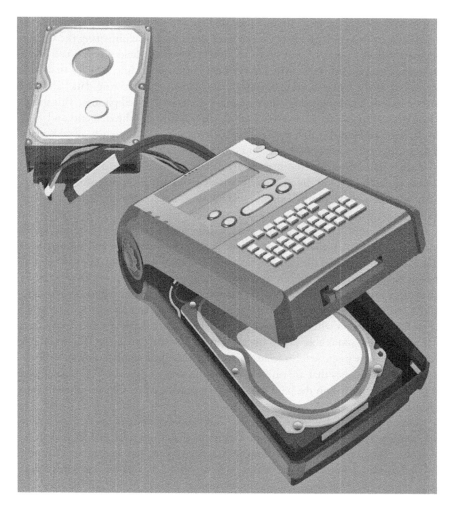

EXHIBIT 3.5   An Evidentiary Hard Drive Physically Attached to a Write-Blocking Data Acquisition Device

The Logicube Talon contains a master forensic hard drive in its interior. Here the Logicube is shown in the open position just prior to the actual data capture process.

law enforcement, military, government, and corporate security organizations. The device comes equipped with a variety of field-ready components and tools in a specially designed briefcase, which is an affordable choice for deployment across corporate security departments or foreign, entry-level computer forensic examiners who are beginning their own practice. In addition, Logicube produces devices called the Forensic Dossier, the Cell Extract, and the Net Connect.

With the limitations of space I'm unable to provide all the features of all of these unique tools but I can provide a few highlights, including those of the

Forensic Dossier. One of its unique features is that it allows for the capture of one hard drive to two evidence drives at the same time, thereby eliminating the need to separately create a master copy and a working copy in the field. Or you can create two master copies from two evidentiary targets at the same time, which can double the speed of the forensic examination in the field when collecting data. The Cell Extract is a device designed for the extraction of data off of cell phones. This stand-alone device has a touch screen that is designed to withstand the elements and work in the field and has the ability to collect data from Android phones, BlackBerries, Palms, Apple phones, and some 2,000 other mobile devices. It also has the ability to extract data using Bluetooth or IrDA if you are unable to connect to the cell phone via cable. One of the nice features is that you can customize and specify exactly what part of the phone's memory you wish to extract, thereby increasing your ability to target relevant data.

Another important device from the Logicube firm is called Net Connect, which provides automated high-speed network access to evidentiary data and allows you to quickly share or transfer the data to a network location for further analysis by forensic technicians. Connecting data from networks and from servers presents a variety of challenges; using a device such as Net Connect can help to automate, systematize, and speed up these types of challenging connections and can also serve as part of a compliance program within the corporation. Net Connect has the ability to conduct live acquisitions and is able to capture a computer's volatile memory. This important feature will allow forensic technicians to access critical data such as passwords, IP addresses, and processes that are running during the time of capture. This type of data is not typically stored on the hard drive and can provide a forensic examination with great advantage.

A competing device to the Logicube Talon and its family of products is a suite of products developed by Intelligent Computer Solutions available at www.ICS-IQ.com. These systems provide similar functionality as the Logicube. Presently, ISC offers a tool known as the Image MASter Solo 101 forensic hard drive data acquisition unit. This device allows for high-speed transfer of SATA IDE and USB 2.0 connectable drives on a budget and with much of the same functionality as the Logicube. ISC also produces the Image MASter Solo-4 forensic hard drive acquisition and analysis unit. While double the price of the MASter Solo 101, the Solo-4 has numerous additional features and includes a color touch screen for navigating the operating system of the unit.

Among Image MASter's additional capabilities are hard drive and cell phone acquisition speeds up to 18 GB per minute, capture of up to two hard drives simultaneously, hash verification, algorithm hash verifications of MD5, Sha-1, and Sha-2 standards, encryption, and the ability to capture Linix-based machines, Macintoshes, and all Windows-based machines.

Most larger computer forensic labs will maintain both the Logicube and the Solo MASter devices as well as additional forensic imaging hardware that I do not have the space to mention here; however, smaller operations will generally standardize one of these platforms, thereby gaining efficiencies in training, capital investment, and risk management.

X1 Discovery

There are such a wide variety of tools that are required by the computer forensic lab that I do not have space in this volume to list them all, so I have selected a few and have unfortunately left out many. I hate to give short shrift to any tool that is required by forensic examiners from the lowly Phillips-head screwdriver and mini-screwdriver kits to the expandable magnetic mirrors and tweezers, which can be placed deep into a computer whose panel has been removed to find a missing screw that has fallen to the bottom of the box. Tools in the forensic lab run the gamut from the investigator's magnifying glass all the way to masking tape, flashlights, zip ties, Sharpie pens, and a plethora of sophisticated software. Among the more sophisticated recent software entrants is a tool known as X1 Discovery, which allows for the forensic identification capture and analysis of electronic data that lives on social media websites and the cloud. Coming in two flavors—X1 Social Discovery and X1 Rapid Discovery—this new entrant has revolutionized forensic data capture of dynamic live content in a way not seen since the advent of EnCase. The social media application allows forensic technicians to leverage a unified platform for the collection, authentication, search and review, and finally production of data from LinkedIn, Twitter, and most important, Facebook. The platform provides a workflow much in the same way that EnCase and FTK do as it relates to static media and evidence acquired from hard drives. X1 allows for that predictable process of collecting data in a forensically sound manner with the appropriate controls to ensure that the tweets and Facebook posts and other dynamic web-based content collected off the web that is presented as evidence in a court of law will be preserved in an unaltered yet fully interactive state. The X1 Rapid Discovery tool allows for cloud-based data collection and identification in a highly scalable and distributed fashion without the traditional investment of significant hardware costs and centralized management. In fact, the Rapid Discovery Tool allows forensic technicians to quickly identify, search, and collect distributed data wherever it is on the cloud or within the enterprise and whatever its type, a challenge whose time has come.

NetAnalysis

Another such groundbreaking device or software tool that should be present in any computer forensic tool kit is a product known as NetAnalysis, which is built by Digital Detective. This tool, which in many ways is becoming an industry standard for the recovery and analysis of Internet browser artifacts, was developed in the United Kingdom and was initially used by law enforcement. Now it's being used around the world by both law enforcement and private interests for the purpose of quantifying all of the data associated with Internet use. This data is often collected by using EnCase, FTK, or other tools, but then NetAnalysis is applied to learning additional statistics and information about the URLs (universal resource locators), rebuilding HTML web pages from extracted cache, adding the correct location of graphics so that you can view the pages where they actually appeared when the suspect viewed them, and providing easier viewing of image files such as JPEGs as they were viewed by the suspect. The tool also allows for reconstructing search criteria that was typed by the actual user of the website or a browser, and in some cases passwords and user-names are recoverable.

This NetAnalysis tool, which also allows you to create timelines, can be further enhanced by HstX version 3, which is a tool that is designed for the recovery of deleted data from Windows-based systems. This tool recovers browser artifacts and Internet history from a wide variety of evidence types and supports all of the major forensic formats. The purpose of using HstX 3 can be to gain further insight into the unallocated clusters, cluster slack, memory dumps, crash dumps, page files, system files, hibernation files, and the system restore points that are maintained either in the allocated space or within the Windows operating system itself. This illustrates that there are a number of ways to examine and parse data that is captured from a suspect machine. Although one may use Logicube or an Image MASter to forensi-cally collect the drive, one may also use EnCase or FTK for the initial analysis. Yet further analysis may take place using tools such as NetAnalysis, X1, or even other products built by Digital Detective, such as Blade, which in some cases can allow you to intelligently carve out validated routines such as in the recovery of JPEGs or other known file formats from the allocated space and reconstruct those otherwise unrecoverable files.

Building a Team and a Process

When a computer forensic laboratory is being set up, teamwork is required to sup-port and establish a process for handling electronic data and for managing the work flow of the cases that are received by who lab. Establishing this work flow process will assist in identifying those team members who should be deployed within the lab. In some cases, laboratories, particularly those that are embedded within existing cor-porations, need to rely on outside resources. For instance, the records, such as audit or security records, in the information technology department of the company will assist in establishing clear procedures and processes for the management of electronic data and will ensure that those individuals who are brought onto the team on an ad hoc basis are properly deployed. See Exhibit 3.6.

A typical small-size laboratory will generally consist of a lab manager and a number of forensic technicians. These technicians may have different skill sets. Some may be focused on the collection of electronic data in the field, and others may be focused on the analysis of electronic data. Still others may be focused on certain subsets of the field of analysis, such as analyzing network or dynamic data, including the data that is contained in network log files or router log files or the dynamic data that can be pulled off of hard drives and flash memory while the devices are in use.

EXHIBIT 3.6 An AntiStatic-Sealed Evidence Bag Containing a Hard Drive and Used for Transporting and Storage of Hard Drives

Every precaution should be taken when managing evidence to ensure its safety, integrity, and reliability.

Other specialists include individuals who are familiar with e-discovery production protocols that are focused on both keyword search data management and the production of electronic data. These protocols must be implemented in such a fashion that the data can be reviewed within the context of an online e-discovery review tool or manually reviewed by attorneys or investigators downstream. Other individuals who may be full-time employees (depending on the volume of work) in the lab are the investigators. Expert testimony may be required to certify and/or testify as to the findings of the lab technicians.

Processes that must be included in the lab are the manner in which electronic evidence will be received, which is covered elsewhere in this volume. Chain-of-custody and data acquisition forms, as well as evidence inventory systems, are important components of those processes. Also important is the establishment of a procedure for the physical handling of the drives and/or evidence that are brought into the lab. This includes procedures for how these items will be transported from the intake area to the analysis or collection area and then, finally, to the evidence lockup. Similarly, it is important to establish how items contained within the evidence lockup are to be distributed to analysts, when data review takes place, and whether the evidence is to be destroyed or sent to clients at the conclusion of a matter.

Managing Workloads and Expectations

Forensic examiners are put under tremendous pressure to perform Herculean tasks in very short order. Managing the workload and the expectations of either a client or manager as they relate to this complicated technical work is an important step in ensuring that deliverables are of the highest possible quality and integrity and that they are delivered within a reasonable time frame, without burning out the forensic examiner who is charged with doing the work.

The tasks associated with computer forensic examination, and even computer forensic collection, are frequently underestimated by those individuals who are issuing the orders, as in many cases in which lawyers and managers will demand that the electronic data is processed in an unreasonable time frame. There are a number of things driving this misconception. One is the perspective that computers are simple to work with, just like the Windows or Macintosh desktop sitting on your desk and waiting for you to push a button to make things happen quickly. Other reasons for such misconception include the potential inexperience of the attorney providing the direction and the requirements of the case, for which the timing has been set by the court or regulator and which can create a real pressure cooker.

The forensic acquisition of a computer hard drive requires a set amount of time, which is nearly impossible to modify. Rather, many forensic examiners will provide quotations of the amount of time that it will take to image a hard drive in the field, such as one hour for a 100-GB hard drive or two hours for a 200-GB hard drive. What they often fail to take into account is the set-up time, which includes the time required to identify a location within which to work, to arrive at the facility, to introduce yourself to the parties, to identify the location of the drive that you will be collecting, to disassemble the drive, to remove the drive from the computer, to prepare your forensic equipment for the acquisition of the drive, and to kick off the acquisition. Then, following the acquisition, which in fact may take one or two hours or longer, depending on the size of the drive, time is required to reassemble the computer and reassemble the forensic kit (which now needs to travel back to the lab with the computer forensic examiner), and, even more important, the completion of the paperwork, which needs to be done on-site.

At times, the paperwork can be completed at the same time as the forensic images are being conducted, but in other cases it cannot be completed until the examination is finished. This paperwork includes labels, packaging, chain-of-custody forms, data acquisition forms, and potentially other spreadsheets that are used for tracking the data collections. Finally, it is my recommendation, as a best practice wherever possible, to also collect or create a working copy of the master copy of the image while you are still in the field, thereby eliminating the need to go back into the field to recollect the drive should there be an error, a hardware failure, or some other problem with the master copy. This process doubles the amount of time that is required to collect the data.

Keeping these variables in mind will help set the expectations of the client or the manager when the forensic examiner is either providing a quote for the length of time it will take to collect data in the field or providing the client with how long it will take to complete a particular collection action. The same holds true for the processing and analysis phase of electronic data. Processing of data also has physical and informational barriers that are set by the processing speed of the computers, the software that is being used, the network to which it is attached, and the rotational speed and read/write speed of the hard drives that are in use during the processing phase.

These restrictions require some upfront analysis by a forensic examiner to provide guidance as to how long a particular task, such as indexing a hard drive, running keyword searches, extracting JPEG documents, or searching for particular fragments within the unallocated space will actually take. I have seen far too many unhappy clients over the years because they had underestimated the amount of time that the analysis or processing would actually take, and this has been further complicated by forensic analysts not providing reasonable estimates as to the time required.

When it comes to the analysis phase, it is quite difficult to estimate the amount of time that it will take to conduct an analysis of the hard drive, unless the tasks are highly defined. I liken the exercise to the peeling of an onion. You keep peeling away layer upon layer and you eventually get to the bottom of things, but in the meantime you have many layers to peel away in order to understand truly how many layers there were in the first place. The setting of expectations and timing is particularly important when a forensic examiner is part of a team that is responding to a court order. Judges and/or prosecutors and/or defendants, for that matter, can at times be far removed from the actual physical work that is taking place in a forensic lab in support of one of their cases. As a result, good communication among the manager of the lab, the forensic technicians, and the client is vital to ensure that missteps and missed deadlines, particularly court deadlines, do not happen.

Like the management of any facility or group of people, tasks need to be understood and quantified. The forensic lab setting is no exception, and to the extent that is reasonable, estimates can be provided to clients. However, a forensic technician also has to be able to say, "I just don't know." There are many occasions where I have had to say to a client, "I just don't know. We won't know until we're there." It is similar to what happens when a patient is on the surgery table. You just don't know until you open up the patient and can see inside.

This could not be truer when it comes to the analysis of computers and servers or Internet artifacts and usage patterns, particularly in the case of the theft of trade secret matters, in which you are looking for any evidence that will elucidate how a particular data set moved from point A to point B. It is not uncommon for a good computer forensic examiner to find the proverbial smoking gun within minutes of examining the results of a forensic search, yet it is equally as common for that same examiner to labor for weeks on a particular machine, piecing together disparate clues in order to establish a fact pattern that can be used in an investigative report as evidence in a court of law.

Computer Forensic Certifications

Computer forensics, which is a branch of digital forensic science pertaining specifically to legal evidence found in digital storage media, computers, servers, and other devices, sets a goal of examining digital media and evidence in a forensically sound manner with a purpose of identifying, preserving, recovering, analyzing, and presenting facts and opinions about that information. Although computer forensics is often associated with computer crime, as we have seen in this volume, it is often used in civil proceedings and internal investigations.

Computer forensic analysts often receive certifications in the various tools that they use. Among the most popular certifications are the certified computer forensic examiner program (CFCE) and the certified computer examiner (CCE), along with the EnCE from Guidance Software's EnCase and the ACE from Access Data's FTK. Other certifications include those offered by the EC Council, such as the CHFI certified hacking forensic investigator, and those provided by the educational organization SANS, such as the GIAC Forensic Examiner Certifications (known as GCFE and GCFA), which offers a full complement of options for a forensic examiner to receive technical training, education, and certification in their field.

I should note that, over the years, I've worked with numerous highly qualified forensic examiners who did not have certifications and numerous letters after their name, and these examiners were able to equip themselves to the highest standards of care. So, although there is some advantage to achieving certifications and these designations in the computer forensic space, by no means is it mandatory.

The Human Quotient

The purpose of this section is to discuss several of the various human components of the computer forensic world, from the victims to the clients and from the engineers to the investigators and from the attorneys to the judges.

There is a wide variety of individuals who play a role in the computer forensic space, either as consumers of computer forensic work product, directors of computer forensic activity, or those who rely on the results of computer forensics in either proving or disproving a position.

This section discusses and provides some brief insights into each one of these roles. By no means is this an exhaustive or complete list of the individuals that one would come in contact with. This relates to computer forensics, but it is meant to provide an overview of some of the motivations, interests, and hot buttons of these specific vested interests in the computer forensic space.

As a consumer of computer forensic services, it may be that you have a global vision of the capabilities and positions of each of the players in any given investigation or litigation. If you are like many, however, you may be very focused on your own expertise and may not have a firm understanding of what motivates the forensic examiner or what a defense attorney is trying to achieve through the use of forensic analysis. Spending a little time on this topic will fill in some of the blanks for many of us.

The Client or Victim

The practice of computer forensics is often seen as highly analytical and detached from the human aspect of our world, particularly for the "Forensic Taoist," who stares at a computer screen day in and day out, analyzing the digital aspect or components of electronic files in their pure and most elementary form. But what always needs to be kept in mind is that the work that is being conducted has a human element—direct consequences for individuals and stakeholders who care deeply about the outcome of the analysis. In criminal cases, this can mean the difference between justice or injustice, a victim finding closure or a criminal escaping the rule of law. In the corporate world, the activities undertaken by a computer forensic examiner can easily mean the difference in resolving disputes that are valued at thousands of dollars or even billions of dollars, uncovering massive fraud, or simply ensuring the integrity of the key processes within an organization.

When thinking of the human quotient in computer forensics, I list the client and/or the victim first and foremost, because I am usually working on behalf of a client who may or may not be represented in the form of a corporation but ultimately is found in the form of a real human with a real face and real cares and concerns about the outcome of the matter. This lone human or group of people may care deeply about the consequences of the work or may be impacted unknowingly by the decisions that are made, the judgment calls, the ideas, and the questions that are asked at the desk of a computer forensic examiner. This is true whether your client is a spouse embroiled in a bitter custody battle in which the contents of the hard drive that you are examining will determine the fate of a child where the disposition of the primary caregiver hangs in the balance, or where your work will determine the legitimacy of the claims made by an entire class of people who have alleged the criminal contamination of ground water at a chemical plant. Either way, your work and your conclusions may have a lasting impact on the lives of real people. In the criminal context, victims are the ultimate clients, and seeking justice and truth requires diligence and care when handling electronic evidence and analyzing the data to ensure that the truth will prevail.

In many cases, computer forensic examiners never come face-to-face with their ultimate client because they are submerged beneath multiple layers of decision making. In many cases, the computer forensic examiners never know the true and final outcome or disposition of the case that they worked so hard on, an outcome that was the result of the analysis that they completed. Again, this is because you, as a forensic examiner, are submerged beneath the multiple layers of the process, which ultimately leverages computer forensics as part of its fact-finding mission.

I believe that there is a time and place for informing the computer forensic examiners of the details of the case. In some matters, it can add positively to the process, and in others it does not. There are some matters where true objectivity, without regard for the outcome, can be better served by having a computer forensic examiner operating in the blind, if you will, as it relates to the facts of the case. However, there are judgment calls that need to be made by the computer forensic manager or lead investigator or even by counsel as to whether the examiner should be brought into the loop on the facts of the case.

Often, having a better understanding of the on-the-ground events that are potentially represented by the electronic data being examined will help provide context for the forensic examiners when they are making judgment calls as to what data to examine and how to interpret the relationship between data points. This often overlooked aspect of the relationship between the computer forensic examiners and those who are directing their actions is an important one and is best judged by seasoned practitioners who have the ability to make these calls.

I would also note that as part of a postmortem of any investigation or forensic analysis, it is important for the manager, client, or director of the project to take the time to inform the forensic examiners as to the results of their work, including the impact that they may or may not have had on the case and the reason for their utilization in the first place. Better examiners are made when they are included in the information loop—if not at first, then certainly at the conclusion of the matter.

The computer data that relates to the activities of the victim or client, when examined in a forensic manner, is a unique window into a place and time, frozen like a photograph for inspection, but often with so much more depth. This is because often the activity taken by an individual through the use of e-mail or web browsing or leaving a voice mail is the actual action itself, and in preserving and capturing that activity, you are capturing the specific act as if you were freeze-framing not only a point in time, but multiple points in time with each of these data points having a relationship to the many other interrelated data points that are also captured during the exercise.

The result is that you can replay for a jury the actual events as they happened while the criminal was undertaking them—not as a fuzzy CCTV camera recording, like those that you would see from a bank robbery, but more from the first-person viewpoint, seeing exactly what the criminal saw and, perhaps, created or acted on. In the case of the bank robbery analogy, it would be as if you were able to capture the look on the face of the teller when the note is passed to her that says, "Give me all the money in the drawer or I will shoot." The capture of electronic evidence has moved the analysis of evidence into the first-person viewpoint and forensic evidence is no longer only residual, but is now often a complete and intact synthesis of the actual crime or action one is looking to re-create.

The Computer Forensic Examiner

The computer forensic examiner's role is to collect and preserve, identify and analyze, and store and present electronic evidence from a wide variety of devices. These devices run the gamut from computer hard drives, both spinning disc drives as well as solid-state drives, to portable memory devices, such as thumb drives, flash drives, or even external hard drives. We must also remember cell phones, laptops, desktops, servers, and even the electronic data off household devices, such as alarm systems, voice mail systems, or automobile-based systems. There is such a wide variety of data collected from sensors throughout modern life that a computer forensic examiner may be faced with the job of collecting electronic data off a standard laptop one day and the next day collecting data that comes off a hard drive that is recording video from a 7-Eleven convenience store.

As a result of the wide variety of data types, as an examiner you must be confident that you are familiar with the role. The experience that the examiner has for his or her professional career is one that includes a good deal of education, including educating him- or herself on the presumed and actual functions and processes employed by all of these various new devices as well as legacy devices.

A legacy device is a system that either is outmoded or was deployed in the past and is generally not deployed as often in the contemporary world, but which still maintains electronic data that for one reason or another must be examined. An example of this would be when, during an investigation, it is necessary to examine backup tapes from an older mainframe computing environment. A mainframe computing environment may be considered a legacy data type, or it may be considered to hold what we consider to be legacy data, which may be data that is present in programs that are no longer accessed or used in the ordinary course of business. These types of legacy data present unique challenges for computer forensic engineers, particularly the younger engineers who, in some cases, had never even seen a mainframe computer, any computer reel-to-reel tape, or even a punch-card machine.

Computer forensic examiners and engineers often find themselves intrigued not only by the mechanics of the systems they are reviewing but also by the historical legacy of the applications and hardware that they are entrusted with examining. I have seen many computer forensic labs that contain a variety of software spanning decades, software that is certainly no longer used, but that may come into play during the forensic examination of an older device.

A case in point would be when a forensic examiner is required to restore data from the backup of a computer from 10 years ago, or even 20 years ago, which has been sitting in a storage unit, but that is evidence in a murder trial. This means that it is required for that individual to bring up the data backup in its native environment to show how the user may have accessed and used the application and interface. It is not inconceivable that these data points would be relevant and that a prosecutor can use them to show how a potential criminal took certain actions on a computer at a given time.

Quite frankly, part of the fun for forensic examiners is the sleuthing and investigative work that they are entrusted to undertake, either on their own or at the direction of counsel. Even for seasoned traditional investigators who leverage the skill set of the forensic examiner, it is fun to find the digital smoking gun.

The Network Engineer

The role of the network engineer in computer forensic examination can be of vital importance. In most cases, computer forensic analysts and acquisition specialists are not trained in the deep complexities of network topology and network systems. Naturally, there are exceptions. However, what I have found in practice is that most computer forensic specialists or analysts have primarily been trained in the forensic acquisition of computer hard drives and the usage of primary computer forensic tools, such as EnCase and FTK, for the required digital analysis of files found on a computer hard drive.

In cases where computer forensic analysts also have network engineering or equivalent training and experience, the value that they can bring to a project that requires that skill set can be immense. Network engineers are individuals who are usually in charge of managing the components of a network, in other words, ensuring that communications between computers and routers, servers and systems, take place in a predictable and defined manner.

These networks can exist within the context of a room, a building, multiple buildings, the city, multiple distributed facilities, or even the entire planet. Also, let's not forget about satellites, which clearly rely on network engineering and technology for their transmissions to and from land-based systems while managing data reception.

The most common network engineers are those who will manage mail servers, file servers, firewalls, routers, and other application servers within the context of the corporate network. These engineers have a wealth of knowledge about the manner in which data traverses the network, how it is saved, how it is stored, and the various protocols used by the data traveling along those networks during and after their creation. On numerous occasions, I have found that to properly reconstruct the events that took place on multiple computers of users from a corporate environment, an analysis of network logs and network applications was required to triangulate the meaning of the activity and the evidence itself.

In many cases, the network engineers simply give you the ability to access mail servers. In other cases, they may have the ability to provide you with remote real-time monitoring of data as it flows across the network by using specialized tools. In still other cases, network engineers may provide you with an analysis of router logs so as to better understand how an individual or individuals accessed network systems internally or externally, either with permission or maliciously.

The role of the network engineer in a computer forensic laboratory, whether specifically focused on network-related issues or as a computer forensic examiner who also has network engineering capabilities, should not be overlooked or understated.

The Cyber-Investigator

Cyber-investigators are a unique breed, in so far as they have a broad skill base encompassing, in most cases, strong computer forensic skills for both the capture and analysis of electronic data from hard drives and other equipment, as well as strong network engineering capabilities, with a deep understanding of the processes and procedures used in managing firewalls and routers, servers, and other online applications both of the traditional and the contemporary, including what we now call cloud-based services. In many cases, these cyber-investigators also understand the mechanics of software development and code development and may have a background in coding with languages such as C++, PERL, HTML, and Java. A good cyber-investigator may also have a strong knowledge of the development and manufacture of malware, also known as *viruses, Trojan horses, spyware, spam,* and other dastardly devices that permeate the Internet.

I should note that the development of many of these types of malicious software tools, which are used for the extraction of personally identifiable information and other protected information and behavioral stats, can be as simple as creating a new device by using a prepackaged malware development tool set, or may be as complex as the recent STUXNET virus/worm, which was developed using line-by-line written code in a formalized software development process involving multiple teams, perhaps in the dozens, if not more.

A good cyber-investigator will not only maintain all of these hard skills from the technology space but will also have strong soft skills, dealing with humans in what we call *social engineering.* This is a circumstance where the cyber-investigator is able to overcome real and artificial obstacles that have been developed, or at least maintained, by humans, such as the secretary sitting at the front desk of an office, who does not allow access to the office of the network admin, who in turn refuses to give up the password for the e-mail system. These human obstacles are often overcome through the use of the skill set known as soft skills.

Cyber-investigators with whom I have worked over the years often find their roots in the hacking community and have developed a sense for both the technical and human aspects of an event or investigation. These are naturally curious people who have evolved to the point where they've chosen to apply their skill sets in a positive fashion, as opposed to benevolent hacking or worse. The cyber-investigator plays an important role in a computer forensic examination or investigation in so far as they may lend real-world understanding and knowledge to questions that are being asked as a result of the evidence that is being examined. They can also assist in the real-time investigations, which require more sophisticated skill sets that need to be deployed in real time and outside of the laboratory.

The Traditional Investigator

There is often a role for the traditional investigator in a computer forensic examination or investigation. I've worked with numerous fine investigators over the years who have had little in the way of computer forensic or even regular computer skills or experience. However, these investigators have lent vital support to an investigation because of their knowledge of the investigative process, their understanding of human nature, and their ability to distill fact from fiction when the witness is speaking to them or when they are reviewing documents that don't meet the smell test.

I find that if you can properly leverage traditional investigators in the process of working hand in hand with cyber-investigators, computer forensic engineers, network engineers, and others on the team, then these resources will prove that the technology, as important as it is, is not driving the boat in the quest for knowledge, truth, and human failings that a good investigator can often ferret out. I should note that traditional investigators also play a role in managing the traditional investigative methods that need to be used to buttress many a cybercrime or cyber-investigation.

We have to remember that humans still exist in the real, tactile world. They drive cars; they enter homes; they ride elevators; they have conversations in parks; they purchase things in markets; they withdraw money from banks to fill up their cars with gasoline; they speak to their secretaries; they undertake activity that, in many cases, must be observed in the here and now in such a way that does not require any newfangled technology whatsoever and may simply require a good set of eyeballs, a notepad, and perhaps a car or a cell phone.

In many cases, traditional investigators should also be used to assist the computer forensic examiner in reviewing data and documents and making the judgment calls on how to search for data on the Internet when one is conducting a background check or looking to learn information about a particular subject for the purposes of either an investigation or due diligence or any other fact-finding mission. These traditional investigators will, more often than not, see something in the data set or connect the dots on websites in a manner that may not be self-evident to a computer forensic or cyber-investigator who has spent most of his or her career staring at a computer screen.

The Forensic Accountant

Forensic accounting is a field that has emerged in the past 20 years as an important adjunct to almost any investigation, particularly because so many investigations today revolve around financial fraud. Although the world of forensic accounting is relatively new, over the last many thousands of years accountants have, from time to time, had the task of reverse-engineering or looking at historic records to try to piece together what may have happened in the past from a financial perspective. Today, forensic accounting has taken hold in the United States, and in numerous nations abroad, as a field of study and practice that is accepted within the business community and that has been acknowledged to be responsible for the successful uncovering of fraud, both large and small, ranging from a few thousand to billions of dollars.

Today, numerous universities have added forensic accounting to their curriculum and there are industry associations through which you can take continuing education or even become certified in one of these fields. Among them are the Association of Certified Fraud Examiners (ACFE) and the American Institute of Certified Public Accountants (AICPA). In addition, these organizations run educational programs throughout the United States and elsewhere to inform practitioners of forensic accounting about new methodologies and updates in the field, as well as to allow them the opportunity to sharpen their basic skills.

Forensic accounting involves the historic review of accounting data for any purpose required. That purpose may be as benign as assisting a company that is looking to purchase a rival company and who requires forensic accountants to reconstruct numbers and accounting data for the purpose of due diligence. In many cases, forensic accountants are used to study the financials of foreign companies, where the accounting standards applied to the management of that company may not be consistent with the standards that are applied in the United States. A case in point would be when a U.S. corporation is looking to purchase a Chinese corporation and it is necessary to review the Chinese accounting. For instance, there have been several recent transactions in which U.S. purchasers of foreign-based companies were rudely awakened post-transaction by the reality that the value they had calculated was in fact not there. (For specific examples, look up the HP/Autonomy transaction and the Caterpillar/ Zhenghzhou Siwei transaction in any online search engine). While more effective early due diligence on the part of forensic accountants may have revealed these deficiencies earlier, it is also true that forensic accountants can and are often used after the fact to establish the true value of the entity of the damages sustained.

In some cases, accounting standards and accounting procedures may have differences. The company management, and a forensic accountant in some cases, may assist the traditional accountants in forming their conclusions and opinions. However, for the purpose of investigative computer forensics, a forensic accountant ordinarily comes into play when there is a financial aspect to the fraud or the crime that is being investigated. Often, it is necessary to bring in forensic accountants to review the electronic records that are recovered by a computer forensic specialist or simply provided in written form.

When computer forensic analysts are pulling electronic accounting records from computers and servers, these records are usually held in what are known as *databases* or *structured data formats*, such as QuickBooks, Peachtree accounting, or other accounting packages that maintain the data in a highly structured database format. The standard computer forensic process is often challenged by structured data that is found in a data set and needs to be reviewed. Most computer forensic tools are quite adept at analyzing what we call *unstructured data*, which would constitute e-mail, PDFs, Microsoft Office documents, and other miscellaneous documents and communications that may exist on a computer or a server. However, structured data, if it is retained inside a "container," is not as easily reviewed and often requires manual extraction of the data set in order to properly view and reconstitute the data.

When forensic accountants are a part of a team charged with reviewing accounting data, they generally work hand in hand with forensic analysts to identify the accounting data and/or the accounting software that may have been used by the company and to devise a defensible methodology for the extraction and reconstitution of the data in such a format that the forensic accountant can review it. Forensic accountants have the ability to quickly assess and analyze accounting data and to compare it to other accounting records that may be found in the company or accounting data that is provided by third parties, such as banks, regulators, vendors, and other potential partners, companies, or shareholders.

The forensic accountants provide a highly useful service in determining whether fraud took place as the result of the inconsistencies or inequities that are found. Many of the large financial fraud cases that have been in the news in recent years, including Enron, Bernie Madoff, and WorldCom, have, in some fashion, required the services of forensic accountants to understand the complex fraud or financial fraud and to determine the losses to the victims and what damages were sustained.

During litigation, one party generally needs to calculate the damages that will be offered and often the expert testimony of forensic accountants is required to assist in building the models to support those calculations. So when a forensic accountant is assigned to a project with a forensic analyst, and potentially a standard investigator, cyber-investigator, and some of the other types of individuals whom I mentioned previously, it is important that forensic accountants are integrated into the team as early as possible so that they receive the full benefit of the knowledge transfer and the institutional understanding that the team will glean from the forensic accountant.

Often, the forensic accountant can help guide the team members to where to concentrate their efforts and focus their resources, whether it be in certain accounting packages, or perhaps even third-party business applications that would result in exporting data or numbers that can help validate the assumptions that are being made in the investigation. I can hardly think of a complex fraud that has not, at some point in time, required the expertise of a forensic accountant, and I would note that in those investigations in which we have brought forensic accountants in early and who have been consulted as part of the core team of investigators, the client has benefited and the investigation has yielded more concrete results.

Interestingly, forensic accountants do not require any specific licenses or training in order to call themselves forensic accountants. It is a relatively unregulated space. However, even though you may have forensic accountants who are quite adept at what they do, based on prior experience and their career path, for the most part I would think it would be relevant to find forensic accountants who have certain certifications, such as the CMA (Certified Management Accountant), CFE (Certified Fraud Examiner), and CIA (Certified Internal Auditor). There are many forensic accountants who simply have a CPA, but I can say that the world of forensic accounting is limited to standard accounting issues. Therefore it's important to be able to verify a standard CPA's successful experience in reconstructing fraud or historic accounting records in prior engagements.

Forensic accounting requires an inquisitive and investigative mind-set to challenge assumptions and challenge the numbers as you see them. This is generally for the more curious types and I find that traditional investigators who have gone out and acquired the financial certifications to understand accounting data have fared well in the forensic accounting space. Similarly, standard accountants who have spent the time to understand the investigative world, and perhaps even the computer forensic world, have also fared well as forensic accountants because they've rounded out their knowledge base and are able to pull from these various disciplines.

Among the types of cases with which forensic accountants can assist, particularly when it comes to cases that have computer forensic investigatory components, are inventory and fraud cases in which forensic accountants are looking to reconstruct the usage of inventory or whether there was a divergence, a misclassification, a counterfeiting, or other types of inventory issues. Another area of focus is the problem of revenue recognition, which will often be kicked off by a regulatory action of some sort and where you will need to reconstruct quarterly revenue within an organization to determine whether revenue is recognized correctly. This type of work is often a historic exercise in which you are seeking to reconstruct books and records going back quarters, months, and years, and where the forensic accountant needs to work hand in hand with the investigative computer forensic analysts to reconstruct the data.

Other areas in which forensic accountants are playing a role in this type of work include financial statement fraud in which there is a fraudulent representation on the financial statements and where the financial statements need to be reconstructed using various data sources. Securities fraud is another area that has been in the news of late, and within which there is continual scrutiny, and that will see additional opportunity for forensic accountants to focus.

Forensic accountants often find themselves dealing with real estate fraud and real estate transactions, reconstructing the books and records related to everything from false deeds to mortgage fraud to unnecessary repairs that may have been conducted and all the way to landlord and leasing issues over rents that they may collect.

Finally, forensic accountants will sometimes be beholden to a domestic dispute and matters such as divorce in which a reconstruction of historic assets and the placement of those assets by your side of the divorcing party requires the backing and investigative skill set of a forensic accountant to reconstitute the numbers and develop an equitable solution. I would also add estates and trusts and the protection of the elderly as an area in which forensic accountants can, and often do, play a role, reviewing everything from life-insurance claims to the unintentional modification of wills or trusts and other issues that people in today's world and in the past have faced.

The bottom line is that the forensic accountant's role in the analysis of the financial records that are made available by computer forensic investigators is to follow the money, from where it came, and what is the disposition of it. It is a fascinating area of intrigue and study and there is tremendous opportunity for closer cooperation on these matters between forensic accountants and computer forensic analysts.

The Plaintiff's Attorney

The plaintiff's attorney or the prosecuting attorney, depending on whether it is a civil or criminal matter, plays an important role in the process that requires computer forensic evidence analysis and investigation to take place. The plaintiff's attorney is often the catalyst that kicks off the requirement or need for investigative computer forensics professionals to be engaged.

There are numerous scenarios to contemplate, in which activities undertaken by the plaintiff's attorney will require investigative computer forensics to be deployed on a matter. These include a preliminary internal investigation within an organization prior to the filing of plaintiff-based litigation, whereby the plaintiff's attorney, in preparation for that litigation, will kick off an internal investigation to determine what the potential involvement, downside, or risk level is of the plaintiff's company should litigation fail or should there be a counterclaim, which the client has some level of risk in sustaining.

Another manner in which the plaintiff's counsel will kick off the need for investigative computer forensics is, quite simply, the response that will be required by the receiving party of the lawsuit to conduct internal investigations to determine the level of exposure they may have. These internal investigations that take place at the inception of litigation and prior to the discovery process often require very specific computer forensic skill sets and an investigative team. A new field of work known as *early case assessment* has evolved around this area of the litigation process, where a company that is in receipt of a lawsuit performs early diligence and early investigative work to determine the extent of its exposure, its ability to respond, and to assess whether it is in its best interest to settle the lawsuit.

Many plaintiff's attorneys, particularly those representing class-action lawsuits, understand that large firms will generally undertake this early case assessment review to determine whether they're prepared to fight the claims as charged, and with that knowledge in hand, will come to the negotiation table hoping to either force or promote a settlement based on their own analysis of the merits of the case or be prepared to fight the case in court. Computer forensic investigators are often at the forefront of this early work, using tools such as Wave software's Trident, Zylab, Nuix, Clearwell, EnCase, or FTK, or even internal IT systems to coordinate among various departments.

The purpose of this is to assemble data in the form of either accounting data, e-mail, transactional data, or other documents that can undergo preliminary review by defense counsel, in-house counsel, or the executive management of the firm. This will help them make the determination as to whether they should move forward with the defense of their company. Plaintiff's attorneys also deploy computer forensic investigators at various times during their initial internal investigations. In some cases, the plaintiff's attorney will have access to a whistleblower or to an individual who has highlighted some wrong deed. These people may have at their disposal electronic records that they have preserved, in which case the plaintiff's attorney will more than likely seek the advice and assistance of a forensic expert to analyze that data and help determine whether the claims that are being contemplated are in fact true.

Once litigation is well underway, the plaintiff's attorneys will often assign their own computer forensic consultants and, potentially, computer forensic experts, to assist them throughout the process of litigation. In many cases, there is a separation between the testifying forensic expert and the consulting forensic expert. In this separation of duties, counsel is able to test theories and review multiple work streams with the consulting forensic expert to which the testifying forensic expert may not be privy. Testifying forensic experts will have very specific tasks to perform and will, at times, leverage an entire team of their own, consisting of technology specialists, forensic accountants, or other experts, to help formulate their expert opinion, to which they will eventually testify.

The plaintiff's attorney will also frequently reach out to third-party neutral forensic experts, as a result of the agreement with the opposing side. A neutral third-party computer forensic investigative expert or technician should be deployed to deal with specific issues that would benefit from having a neutral party conduct work, as opposed to a party who has vested interests.

Plaintiff's attorneys often find that working with their investigative computer forensic experts is a central theme to an important component of the case, particularly when the case is resting on either the actual evidence that is in hand at the time of filing or the presumed evidence that they expect to find during discovery. It is incumbent on plaintiff's attorneys to work hand in hand with their forensic experts and allow them a seat at the big table, if you will, for the purpose of crafting, analyzing, and preparing the strategy of the investigative work that needs to take place in preparation for discovery, further work, or for expert testimony at trial.

I have found in many cases that inexperienced attorneys have failed to engage the forensic experts appropriately at these early junctures, when they can provide the insight that is necessary to properly formulate strategy and case planning. This is often the result of plaintiff's attorneys not fully appreciating the significance that the electronic data will play in the case or the failure of the client to properly value the implication of the fees that will be spent on such an expert in the pursuit of their claim.

As a computer forensic expert or as an investigative computer forensic technician, it is vital that throughout the process of your engagement with plaintiff's counsel, you maintain meticulous records of the activities you undertake and that you communicate regularly and clearly with the plaintiff's counsel as to the direction in which you are going, given the findings that you have established and the risks and challenges that need to be escalated for counsel's input.

I have found that good computer forensic examiners, the ones who really make a difference in winning the case, provide their own intellectual capital to the process. They ask the deep and searing questions, pose the queries that aren't asked by others, ask the obvious or seemingly dumb questions, which perhaps may not have been considered by counsel at the time, and work with counsel to formulate a strategy and bring true value to the process. It is in those cases where the computer forensic investigator has brought value to the case and has assisted the client and/or counsel in making the right decisions that the relationship between counsel and examiner has been maximized.

I feel that the plaintiff's counsel who engages computer forensic experts and investigators in this manner and is diligent about finding the computer forensic investigators who have this capacity, can be well-served. The converse of this is to fire the forensic examiner who simply pushes the buttons and moves the data forward through the forensic applications without questioning the intent or the conclusions.

After all, even the questions that are drawn through the process are not cut and dried. That data, contrary to popular opinion, is not as black and white as we like to think, and there are nuances, both implied and real, that can be interpreted from the data and its interrelationships with other data points. These nuances can be ferreted out through questioning by both the forensic analyst and the plaintiff's counsel, or for that matter, the defense attorney, throughout the process.

This give-and-take back and forth between the parties will invariably increase the hours and the time that are spent on the case and ultimately may cost clients greater sums of money, but the net result will almost entirely be a more well-established and well-thought-out product and, generally, a more winning argument.

The Defense Attorney

Defense attorneys are initially in a reactionary mode when they receive from the plaintiff's attorney a complaint or notice that there may be a complaint. Defense attorneys' job is to quickly establish with their clients whether they're going to defend the action, how they intend to defend the action, and what resources they have at their disposal. Along with this activity, the defense attorney needs to formulate a response to the plaintiff's action in coordination with the client to ensure that electronic data and evidence that the defendant has access to or control of is preserved. This action is initiated by what is known as a *litigation hold* where counsel works with the defendant to identify all sources of potentially relevant and responsive documents or evidence and ensures that steps are taken so that these items are not modified or destroyed. A defendant may be an individual or corporation or even a government agency. In either case, the evidentiary obligations and duty to preserve are clear and must be taken seriously at the outset of the litigation.

I believe that computer forensic investigators can and often should be deployed to assist defense attorneys and their clients in formulating a response that will be consistent with the expected evidence and that they work to defend the case and assess the matter. In this respect, the early case assessment activities the plaintiff's firm might take in preparation for a lawsuit also apply to the defendant's case. The clients may need to undertake an early review of electronic data and physical records and potentially hold interviews within the organization to determine their position, their culpability, their response, and their risk profile.

This activity is often going to be led by information technology professionals that are already engaged within the organization, and to that effect, if there are computer forensic specialists or investigators or other investigation-minded folks within the organization who can be brought on board, this is often preferred. Sometimes, it is also preferred to bring in third-party experts who can review the electronic data and potentially review the early case assessments with an objective eye, with the goal of finding the relevant documents and maintaining absolute objectivity. I note this because, in some cases, organizations will have vested interests that are controlling certain pockets of information or processes, and as a result, the outside counsel, the defense counsel for the board, the senior executive management, or, for that matter, the in-house counsel may not always be receiving the true objective knowledge of what is taking place within the organization. This may be because these vested interests wish to protect their turf, their reputations, their jobs, and their families.

Computer forensic investigators can assist with this early case assessment work by providing objective insight into the disposition of electronic data and assist the team in formulating its conclusions so that a proper response to the lawsuit can be formed, whether it be a settlement offer or the response will take the company into full-blown litigation.

Following this early case assessment work and moving into the nuts and bolts of the litigation life cycle, the computer forensic investigators will be working closely with defense attorneys and, potentially, in-house counsel who are supporting the defense attorney's work. Computer forensic investigators work to preserve electronic data, analyze it, and scour systems for relevant data points that will help formulate the defense of the company and potentially even a counterclaim.

Defense counsel would be wise to engage these professionals as early as possible if the dispute relates to an electronic data issue. It is hard to think of disputes that don't have an electronic data component, being that almost all individuals today are communicating by e-mail, text messaging, voice mail messages, computer dialogue, and a host of other integrated technologies from smart chips to card readers and databases. As a computer forensic investigator, I have found that there is a significant volume of work available when focusing on corporate defense work. These corporate defense attorneys and white-collar criminal defense attorneys understand the significance and value of managing electronic data appropriately, both in a defensive and offensive posture, and will often rely on the advice and counsel of investigate computer forensic professionals to formulate the game plan and get ready for battle.

Much like the plaintiff's attorney, defense attorneys will sometimes divide their computer forensic professionals into consulting experts and testifying experts, in order to maintain some boundaries between the knowledge base of the two sides and to give the defense attorneys the flexibility to work with the data set from a forensic perspective and to draw certain conclusions without tainting the opinions of the testifying expert. To this end, the testifying expert plays a vital role in the defense of organizations and is required to work with defense counsel in preparation for expert testimony in a highly collaborative manner.

The relationship between defense counsel and investigative computer forensic professionals will vary, based on the type of case it is, the geography, as well as the budget that may be available to the defense counsel for managing the tasks. Often, corporations will insist on using their own internal forensic specialists. There are risks when going this route, of which the defense counsel should be aware in order to help the client make the right judgment call.

The E-Discovery Expert

The e-discovery expert works on many cases, particularly large complex litigation, and assists in the process of collecting and managing electronic data in cooperation with the investigative computer forensics specialists. These e-discovery experts may have expertise in a specific discovery review tool or certain methodologies, which will help streamline the process that the plaintiff or the defendant needs to implement to meet your discovery obligations.

In large, complex cases, it is not unusual for each side to have to produce millions of documents. Although these documents are electronic and one would think that there should be computer tools that would allow for the automated review of these documents, that is not the case. Although it is true that there is a new burgeoning field we call machine-assisted review, technology-assisted review, or predictive coding, where certain intelligence has been embedded into the software code and algorithms of these machines, allowing for a partially automated review of large volumes of documents, particularly for first-pass review, the reality is that, for the most part, most documents need to be reviewed by human eyes and this is an expensive proposition.

The role of an e-discovery expert is to assist in the process of managing significant volumes of data that are acquired by the investigative computer forensic specialists, so that you can leverage that data in such a way that it can most effectively be searched, processed, deduplicated, and organized for attorney review. In some cases, the e-discovery expert will also manage the attorney review, which will ordinarily take place on an online e-discovery platform.

There are many e-discovery platforms in the field today, including Concordance, Summation, Relativity, and others. This is a field that has grown exponentially over the course of the past 10 years, and there are now multiple companies offering excellent solutions for posting electronic data for attorney review.

However, the attorney review is also fraught with potential risks and pitfalls, not the least of which is the cost associated with managing such a large volume of documents that need to be reviewed by a group of attorneys for either privilege or issues. Some of these reviews can be accomplished with as few as one to three paralegals. Other cases need to be responded to in short order and can contain millions and millions of documents. In these instances, it is not inconceivable that a review would occupy the efforts of hundreds of review attorneys, operating in shifts around the clock, reviewing all documents off the same database, which is available online. This needs to be managed by an expert who knows where the pitfalls are and where the problems exist. This person must also manage challenges as they arise and must be able to testify in court as to the processes and procedures that were deployed during the data review and management, should the opposing side challenge the methodologies deployed and move for sanctions.

There have been hundreds and hundreds of cases in recent years where the plaintiff side or the defense side has moved for sanctions against the opposing side for what is known as *spoliation*. Spoliation claims occur when one side argues that the opposing side either intentionally or unintentionally destroyed, removed, or modified documents in such a way that they cannot be made available to the requesting party for review. In these spoliation cases, there have been tremendous outcomes where judges have ruled against one side or the other on the entire lawsuit as a result of the spoliation claim. In other matters, the spoliation claim has resulted in sanctions and monetary damages against one or both parties. Therefore, the issue of maintaining the integrity of the data from the point in time that the computer forensic investigative specialist acquires it and does the initial analysis all the way through to the processing, review, and eventual production has never been more important. To that effect, e-discovery experts can often carry their weight in gold by ensuring that those processes are followed in a manner that is consistent with the standard of care as dictated by the discovery industry and the various organizations, such as the Sedona Conference (www.thesedonaconference .org), that have proffered practices that in many cases represent the industry standard.

In some cases, the e-discovery expert will also take the form of an independent third-party e-discovery neutral, whose job it is to coordinate between the plaintiff and the defense on e-discovery issues, so as to both minimize the tension between both sides and minimize the costs associated with the electronic discovery collection, processing, review, and production. Discovery experts can also fill this role for the purpose of moving the case along without it getting bogged down in a costly and protracted review, something that is certainly not out of the question and that has been felt by law firms, plaintiffs, and defendants the world over for the past 15 years.

These neutral independent discovery experts, who are sometimes called *neutrals*, and can be appointed as a special master by the court, provide a valuable service to the litigation process, and specifically to the discovery process, by harmonizing the methodologies that are used between both sides, reducing the overall cost and tension associated with the discovery requirements, and allowing the parties to have their cases heard on the merits of the case as opposed to the fight that is, at times, artificially created during the e-discovery process.

I should note that there are a number of emerging standards for the e-discovery process. The Electronic Discovery Reference Model (EDRM) available at www .edrm.net is an important reference point for the emerging standards in this space. And although the Sedona conference (www.thesedonaconference.org) is potentially the gold standard for this space, there are others that are seeking to create certifications and education around the e-discovery process. One such organization, the Association of Certified Electronic Discovery Specialists, maintains and administers an accreditation for this space called CEDS, or certified electronic discovery specialist (www.aceds.org).

The Data Privacy Expert

The data privacy expert is an individual or group of individuals who can, from time to time, be deployed on a matter in which investigative computer forensics is required. I have seen this most frequently taking place during investigations in electronic discovery and litigation matters that involve a foreign jurisdiction outside of the United States that has a data privacy standard that is different from what is practiced in the United States. These data privacy experts will have expertise and working knowledge of the foreign jurisdiction's privacy standards and statutes and will assist the investigative computer forensic professional team and the electronic discovery team in collecting, reviewing, and processing that electronic data in a fashion that does not run afoul of the statute or standard of the country in which the data was acquired.

Case in point, in the European Union, there is a privacy directive that governs the manner in which electronic data can be collected, processed, produced, saved, destroyed, and managed in general throughout the European Union. In addition, each member state of the European Union has its own privacy statutes and regulations, which further define the manner in which data can be accessed and managed in the context of the ongoing operations of an organization and investigation, litigation, and other activities.

Some of the statutes are quite severe and will call for criminal penalties against the individual or company that breaches the standards. One of the fundamental tenets of the European privacy directive, which differs from the U.S. standard of privacy, is the notion that data that is created by an individual who lives and works in the European Union is the property of that individual, and data about that individual that is created by an organization is also the property of that individual. Therefore, if an individual and a European company create a document on their company computer, then the statute essentially states that that document is the property of the individual or at minimum that the individual has certain inherent rights over its usage. This is particularly the case if the document in question contains any personal information related to that individual. This is the manner in which rights are managed in the European Union as they relate to electronic data that may contain personal information regardless of the fact that the individual created the data on a company computer at the direction of the company while employed by the company.

In addition, records about that individual that are maintained by the company, such as human resource records, health records, or other business records, may also fall within the notion that the data is the property of the individual and not of the company. If, by chance, it does not rise to the level that it becomes the property of the individual, then it will at least rise to the level that it is within the right of the individual to determine and dictate how that data will be accessed and used. Therefore, if a U.S. company is investigating a case of fraud at one of its European subsidiaries, it must take great caution and care in collecting the electronic data of the individuals who are at the center of the fraud in the company's foreign operation, for should the company run afoul of the statutes, it may find itself in hot water up to the point of criminal prosecution.

There are a number of constructs that have been developed over the years to help organizations overcome these institutional barriers. One of them is the U.S. Department of Commerce Safe Harbor, which allows European companies and U.S. companies to self-certify that they have a process in place for the management of this electronic data that is subject to European privacy statutes and that will allow for its proper collection, preservation, and destruction when it is no longer required. The Safe Harbor, and other institutions like it, as well as a general knowledge of the privacy risks that organizations face in the collection and management of data, particularly in an investigation or litigation in the European Union, Asia, the Middle East, Africa, South America, or even as close as Canada, must be observed and reviewed by what I call a *data privacy expert.*

A data privacy expert can often form an important component of the overall computer forensic investigative team, chosen to ensure that the investigative analysts are not running afoul of those regulations during the collection and review of the data and other domestic privacy issues, such as the Health Insurance Portability and Accountability Act and state statutes governing how companies respond to data breaches and the inadvertent disclosure of personally identifiable information. Privacy experts can also potentially serve as a checkpoint for counsel to raise a red flag should it be determined that the opposing side is in fact running afoul of those very same regulations in the manner in which they are handling electronic data.

Data privacy experts are often certified by the International Association of Privacy Professionals (IAPP), available at www.privacyassociation.org. This organization holds conferences and regional meetings throughout the world and provides thought leadership on the topic of privacy.

The Data Reviewer

The role of the data reviewer in a computer forensic investigation or litigation matter should not be overlooked by the parties that are formulating a strategy for the data analysis and data collection, nor should the role be ignored by the forensic technicians who are charged with actually capturing and processing that data. As I said elsewhere in this volume, communication between team members is vital, and it is important for each component of the team to understand what the other components' responsibilities are so they can more effectively guide their own performance in relation to the work product that needs to be managed by other folks, either upstream or downstream, in the investigation.

One example is the sensitivity that needs to be applied to the data reviewer. A data reviewer is an individual, a group of individuals, or, in some cases, a machine, that is going to review the electronic data that has been processed and presented for analysis. In a small case, that very well may be the same individual who is conducting the computer forensic data collection, processing, and analysis, but in more cases than not, the data reviewer will be the attorney whose job it is to review the electronic data.

This data review is done for two reasons: (1) for privilege and (2) for issues.

It is done to flag certain documents that need to be either produced or held back for privilege, for further review, or for case strategy and analysis.

In a simple case where there are only a few hundred or perhaps even a few thousand documents, it is quite conceivable that the electronic documents that are produced would be printed out and placed in binders for review by data reviewers, or they could be burned onto a DVD or a CD or perhaps even e-mailed to an individual or group of individuals for review. This type of data review takes place day in and day out throughout the legal and investigative spectra. However, large-scale investigations and electronic discovery projects require dozens, hundreds, and, sometimes, thousands of individuals to review electronic data in order for the investigators, the regulators, or the plaintiffs and defendants to find resolution to their issues.

A data reviewer requisite is required, so the manager of the project can document the level of skill that is required by the data reviewers prior to that data review taking place. Some data reviewers are more adapted to reviewing financial documents, as they may have an accounting background or forensic accounting background, and data reviewers may have an easier time and be more familiar with using online data review platforms, such as those that have been described elsewhere in this volume. These may include Relativity, Summation, and Concordance, and data reviewers may already have the training necessary to be able to leverage these online review repositories; in other cases, reviewers must be attorneys.

The largest reviews will generally leverage what are known as contract attorneys, which are attorneys who are willing to work on a contract basis, usually on an hourly basis here in the United States, or in some cases overseas, for a first-level review of electronic documents for a very specific issue. The second-level review, which would often take place after those first-level reviewed documents have been collected, will then be undertaken by subject matter experts or counsel for the plaintiff or defendant, whoever is required to review the document, or perhaps even executives or management within either the plaintiff's or the defendant's company. These documents must be seen by folks who may have the ability to further understand comments on the documents that have been flagged for a particular issue, subject, or requirement.

The process of data review can, at times, be tedious and challenging because of the sheer monotony of reviewing hundreds and hundreds of documents per day, particularly on the online platform and particularly when one is reviewing electronic e-mail correspondence between employees of the company day in and day out for weeks or months. Because of this, it is important that supervision is taken seriously and that individuals are circulated or rotated between subject matters and data types as necessary so as to not burn them out during the data review.

Contemporary electronic data review systems have the ability to monitor the effectiveness, speed, and accuracy of the data review, and as such, managers have the ability to more accurately manage the data review team so that they are getting the most out of each one of the contract attorneys or other individuals who have been assigned for the review. In many midsize cases, where there has been a requirement to review several tens of thousands of documents during a period of a few weeks, a technique that is used to post those documents to an online review platform is preferably a robust and scalable one such as Relativity. You can then provide access to a group of individuals whom you have trained to review these documents for specific issues that may be privileged, or maybe more complex issues, such as documents that relate to specific conversations within a group of employees or a particular issue that may be at the heart of the subject for the plaintiff or defense lawsuit.

Often, once these individuals have been properly trained, are able to collaborate on the online review platform, and have been assigned their share of documents to review on a daily or weekly basis, these individuals would be well served by being located within one large room, such as a conference room or what is commonly known as a war room, where 8, 10, 12, or more computer terminals that are connected to the Internet and have access to the database are set up. These individuals can work in this room in shifts, under the supervision of a data review supervisor who will ensure that questions are answered as they come up, challenges with specific documents are dealt with, and that the work flow is proceeding with the level of speed required to meet the time frame of the particular discovery order.

It is not unusual for the data reviewers to highlight or flag documents that need to be sent back to headquarters and an investigative computer forensic professional for further analysis. An example could be to review the metadata of a particular document or to find the linkages between a particular document and other documents of interest. This is often an important component of the overall investigative or discovery strategy. Therefore, the role of the data reviewer should not be overlooked or underappreciated.

The Project Manager

During an electronic discovery investigation, and specifically during a forensic investigation, project managers play a vital role. Project managers ensure that the delivery of the work product is consistent with client expectations. They ensure that timetables and deadlines are met and that the team is on budget. These issues are flagged and escalated when the team looks to be approaching a budget constraint that needs to be overcome or for other technical issues that need to be addressed, such as the requirement that additional expertise in some specific field of study be brought onto the team.

I often have push-back from clients on the project management fees. However, I have found that when solid project management on the engagement is involved, particularly by project managers who have deep experience in electronic discovery, computer forensic investigations, and litigation, and even more particularly, project managers who are certified project managers, the project will stay on track and operate more smoothly overall.

Many large organizations even go so far as to institute an office for the project manager, whereby the project management and administrative features and functions of a particular project are centralized not just with one individual but with an entire team of individuals who are responsible for issues as far-reaching as time and billing, compliance with regulatory and privacy issues, staffing, the logistics of moving teams from point A to point B, client communication, and reporting functions. These project managers serve a vital role throughout the process, and it is my recommendation that, on any decent-size investigation, you indicate who is the project manager you have assigned the task of project management and clearly define the responsibilities and roles of that individual to ensure that the individual has been integrated into the conversations, the strategy, and the communications among the various investigators, technicians, lawyers, and other players. This way, they will be well-versed in the political and logistical realities of the engagement, so as to help keep things on track, avoid potholes, and fend off problems before they happen.

A good project manager is a good communicator and has excellent follow-through and great attention to detail. However, a good project manager does not allow that attention to detail to skewer the more nuanced needs of some of the investigators, who require some latitude to be able to conduct their work without having artificial constraints of either logistics or time frames clouding their judgment or their ability to act. Now, it is clear that in cases where you have well-defined analytical work, it needs to take place where you can keep a short leash on individuals, particularly when it is highly quantifiable, such as data reviewed by data reviewers or review contract attorneys.

When you have individuals who are charged with surveillance of individuals in the field and they need to report back their findings on, for instance, wireless communication or keylogging observation or other activities, project managers need to be flexible enough to be able to give these individuals the space and time they need to operate in the field. I often find inefficiencies in cases where the individuals charged with conducting some very specialized tasks, such as data analysis or data collection, are sidetracked by project management with other responsibilities. In this case, the client is being shortchanged by paying higher fees for skilled technicians who have been relegated to conducting administrative work that could be better centralized by a project manager who would be more efficient in the execution of those duties and would free up the technicians to do what they do best.

The Interviewer

Interviewing skills are an important component of any investigation and are often needed at the inception of the investigation. Investigative computer forensic professionals can often serve as interviewers, particularly technical interviewers when they are in the field and are required to ascertain the characteristics and components of a computer network at a site that is under investigation or to understand the user habits of individuals who are working on the computer network so as to better structure an investigation plan. However, interviewers with specific interviewing skills may be required.

There have been numerous occasions in which, even though I am conducting a computer forensic acquisition, it is important for me to have on staff and as part of the team seasoned investigators who have a keen sense of observation and strong interviewing skills. I have found particular luck with retired FBI agents whom we are able to deploy on investigations, as they are trained in interviewing skills by some of the best in the industry and are able to quickly ferret out information from individuals based on what they say and what they don't say, by their body language and other movements, and by many other intangibles that are difficult to quantify, specifically for forensic investigators or forensic analysts who spend most of their time staring at a computer screen as opposed to the human body and human face.

The role of the interviewer throughout the life cycle of the investigation, and sometimes also within e-discovery, can be a vital component of the overall team. So when you are in the process of constructing your team, pay some attention to the need for interviewing skills. In many cases, I have found that the attorneys for whom we were working will ask for an investigating computer forensic professional to assist them during those interviews, and perhaps sit in on the interviews to ask some of the technical questions. This can often help to bridge the gap between legal and technical vernacular.

I have found that many attorneys make fine interviewers. They have been trained in the art of questioning, which is demonstrated through their deposition skills and their trial skills. However, their technique in some cases can prove to be offensive or combative to the interviewee, therefore, having an interviewer who is able to go soft or hard, depending on the requirements of the day, may benefit some cases.

The Researcher

Research is an important component of many investigations. Research can be conducted to find public domain information, or to private data that is located within the confines of a corporation, or even data that is contained within the individual's own hard drive or computers. The techniques that professional researchers use are well-defined and have specific processes that help to classify and quantify information as it is being received. When using researchers, the investigation can become more extremely efficient because they have the ability to distill their findings into a more useful format.

I often must rely solely on the forensic professionals, who are more focused on leveraging electronic data and analyzing computer hard drives, to do the research. Although they may find good nuggets of data that we are seeking, their skill set is not specifically designed for traditional research. Their skill set is more in line with conducting computer forensic analysis, which is a highly granular and detailed type of research into the inner workings of electronic equipment and file types, but it does not necessarily translate well into linking real-world concepts and ideas reflecting the behavior of your target.

It is quite simple to hop onto Google, Bing, or Yahoo and conduct your own research as an investigator, and the level of the low-hanging fruit will make itself quite available to you. You may feel quite good about what you find, but good researchers have the ability to go way beyond what is commonly available on a search engine. They understand how to triangulate data points from different sources that are not on publicly available search engines, and also through the use of databases and private data repositories that store information that is not publicly accessible or are known to the average attorney or even computer forensic investigator who is charged with researching a particular topic.

This is particularly true when conducting background checks, which are often helpful in understanding who your target is, and will help paint a picture of the habits and background of the individual whose data you may be searching. Having this background brief can provide the computer forensic investigator with great insight into the reasons a particular device or particular type of data was used in a particular way and can often spell the difference between a winning or losing point at trial.

Law-Enforcement Officers

Law-enforcement officers often play a role in the computer forensic investigation. Clearly, the role of a law-enforcement officer in a criminal matter goes without saying, particularly when the law-enforcement officer is assisting the prosecuting attorney or the district attorney's office in framing a case and pulling together the relevant electronic data to support the charges that are being made. Often, the law-enforcement officer is required to work with the computer forensic investigator in order to draw out the electronic data that needs to be searched.

On other occasions the investigative computer forensic professional is the law-enforcement officer, as there are numerous sworn peace officers who are focused on computer forensics whom are charged with combating everything from financial fraud to child pornography, smuggling, cybercrime, and other dastardly deeds. Computer forensic professionals will also, from time to time, work against law-enforcement officers when they are charged with defending a particular white-collar crime or a criminal matter in which there is an electronic evidence component and where they are assisting in the defense of an individual or corporation. In these types of matters, the investigative computer forensic professional may be called to testify on the findings in support of the defense, in which case he may find himself in a courtroom offering testimony that is in direct contradiction to the testimony that is being provided by a sworn police officer or officer of the law.

These cases can be quite challenging and trying for computer forensic investigators, specifically because the computer forensics industry by and large has been given short shrift to denote the world of computer forensic defense work. In fact, the organization known as the HTCIA, or the High-Tech Crime Investigators Association, has a dominant position in the training marketplace and has made it a tenet of membership that if you are to join and be a bona fide member of HTCIA, then you cannot take on criminal defense work as a computer forensic investigator. Certainly, there is a rationale for an organization to be formed that would support the computer forensic analysis work conducted on the behalf of defendants, so as to ensure that the standards that are being applied to the prosecution are being upheld for the defense as well.

The Prosecutor and Magistrate

The computer forensic professional or investigator may at times work for a prosecutor or magistrate as an expert. Prosecuting attorneys' role is to ensure that they are prosecuting cases on behalf of the entity that they represent, whether it is the city or state, a government agency, or a nation. They will enable computer forensic techniques and technologies on behalf of that agency or entity in order to make their case, just as the plaintiff's attorney will.

The e-discovery rules in the federal criminal world are somewhat different from those in the civil world, and when a prosecuting attorney is in receipt of computer forensic evidence, the responsibilities for sharing that data with the defense are very different than one would find in the civil arena. As a result, the defense attorneys and defense technicians, in many cases, do not have an opportunity to do a complete computer forensic review of the electronic data that is being brought against them as evidence during an action. Therefore, they must seek alternatives to refuting any points being made and try to fill it in later.

The roles that are given to magistrates in the U.S. federal system include the role of managing the electronic discovery aspects of a large federal case. The mandate would normally be to manage and rule on issues pertaining to e-discovery for both the defense and the plaintiff. Magistrate judges will make judgment calls on the discovery rulings and may even go so far as to issue sanctions against the parties should they fail to meet their obligations.

I have found in the federal system that magistrate judges have increased their understanding of electronic discovery and computer forensics to the extent that, in many cases, they are leading the way in best practice. Noted federal judges and magistrates such as Honorable Andrew Peck, Honorable John Facciola, Honorable Lee Rosenthal, Honorable Paul Grimm, Honorable Elizabeth Laporte, Honorable Nan Nolan, and Honorable Shira Sheindlin have all established important rulings and have presented themselves within the discovery and forensic industries as noted authorities on the topic. This has allowed for a more comprehensive and perhaps multilayered set of standards of care and practice to be fostered among the legal community, corporations, and technologists alike. The addition of a growing body of case law, precedent, and judicial commentary has given much-needed certainty and clarity in a space that has often been clouded by conflicting approaches and expectations of how to manage electronic data in this age.

The Judge

The judge has the final word, and as such, when the prosecution or defense attorneys get to the point that they are in front of the judge, their pulse quickens and their wits sharpen, and everybody is on their game. This includes the computer forensic analyst or investigative computer forensic specialist, whose responsibility it is to report on the facts from the witness stand or to support the efforts of the plaintiffs or defendants behind the scenes, while they prosecute or defend against the opposing side in the trial.

Judges come in all shapes and sizes, and one can find judges in rural areas of the U.S. state court who are as well informed, if not more so, than the most sophisticated judges in the federal system in Manhattan. Conversely, you can find federal judges who really don't understand computers any better than the state judge who doesn't know how to use his or her own laptop and must rely on his or her clerk for printing all documents. So, there should be little expectation, or I should say predisposition, when one goes into the courtroom as to how your judge is going to treat you when it comes to electronic- and technology-related issues. It is important to be deferential, clear and concise, educational, and polite and to seek the truth. The importance of the role of the judge in the litigation process cannot be overstated. It would be unwise to presume that your past experience in court could predict the temperament, procedures, or attitudes that you will face. Maintaining decorum and showing deference for the sanctity of the courtroom is an obligation that any forensic investigator should feel not only toward his or her client but also to the institution itself.

Judges are often appreciative of a forensic expert who is prepared to explain the details of how a particular investigation or a component of an investigation was performed, simply and clearly and without unnecessary complicated technical language, in a way that prepares the jury, the judge, and the other parties in the litigation to discuss, reflect on, and argue the point with clarity. The role of investigative computer forensic experts, when testifying, is often to provide guidance and to illuminate the tasks that they were assigned and to clearly state what questions they were tasked with answering and what conclusions they may have reached as a result of analyzing the available evidence.

The Jury

Another component in many cases involving investigative computer forensics is the jury. This is particularly true when the case that you have investigated or of which you are part has made its way through trial and is now going to be decided by a jury. The jury is generally composed of 12 individuals, who are peers from the public and who will consider the facts of the event that are presented by both the plaintiff's and defendant's side. They will also take into consideration the instructions from the judge and ultimately will have to render their opinion.

When considering the jury makeup, remember that the jury is going to be made up of randomly selected individuals. They will have undergone some scrutiny during the voir dire process. Nonetheless, they can represent both novices of computer use, as well as experts in computer use, and can have certain predispositions to how computers work and how data is stored, what acceptable policies and procedures should be, and how an individual's privacy or responsibilities can be impacted by the reach of corporations, individuals, laws, government regulations, and so on. As a result, it's always going to be a mixed bag, and you never know what kind of jury you will get.

My advice has generally been for testifying examiners to stay clear of courtroom disputes and focus on the facts as they are. Direct the responsibility of the computer forensic examiner, who is testifying in court, to present the facts; to represent them accurately; to represent the procedures, policies, and techniques that were used; and, if called on, to relay the conclusions that were reached during the investigation.

The Public

One of the final elements in the human quotient is a little wild card called the *public*. For cases that involve the disclosure of testimony or production to the public and in which the public has the ability to comment or to weigh in, it is possible that this discourse will have the ability to sway or influence the actions of members of the defense or prosecution team. For the most part, this needs to be avoided and team members need to stay focused on their mandate and their fact-finding mission, but wild cards can appear out of nowhere, and from time to time, a member of the public can offer information that can assist the fact-finders in resolving roadblocks that they may have in analyzing the available data.

Case in point would be whistleblowers who have come out of the woodwork once a case has been brought to the attention of the public domain. These whistle-blowers may provide additional evidentiary media to examine and they will point individuals in the right direction. That direction may simply be a posting on a blog or an entry on a website that needs to be captured to assist in the investigation. In international investigations, one also has to take into consideration the response or uncertainty of the public, particularly in environments in which one is not entirely aware of what the rules of the road are. For example, if you are sent to a foreign country to conduct a forensic investigation and there are cultural taboos and rules of which you are not aware and that you breach, this can create problems and challenges for the investigation, from a practical standpoint.

By example, if one is collecting electronic data in Japan, then it is expected that you treat the actual computer hardware with a degree of respect and care, to the extent that most computer forensic examiners in Japan will wear white gloves when they are receiving, disassembling, assembling, touching, and returning the computer. This active donning of the white gloves as a sign of care and respect and conveys a message to the custodian that you are being careful and attentive to your work. Should you fail to observe cultural norms within the nation in which you are operating, you run the risk of having uncooperative custodians, more challenging interactions with your client or with the operators of the target facility, and potentially even more challenging interactions with regulators, law enforcement, or other persons in a position of authority.

This can run the gamut from local police officers who may or may not take an interest in what you are doing in their town with computer equipment from a foreign nation, to the reaction that you may or may not receive from customs officials or security officials at a border checkpoint or airport when passing through with multiple hard drives and computers, an event that they may never have seen before. Therefore, keep in mind that the public at large and the cultural proclivities of any number of groups of people, whether they be nationalities, corporations, clubs, associations, unions, or any other construct, can have an impact on the investigative work that the U.S. computer forensic examiners are conducting. While deployed in foreign jurisdictions or even geographies that are somewhat removed from your normal area of operations or comfort zone, you as the individual leading the investigation, need to be aware of the localized nuances and sensitivities when managing and guiding your resources.

The Bad Guy

Bad guys are everywhere. They may be sitting next to you in the cubicle or standing behind you waiting to use the ATM. The bad guy may have sent you an e-mail requesting an introduction or challenge you to a fight at the bar. The bad guy might be the corporation that shredded the auditor's notes, eliminating evidence of financial fraud, or he or she may be the reclusive 18-year-old maladjusted hacker who is looking to deprive you of your privacy by inserting keylogging software on your computer. See Exhibits 3.7 through 3.9.

The reality is that there is no end in sight for frauds or crimes that are being perpetrated on users of the global networks or computers. Regardless of the bad guys' motivation—whether it be for profit, retribution, revenge, anarchy, politics, mayhem, or vandalism—they are bound to leave a trail of digital evidence, which, if pieced together effectively, can help bring them to justice or can assist in providing the victims with some measure of peace.

Newspapers, television shows, films, fictional books, and Internet websites are filled with stories today of how bad guys have hurt the innocent by leveraging the Internet, and it is clear that this trend will not abate as long as people are free to do as they wish. Obviously, the extreme solution of enslaving all people and preventing communication is something no people in their right mind would desire and thus societies are required to manage the sober reality of cybercrime and fraud as best they can. Because of the ease with which the bad guys today can disguise themselves behind the mask of anonymity, the role of the investigative computer forensic examiner is all the more relevant and needed in both the public and private sector.

EXHIBIT 3.7   Interior View of Crashed Hard Drive Platters and Actuator Arms

This hard drive was used by a hacker who thought by damaging the hard drive with a hammer and thereby forcing the heads and the actuator arms to dislodge from their standard position that the data would be irretrievable. (Arms are now resting near the spindle of the platters.) In fact, through a combination of clean-room work by hard drive reconstruction specialists and examination by computer forensic investigators, the data implicating the hacker in the writing of vicious malware and viruses was preserved and presented to law enforcement.

The Devil Is in the Details

As a parting thought on the fundamentals of computer forensic investigations, I would submit that the devil is in the details. It is necessary to treat the evidence; the policies, procedures, and practices; the technological systems; and the human beings who are involved in the process with care, thought, and attention. It is also important to ensure that your work product is thorough and complete, that it has met the highest standards of which you are capable, and that it is objective, sincere, and meaningful.

It is the responsibility of the computer forensic investigator to report on his or her findings in a factual and professional manner, using language that can be understood, using structure that is proper, and using conclusions that are sound. I've seen too many computer forensic professionals sliced and diced by an effective opposing counsel who knows how to ask the stinging and penetrating questions about their processes and procedures, both during deposition and in trial, and the results can be devastating. Ill-prepared

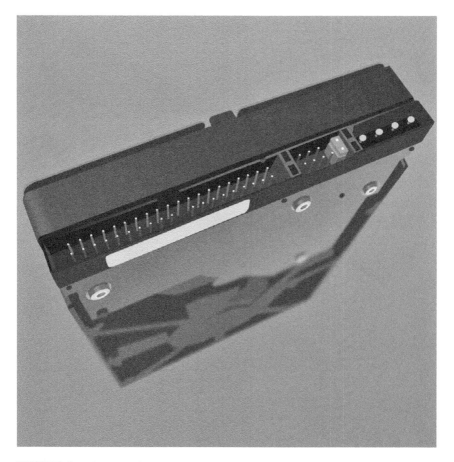

EXHIBIT 3.8   Close-Up of the Connection Points on an Internal Computer IDE Hard Drive

This is the connection that employs pin metal wire connectors to connect via ribbon cable to the motherboard of a computer. This was the common hard drive interface that was used until the introduction of SATA connectors. One of its vulnerabilities was that the pins on the drive could snap off or break with frequent wear or if an examiner was too rough with the installation or removal of the corresponding ribbon cable.

forensic practitioners or those who have taken shortcuts because of the demands of their client, their job, or their own unwillingness to see through all potential avenues of investigation are certain to find their day at the "O.K. Corral" a less than fruitful one.

Resisting the temptation to reach conclusions because they appear to be obvious at first blush is an important hallmark of a good forensic investigator. One has to back up the conclusions that are reached by the evidence that is found in the data, and should the conclusion have challenges or holes that cannot be explained, then the forensic examiner must be upfront about those challenges with the attorney, executive, or manager at whose direction they are working.

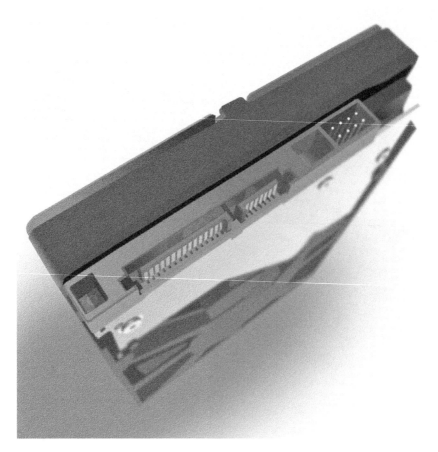

EXHIBIT 3.9   Close-Up of the Connection Points on an Internal Computer SATA Hard Drive

This connection employs a prefabricated and integrated male plug to interface with a SATA cable to connect to the motherboard of the computer. SATA components are modular and allow for easier and less risky connection and disconnection while also improving data throughput and reliability.

Good computer forensic examiners will not know where those holes are unless they have gone through the hard work of "running all threads to ground," as one of my colleagues, David Knutson, likes to say. Seasoned forensic investigators, like Knutson, who hail from a frame of mind that is analytical, stout, and unforgiving, are able to provide analysis that is solid and will stand the test of direct challenge. I've seen other investigators over the years who are willing to take shortcuts, or perhaps have not completed the necessary training or education (whether on the job or formalized) that they require to know that the pitfalls even exist, and when the time comes to go to trial, not only are they left holding the bag, but the client pays an enormous price as a result. So, as my old partner at Online Security, Charlie Balot, would always say, "The devil is in the details" and if you don't pay attention, he will take you down.

CHAPTER 4

Investigative Fundamentals

This chapter deals with some of the primary investigative fundamentals that are required to develop a sound investigative plan and to achieve success in the fact-finding mission with which you are charged or with which you are charging your computer forensic investigators. In the classic investigative world, long before the advent of computers, when investigators were required to review volumes upon volumes of paper data and research material from public records in halls of administration and also were required to trail suspects physically, many of the attributes of a successful investigator could be easily defined.

The Investigative Mind-Set

Among the primary attributes of a successful investigator is a natural sense of curiosity, having a desire to understand things that are out of your reach and to learn the truth to questions that come across your field of vision. These are essential elements of the investigative mind-set. Suspicion is also an important aspect of the investigative mind-set. Good investigators have natural suspicion of things that are presented to them, stories that are told to them, or even the observations that they themselves make. The five senses of the human experience allow investigators to observe. This ability to observe and to have an acute sense of observation is a key ingredient to being an effective investigator, regardless if it's in the days of Sherlock Holmes or in the twenty-first century, when one must observe the activity of individuals on the Internet.

Remembering patterns of unusual behavior about an individual, such as what the individual ate while in an interview with you, how an individual walked, or the type of clothing that the individual was wearing—these little clues reveal the makeup of an individual's behavioral traits can pay dividends down the road when the investigator must deduce patterns from a broad set of disparate observations. It is important for an investigator to remain as unbiased as possible, without a predisposition to a particular outcome in the investigation. When the investigator has bias or prejudice, it may result in false findings and can have disastrous consequences for the subject of the investigation, the parties who are seeking the investigation, and certainly for the investigator themselves. In some investigations, on the Internet in particular, it is important for the investigator to have the ability to assume a new identity or to role-play for the purpose of ferreting out information that may be useful to the investigation, such as when an investigator populates an Internet chat room with a false identity for the purpose of learning more information about activities of a particular individual or group of individuals.

A good investigator is resourceful, inventive, and has the ability to think outside the box. The investigator also has the ability to work with other parties and to seek out and achieve cooperation in the activities that they are managing or pursuing. Whether the investigator is conducting online or in-person interviews or is observing data, there is a need for strong listening skills. These include audible listening skills, but much can also be learned by simply paying attention to the activity around you, from the body language of a suspect to the manner in which you found a particular computer at a suspect's site. Listening carefully with an open, yet focused mind is a skill set that cannot be overlooked; a dogmatic, bombastic, or confrontational investigator will almost always push away potential leads and suspects.

Nearly all of the effective investigators that I have met during my career have been clever, open-minded, intuitive, and confident listeners who have the ability to put people at ease and address nearly any audience with a sense of purpose and intellect. These foundational skill sets will make or break investigators, regardless of the century in which they are operating. In fact, it could not be more important today to have these same skill sets because investigators are required to traverse so many environments and communication platforms, many of which they will not be familiar or comfortable with, but if these foundational skills are in place, then a good investigator will have the resources to work through the most challenging circumstances.

Case Management

There are a wide variety of investigations that may be undertaken, including witness location; employment investigations; workers compensation claims; private family investigations; homicide, suicide, and missing persons investigations; personal background checks; corporate investigations; civil investigations; negligence or criminal investigations; drug-related investigations; reconstruction of accidents; trademark and patent infringement investigations; slip-and-fall accident investigations; divorce cases and other domestic issues; and even undercover investigations. Sources of information that investigators will need to rely on include physical evidence, actual objects and traces of objects that are left at a crime scene or the scene of an event, everything from photographs to Post-It notes to tools, credit cards, personal information and articles, and in the case of criminal investigations, forensic evidence such as fingerprints and DNA. Additional sources of information include records and documents, data from informants who may be working on the investigation and who can identify behavior from within an organization, and information from people who are witnesses or observers of behavior of possible suspects over time, including family members, coworkers, shopkeepers, teachers, friends, neighbors, and the list goes on.

In using the fundamental characteristics of investigating coupled with an understanding of computing processes, networks, and systems, computer forensic investigators must also use good judgment in the preparation of their case and have strong organizational skills. This is to make certain that over time, as the case develops, new information is learned, and changes in direction take place, the investigator is able to manage the information that is processed and received in an effective manner and in such a way that it can be made readily available to outside counsel, other investigators, or other interested parties without losing the dynamic nature of that information.

Proper filing mechanisms, both electronic and physical, as well as clear note taking pay dividends over time. I have seen numerous investigations in which investigators have failed to take regular and appropriate notes, both during interviews and during the analysis of the data, and as a result, have lost key information that would be useful months or even years down the road. In modern investigations, where data is flowing from multiple sources, often in real time, this note taking is very valuable so that a reliable and accurate reconstruction of events and observations may take place.

Fraud and Investigative Analysis

Finding and tracking fraud requires special skills and the ability to interpret clues and information that may be provided by tipsters and whistleblowers or through the observation of day-to-day activity in which there may be anomalous behavior.

Fraud can also be exposed as the result of the review of electronic data by computer forensic investigators. There are a wide variety of frauds that computer forensic investigators may be tasked with reviewing, from corporate espionage to securities fraud to pyramid or Ponzi schemes, insurance fraud, vacancy fraud, and other financial scams.

Today, it is also not uncommon for computer forensic investigators to be tasked with reviewing data related to the Foreign Corrupt Practices Act (FCPA) of 1977: frauds, money laundering, or other issues related to bribes and kickbacks. More often than not, computer forensic examiners will be working at the direction of either investigators or certified fraud examiners or forensic accountants who are examining financial data and other electronic applications for clues to how the fraud was perpetrated. Forensic examination of server data and desktop computers can allow for the extraction of financial transactional database-driven evidence that can be correlated or cross-compared to other data sets to help establish whether a fraud has indeed taken place.

Computer forensic examiners are for the most part not particularly well-versed in financial and accounting rules and procedure; therefore, when examining data in pursuit of resolving a financial fraud, it is recommended that forensic investigators partner closely with forensic accountants and other financial specialists who can help to not only interpret the data but also guide the forensic examiner through the applications and systems that they are retrieving, recovering, and reconstituting for the investigation.

Information Sources and Records

A vital component of any investigation is access to information sources and records. These information sources in the computer forensic context are the obvious computers, hard drives, cell phones, servers, backup tapes, and other components of a network that would contain electronic data belonging to an individual; however, in the traditional sense there are a wide variety of other sources that will prove useful and that can be correlated against sources that are managed by the computer forensics professionals. These include internal corporate records both in paper form and electronic form, such as accounting system data financial statements and tax returns sales, accounts receivable records expense documentation, and other data sources that would be relevant to the investigation.

But there are a wide variety of other native sources outside of the corporate environment that may be relevant in any given time, particularly when investigating individuals. These include credit reports, medical records, tax records, and even public records that can be pulled from public domain sources, such as court filings and records, arrest records, voter records, incarceration records, Uniform Commercial Code filings, real estate records, Department of Motor Vehicle records, academic records, tax lien information, professional licensing information, ownership of intellectual property records from the U.S. patent and trademark office, and business and industry databases proprietary to the specific industry that is in question.

And most effective these days is Internet-based records that are available to trained researchers. These Internet records may be in the form of listings included in databases, which are accessed on a per-use basis for a fee or they may be as simple as searches on Google. The noted computer forensic expert and educator Chad Tillbury has said, "Google is the ultimate forensic resource."

Investigative Techniques

Although the list of investigative techniques deployed by any investigator is long and voluminous and there are any number of subtle nuances to each of those techniques and how they are deployed by the individual investigator given the circumstances that he or she is faced with, this volume does not presume to analyze all of them or even a large number of them, but rather will highlight a few of those techniques that are used during the course of the forensic examination of computer data by the investigator. There is a wide variety of forensic investigative tools available to the computer forensic investigator. Some of these tools are specific to law enforcement, while others are commercially available. Depending on the country and jurisdiction in which one lives, one may have access to specific tools that have been developed for applications that are in use within that jurisdiction, or may be restricted from using certain tools because of export controls from the country in which they are built. See Exhibit 4.1.

There are a number of forensic tools that would fall into the category of forensic platforms, forensic environments, or forensic suites of tools, and I covered some of these earlier in this volume. They include EnCase by Guidance Software Corporation; FTK or the Forensic Toolkit by Access Data Corporation; iLook Leo and iLook PII, produced by Roe Corporation, P2 Commander by Paraben Corporation; X-Ways Forensics, manufactured by X-Ways Software Technology AG; Mac Forensics Lab, manufactured by Mac Forensics Lab Inc.; and Black Light Mac Analysis, produced by BlackBag Technologies.

EXHIBIT 4.1 The Digital Smoking Gun

A euphemism for the electronic needle in a haystack of billions of bits and bytes that the computer forensic investigator is often charged with finding. A challenge that requires a combination of skills ranging from the technical to the intuitive, from the analytical to the skeptical, and which also can at times favor the creative and the lucky.

There are also a number of tools that are task-specific and have been developed to accomplish a specific aspect of forensics, such as products that are developed strictly for the analysis of e-mail, including E-mail Examiner and Network E-mail Examiner by Paraben Corporation, E-mail Detective by Hot Pepper Technology, or Mail Analyzer by BelkaSoft. There is also chat program forensic analysis of services and systems such as Yahoo! Messenger, MSN, and Skype. These tools include Forensic IM Analyzer, made by BelkaSoft, and Chat Examiner, developed by Paraben Corporation. Another task-specific product is NetAnalysis, produced by Digital Detective, and Browser Analysis by BelkaSoft, both of which were developed to review the Internet history of the machine.

Within the world of mobile device forensics, which includes smartphones, iPads, iPods, GPS units, personal data assistants, and other unique handheld devices, there is a wide variety of systems that have been developed for this purpose, including Deployable Device Seizure by Paraben Corporation, Cell Brite by Cell Brite USA Corporation, CellDek by Logiccube Inc., Mobilize by BlackBag Technologies, and IT PIM by Open Circuit, which is an open-source free application.

Surveillance and Interviewing

Computer forensic professionals are often called into the role of conducting real-time surveillance on electronic targets through monitoring of behavior on networks. This is where computer forensics and network security professionals often collaborate, as the network security professionals may be charged with installing the tools and systems that allow for the capture of electronic data, such as keylogging software, network sniffing tools, and other clandestine line devices designed to capture electronic data as it is traversing the network.

The computer forensic professionals who would work with these network engineers or network security professionals would then be in receipt of the output of the data from these tools and would be charged with analyzing the behavior-formulating conclusions and potentially authoring reports so as to help the investigative process along.

Surveillance runs the gamut of monitoring individual machines, routers, and servers, including e-mail servers, web servers, and transactional or application servers, but also includes the monitoring of such mundane systems as voice mail systems or video monitoring systems, commonly known as DVRs (digital video recording devices). In recent years, my practice has seen a significant uptick in the requirement to reconstruct digital video from DVRs for forensic analysis review and potential replay in a court of law.

In some cases, these DVRs recorded the movement of individuals in a particular confined space, such as a bank, a nightclub, a convenience store, a department store, or even a moving bus or train, which sometimes required the reconstruction of overwritten video or the stitching together of numerous camera angles into a cohesive view that will allow for a trier of fact to reconstruct a chain of events that has been captured by these time-lapse cameras. Interviewing is another important skill set that computer forensic investigators are often tasked with managing. Interviews may be as straightforward as an IT interview with individuals within an organization who understand a particular set of systems or an IT director who understands and can articulate the policies and procedures that a target company has undertaken to either preserve data, manage data, or in some cases even purge data. Interviewing skills also are sometimes required by computer forensic investigators when collecting electronic data in the field because an interview of the custodian of that data is often a required component of the investigation.

For instance, when I send my team into the field on a large data collection exercise for an electronic discovery matter, often part of the protocol will include the requirement that the team leaders conduct brief interviews with each of the custodians in the field so that we can collect firsthand knowledge about the usage of various electronic devices by the custodian. What type of computer does the custodian use? What applications on the computer were they ordinarily accessing? What secondary devices were used, such as smartphones and third-party devices, thumb drives, external hard drives, and tablets that are brought into the enterprise? During these interviews, it is not uncommon to collect passwords and other unique data points that will help computer forensic examiners conduct their work and ultimately provide quality work product to the triers of fact or the client.

Trade Secret Theft and IP Investigations

Among the most common investigations that a computer forensic investigator will undertake in today's world—particularly in the corporate world—is that of understanding how intellectual property may have been illicitly accessed and/or ferreted out of a company. Trade secret theft investigations often rely on rapid access to the systems and applications and computers in use by trusted internal employees or ex-employees. These investigations are often clandestine, quiet, and highly sensitive. The fact is that little stands in the way for a trusted employee to walk out the front door with 50 years of intellectual property that belongs to his or her employer and the shareholders copied onto a thumb drive. See Exhibit 4.2.

Countless companies today have been established, or have been built or enhanced, by the introduction of stolen intellectual property. These companies have been built on the backs of victims in the form of coworkers, shareholders, business owners, customers, and other trusting individuals who have been duped by rogue employees who have only looked after their own self-interests through trickery and corruption. Dozens if not hundreds of investigations that I worked on over the past 15 years have focused on this central issue, and more often than not a well-structured investigation led by a team that is prepared to do what it takes can establish a fact pattern that will identify the perpetrators of a trade secret or intellectual property theft of a company. Why, you may ask? Because each of us leaves a significant digital trail in everything that we do on the corporate networks, our own devices, and every

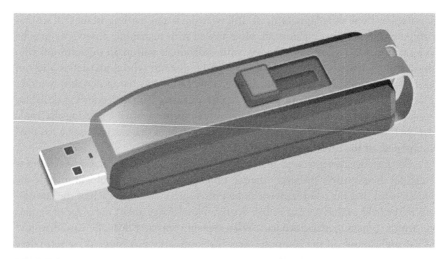

EXHIBIT 4.2   High-Capacity Thumb Drive/Flash Drive/Flash Stick/External Media

Central to many contemporary theft-of-trade-secret matters, this thumb drive was used by a trusted internal employee to raid the company's strategic plans and customer lists before leaving to work for a competitor. Fortunately for the victim, the computers used by the rogue employee recorded the serial number of the thumb drive when it was used. This, combined with metadata recovered from stolen/copied files by computer forensic investigators, was enough to bring a permanent injunction against the competing company.

electronic medium one can think of. Wiping one's tracks only creates new tracks, and a strong forensic investigator—if provided adequate access and cooperation—can often build a compelling case for the victim of such a fraud, which ultimately may level the playing field and deprive the bad guy from profiting by his deception. Many trade secret cases rely on the artifacts that are left in the metadata on desktops, laptops, servers, routers, and handheld devices that are used within a corporate environment. As a result, it is critical to widely and comprehensively preserve this data as soon as the investigation begins.

This is because there is no way to predict what twists and turns the fact pattern may take the investigator on, and without access to the preserved electronic data as close in time as possible to the events that took place, there would be little hope in reconstructing the events. Clients over the years have often fought the upfront costs and pain associated with this process; however, those who have taken it seriously have found that the effort has paid dividends.

Human Resources and Interpersonal Investigations

Some of the most sensitive investigations that computer forensic examiners are required to participate in are those that deal with personnel and human resources (HR). It's also one of the most common types of investigations in which computer forensic investigators are asked to assist, that is, investigations involving employees who may have gone astray, done wrong, or are suspected of some illegal or immoral activity or breach of corporate policy.

In the United States, many computer forensic professionals focus a good deal of their career on reviewing electronic data of employees for pornography, child pornography, or other activities that run afoul of local or federal laws or simply the policies of the organization that they work for. These types of investigations introduce a number of challenges to the investigator, paramount of which is managing the privacy of the electronic data they are reviewing.

Because a computer essentially is a recorder capturing all the activity of individuals in their life or at least while they're on the computer—in some cases 10 to 18 hours a day—it is not unusual for the forensic examiner to be confronted with highly personal messaging and information related to that worker's behavior, personal proclivities, lifestyle, thoughts, ideas, biases, challenges, and other highly sensitive information. I think it's important when forensic examiners are tasked with reviewing personal information from an HR or personnel perspective on one of these types of investigations that they be given a clear mandate of what they are to be examining and what they are not to be examining and where the lines of investigation begin and end. Although there may be a rationale at times to conduct what one would call a *fishing expedition* where one searches all of the data and reviews all possible sources, in most investigations that is not the case.

As an example, I have had numerous cases over the years where individuals have been accused of sexual harassment in the workplace, and the accusations have centered on specific e-mail communications that have been claimed to have been written and transmitted. The question therein lies: Is it reasonable for the computer forensic examiner to be exploring sources of data on the hard drive beyond the e-mail system that reportedly contained the messaging? Is it acceptable for him or her to check the unallocated space and deleted files in case that e-mail has been deleted? The answer may be yes; however, is it also reasonable to check the Internet cache for websites that the individual may have visited that are of a sexual nature or instant messages that the person may have sent to other colleagues? These are questions that need to be asked prior to conducting an examination. I have seen a number of examples of highly diligent forensic examiners following the instructions of overly zealous HR investigators who are looking for anything whatsoever on the computer with which to pin a claim of one sort or another on the custodian.

A pornographic image found in the unallocated space of the computer does not necessarily mean that the individual even searched or browsed for that image. On the contrary one must understand the linkages and relationships between images and data points that are found on a computer with other links and connection points and should be careful not to rush to judgment. I recall a matter where I testified on behalf of an individual who had been accused of child pornography by the cybercrime task force of a major U.S. policing agency. As a result of the accusation alone, the man lost his job, his wife, his family, and his friends, and he was left destitute.

However, on examination of the evidence that had been provided by the so-called forensic experts of this particular policing agency, I was able to conclusively prove that the images that were found on the computer of the custodian/defendant had in fact been deposited on his computer involuntarily as a result of pop-up windows that had been sent to his computer by accessing websites that allow that type of activity to take place. These pop-up windows contained images that could be construed as child pornography. The question always remains: How are you able to determine whether the individual in the photograph is in fact underage or if the photograph has been staged?

But that question was not central to this exercise. What was important here was whether the individual (the defendant) deliberately sought to view and/or save child pornographic information, data, or images on his computer and whether the defendant was even aware of the images. The answer was conclusively no, and as a result the prosecution lost its case. My client limped back to his private life, and although he may not have been able to restore the confidence of his circle of friends and family entirely, at least he was a free man.

HR investigations should be addressed carefully as the initial fact patterns may not always represent what they appear to be on face value. In the electronic world where the digital trail seems to be easy to erase, there are many opportunities for custodians and individuals to take advantage of their coworkers by leveraging electronic data.

One case that comes to mind involved a transgender plaintiff of a large California company who accused his coworkers of sending insulting, slanderous, and sexually explicit e-mail and demanded compensation in the realm of seven figures. On examination of the computers and investigation of the transgender plaintiff and the custodians who had been accused of sending the infringing e-mail, I was able to reconstruct a chain of events that definitively proved that the plaintiff had logged onto the defendants' computers after-hours and had sent the e-mail to himself, trying to implicate the company and its senior management.

What I took away from this and many other cases like it is that what you see is not always what you get in a computer. A forensic examiner should not simply accept the first layer of the onion as representing the true shape of things to come, but instead should use his or her investigative inquisitiveness to examine all the potential options the custodians had at their disposal to impact the evidence in a manner that was inconsistent with the statements that were given. Of course there are limitations as to how far a forensic examination can take these what-if scenarios, and the forensic investigator should not have a predisposition to doubt the claims that are made. I am of the opinion that a fair dose of skepticism coupled with a strong desire to let the facts lead where they may and to find the truth is probably the best combination to achieve balance during an HR investigation.

Reporting and Testifying

When you report the results of an investigation, it is important to keep a clear focus on the mandate that has been provided. For those who are managing investigators, it is always useful to reorient or provide a reset of the engagement by having a frank and earnest discussion about the original mandate, the events that are taking place, and where the investigation finds itself at that point in time with respect to both litigation involving any potential filings and reporting that is required.

This stepping back and reviewing the playing field will help to create a mental and visual thinking zone so that a report—whether it be an expert report or otherwise—can be effectively drafted without the clouding effects of the immediate tasks that had just been worked on or concluded. Sticking to the facts of the case and maintaining precise language that answers the questions posed is the most effective approach.

Injecting your personal feelings, attitudes, proclivities, assumptions, or suppositions in almost every case adds nothing and only serves to detract from the credibility of the reporting party. Objectivity and independence is key, and in order to maintain that, you must think logically and clearly and simply report on the findings. Most good reports will take a linear approach and will begin with background information on the individual who is preparing the report and/or the company that the individual is working for and will then move onto a section that outlines what the original mandate is, followed by the approaches and techniques that were taken to prepare the report. This is then followed by an overview of the analysis or the investigative steps that were followed. In many cases this will lead to conclusions and opinions that may be derived from the analysis. Finally, the report should have supporting documents, exhibits, or even digital files attached as addendums.

Reports, opinions, expert reports, affidavits, and declarations often will end up as evidence in court. As a result, the reports should not only be objective, independent, and analytical, but to the extent possible they should also be well drafted and free of error. Computer forensic examiners who anticipate that they will need to testify on the findings that they have provided in their report—which in many cases can take place months or even years after the report has been drafted—can adequately and accurately opine on the substance of the report at any point in time because there is sufficient detail in the report outlining how they reached their conclusions.

I've seen experts who drafted reports and then six months to a year later when they actually have to testify on the findings are scrambling to review and reprocess their forensic material to recall how they reached their conclusions because inadequate detail was provided in the report and they simply could no longer remember. For forensic analysts who find themselves being deposed or actually providing expert testimony or fact testimony in court, proper preparation critical. Reviewing your materials and the substance of your report and working with either counsel or members of your team on mock questions, sample attacks, and various scenarios that may play out in the deposition or in the courtroom will pay dividends when you are facing the actual task.

CHAPTER 5

The Underpinnings of Investigative Computer Forensics

There are so many areas of study, technology, and experience that go into the making of a strong computer forensic investigator that they are hard to list, and depending on the circumstances of the investigation itself and the needs of the client, one set of experiences and skills that are highly developed may not be appropriate, whereas another set may be. Among the various skills and areas of expertise that I have found to be important within the investigative computer forensic world are a strong understanding of the seizure and examination of digital evidence, which is covered ad nauseam in this volume and in others, and an understanding of data classification and records management and how those concepts may impact your ability to analyze the data you've collected or provide you with insight into the best use of your resources during the collection phase.

Other skill sets that are important include a complete comprehension of deleted data and what data can be recovered, an understanding of backups and systems preservation, a working knowledge of computer crime and its analysis and reconstruction, and an understanding of a wide variety of other technologies, including social engineering, encryption, cyberprofiling, and even a well-developed sense of how contracts, agreements, and third-party instruments are crafted and implemented. These are all important underpinnings of a successful computer forensic investigation.

In this chapter I will review a few of these issues and how they impact the decision-making process. Should any of these processes or areas of expertise become derailed during the course of an investigation, the impact could be significant. Nearly every forensic investigation that I have had the good fortune to be a part of has required multiple skill sets from a variety of professionals, with each one bringing his or her unique perspective and experience in areas that may not be viewed as particularly important when considered separately, but when taken as a whole can be a determining factor in whether a case is won or lost.

Seizure and Examination of Digital Evidence

The most important underpinnings of investigative computer forensics are the proper preservation and examination of digital evidence. I've spent considerable time throughout this volume addressing some of the particular nuances of the identification, collection, and analysis of digital evidence because without deploying predictable and repeatable processes, one runs the risk of tainting the evidence during its collection or modifying the evidence during its examination, which would result in drawing the wrong conclusions, inaccurate conclusions, or incomplete conclusions when reporting on the findings. Therefore, following standard practice and using care and good judgment throughout the process is crucial. See Exhibit 5.1.

Data Classification and Records Management

Due to the explosive volume and complexity of electronic data in the modern era, steps have been taken to classify and manage that data in accordance with standard practices and agreed-on conventions. However, the records management and data classification world often still lags far behind the needs and requirements of those persons, entities, and organizations that use and rely on that data. Data classification can be as specific as managing date and time stamps, extensions, or other metadata fields within any particular class of data, or it can be as complex and sophisticated as data that is produced within very specific formats, with specific languages, and with either automated or human classification points, which allow for those data records to be managed more intelligently by records management software.

Ultimately, the challenge is identifying records, whether they be e-mail, Microsoft Word documents, Adobe graphics files, or any other sort of file, in a meaningful and contextual manner. Great resources have yet to be fully applied to this challenge by the major software companies, but I suspect this trend will change as organizations demand more intelligent real-time analytical capabilities as they relate to their data sets and as computing power continues to evolve to provide software developers with the capability of meeting that need. In the future, I would expect that intelligent data classification and records management will be applied across all data types in a uniform manner so that all data can be recalled with specificity and accuracy in real time by parties that have appropriate rights and credentials.

At present, we all have the capability to access search engines on the Internet, which are able to recall electronic documents that have been made available for public consumption on the global networks, and as smart as they are and as far-reaching as their indexes have become, they are still far from where we need them to be to truly harness the tools of the information age. By this, I refer to the fact that Google.com can instantaneously provide me with tens of thousands of results to any particular

EXHIBIT 5.1   Early External Removable Hard Drive Media in a Cassette Form Factor

This drive has an 88-MB capacity. Now, a dozen years later, current removable media has a capacity of hundreds of times this device with a form factor that is 100 times smaller in volume. Yet computer forensic investigators are still faced with these earlier technologies from time to time and must be well versed not only in what is in use today but also what was popular only a decade ago. Sophisticated investigators have working knowledge of numerous outmoded systems, which may go back many decades.

search. However, what is missing is the contextual relevancy for which I am actually looking.

Granted, the contextual relevancy issue has been improved by leaps and bounds and in most searches on Google, for example, I am able to retrieve with relative accuracy relevant results within the first page or two of links most of the time. However, the filter applied to determine relevancy is my own brain and eyes and it is presumed that within the computer forensics and electronic discovery space attorneys will provide that same function. However, we are getting closer every day to the time when computers will be able to provide that filter themselves, thereby removing yet another barrier between the unification of data in its abstract form and human desire or curiosity.

Today's searches will seem crude and rudimentary to tomorrow's information users, when data will be recalled with exquisite accuracy, instantaneously, and without the requirement of filtering the results with your mind. Oh, and did I mention that we will not be using keyboards but will more than likely simply think of a question and the results will appear either on an integrated display on the surface of our retina, or perhaps, even farther in the future, within the mind itself? As I mention later in this volume, the advent of nanotechnology, supercomputing power, and data classification/records management combined with advances in biotechnology engineering at the molecular and atomic level will allow for science fiction to truly evolve into reality, with a melding of biological and inanimate structures all harnessed by humans on an individual molecular level.

In the electronic discovery space, we are beginning to see the early elementary and rudimentary manifestations of this theme in what is known as *predictive coding* or *machine-assisted review*, where first-level reviews of large volumes of electronic documents, primarily e-mail and office documents, can now be achieved by computers with appropriate software that has been trained to interpret data contextually and subjectively based on its content and algorithms, which are designed to interpret that content in subtle and contextual ways. Because today's litigation requires the review of increasingly insurmountable numbers of electronic documents, it is an absolute requirement that software and computers catch up quickly with the human capability to discern the contextual meaning of electronic documents beyond simple keyword searches, date range searches, and other brute force search mechanisms.

This brings us back to the need to have a more intelligent classification of electronic data so that search and records management can be conducted quickly, predictably, and intelligently by the tools that are established, either within the enterprise, by electronic discovery, or by computer forensic vendors once they receive that data and after it has been forensically preserved. Tools such as Clearwell, Zylab, and Autonomy are among those that have made strides in working with electronic data behind the firewall so as to allow this review of classified documents to take place in a more intelligent manner. This is often called *early case assessment*, although it is really nothing more than applying some of the same search technology and capabilities to electronic data within the environment that it originates, as opposed to waiting to acquire it forensically and have it examined by a third party or within the context of an e-discovery software tool or forensic analysis.

The advantages of leveraging this type of technology within the enterprise are clear. It allows an organization to ferret out relevant documents for the purpose of assessing either the need to pursue litigation, the need to defend against litigation, or the need to settle, or simply to understand the facts on the ground prior to reporting to relevant parties within the organization regarding some event that may have taken place. The world of data classification and records management will continue to play a central and pivotal role in investigative computer forensics, but more generally, in the daily lives of all individuals who are connected to global networks because it is through these disciplines that data becomes more actionable and relevant to a user.

Deleted Data

One of the underpinnings of investigative computer forensics is the notion that deleted data is not necessarily deleted. The transition that the business world has made over the past 20 years in terms of data management is remarkable, as it has impacted every aspect of the individual's world, as well as the business entity's world. While in the past it was quite possible to delete or destroy a business record permanently, today that task is for the most part impossible. In days past, a ledger book containing the records of transactions and sales could be thrown into a fireplace and burned, a filing cabinet's contents could be relegated to the shredder, or an important contract could be stolen from a safe and removed from view forever. In the short span of 20 years all of this has changed. For some it changed 30, 40, and 50 years ago, but for most it has been in the past 10 to 20 years that the revolution has had its greatest impact.

I can remember fighting battles with my employers in the late 1980s over the necessity of having a fax machine in the office. I can also remember fighting battles with my employers, coworkers, business partners, and even clients in the 1990s over the necessity of having a website or having e-mail capability for at least the key employees of the organization. Today, it is unfathomable that an organization would not have the ability to e-mail, access the Internet, or have an online presence of some sort. The entire business world throughout most nations now operates in the early Information Age, where communications take place electronically. The fellow who sought to retrieve the contract out of the safe and ferret it away so as to obscure the agreement between the company and the third party is now confounded by the dizzying array of problems in executing his fraud because the contract that lives on a secure directory on a server in a server farm that is leased by the company that he works for is not the sole copy of that document.

In fact, the document that the fraudster seeks to destroy lives not as a duplicate or even a triplicate, but perhaps there are dozens, if not hundreds, of variants and copies in the active space of the computers that have viewed the document, the servers that have hosted the document and transmitted the document as part of an e-mail, the backup tapes that have preserved this document at various times over the past year and a half, and the disaster recovery site located many miles down the road, which has a duplicate of the server that contains the document. Variants may also exist in the unallocated space on all of these computers.

So how is the fraudster to delete the contract? Quite simply, he or she can't because the document lives in too many locations. Where is the original? Is the original the document that was created by the original author or is the original a printout that was signed and is now on file with inside and outside counsel? Or is the original the document that is received electronically by the countersigning party for the purpose of review and who made modifications that are now reviewable by accessing the track changes function of Microsoft Word or the software in which the document was originally created?

As fraudsters ponder options, they may quickly realize that they cannot remove or delete all of these variants of the document, but they can modify the readily available document or delete the readily available document that the first responders would seek to retrieve or review, such as internal IT staff, internal IT security staff, or internal corporate counsel office. This creates a window of time in which to complete the fraud, but any decent criminal will know that within a short time frame, should the company choose to search its resources for the original document using forensic technology, the document will in fact be found in a wide variety of locations, including, perhaps, the unallocated space of the computer that contained the document that was modified or deleted by the fraudster.

One may ask why, and how, is this possible? Quite simply, computers maintain deleted data on the physical hard drives themselves. Until that data is overwritten, the mere act of pushing the delete button and deleting a document does not remove it from the hard drive but merely removes the reference to it that the operating system would use to retrieve the document should you wish to see it. However, with the use of computer forensic technology, the deleted document that is no longer visible to the operating system may in fact be recovered from the physical platter on the hard drive itself in what is known as the *unallocated space*, should it not have been overwritten. It's also possible that only a fragment of the document would be recovered, or none at all. However, the result of retrieving the entire document, a fragment of the document, or none at all is entirely random, being that the drive itself overwrites the available sectors of the unallocated space in a random fashion.

I have found in past investigations when searching for deleted data, that we have been able to recover documents that were several years old, but were not able to recover documents that were only several weeks old because the documents that were several weeks old were randomly overwritten by the hard drive in the normal course, whereas the documents that were several years old were randomly left unscathed. Deleted data is often at the heart of disputes in which computer forensic professionals and investigators find themselves embroiled. Therefore, the early preservation of electronic data is critical so as to stop the process of the random overwriting of electronic documents that may exist in the unallocated space of the hard drive.

When a computer forensic investigator forensically images a drive or a device, he or she is preserving that data in its form at that very moment and it cannot be modified going forward. Regardless of how much the hard drive itself is examined during the investigation, no further random modification to the unallocated space will take place. In many cases, I have had clients push back on the need for the computer forensic preservation of a hard drive. Often the client has stated that this is a simple electronic discovery case and there will be no need to recover deleted documents. I ordinarily fight back on that argument because, while the need to recover electronic documents that have been deleted may not exist at that moment, facts may change as electronic documents are in the act of being reviewed by attorneys on either side, by the results of the forensic examination that takes place through the investigator, or by the needs and requirements of the judge. I have had many cases where a simple e-discovery matter has ended up hinging on the recovery of electronic data from the unallocated space that was initially unanticipated by either side.

If the computer forensic acquisition of the hard drive or the digital data only includes the simple collection of active data and files from the user and if the case dictates that it is necessary to review or search for deleted data or fragments of data in the unallocated space, or perhaps even in the administration data within the operating system, such as registry files, but that review is not carried out, then it may be too late to turn back the clock. By this time the ship will have already sailed and the computer will have already been put back into use or will no longer be available in many cases, resulting in greater challenges for the fact-finder and perhaps a loss for one of the sides that are trying to prove their case.

Backups and Systems Preservation

Individuals, corporations, and government agencies of every size and sort often maintain backups of their data and/or systems for both data preservation and systems restoration in the event of an emergency, disaster, or failure. These systems can provide a wealth of data and information in the course of an investigation or electronic discovery exercise. Backup tapes, which are often produced on a daily, weekly, monthly, quarterly, or annual basis, can be restored and analyzed, providing investigators with copies of electronic data that has been preserved at a given point in time by users of the system. I have had many cases in which an individual's hard drive has either failed or cannot be found or has been purposely discarded, yet with the analysis of backup tapes all or much of the data can be reconstructed. See Exhibit 5.2.

Backups will not include unallocated space, and therefore, you generally cannot recover deleted data. Often you can recover data that would have been deleted from the computer but that was previously saved as a backup at a particular point in time. The reconstruction and analysis of backup, tape-based data can be rather costly in most cases, and therefore, one of the first steps that we take when we are requested to analyze the backup tapes of a given organization is to extract what we would call a file and directory report from the backup tapes so that we can see what files or directories existed at any given point in time and then more surgically extract data that are relevant.

Although some organizations maintain backup tape collections in perpetuity, others have retention programs that call for backup tape destruction over time. The backup tape destruction is accomplished through recycling, overwriting, or through the usage of new tapes. This is common practice and so understanding your investigative target's backup tape practices early on is important so that you can avoid the challenge of looking for the tapes only to find out that the backup tapes that you are seeking have actually been overwritten. This can be particularly embarrassing if they have been overwritten during the course of the investigation.

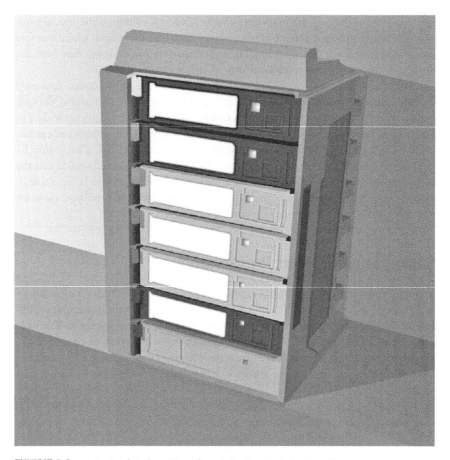

EXHIBIT 5.2   A Stack of Backup Tapes for a Juke Box–Style Backup System

These backup tapes mysteriously reappeared in a cardboard box marked "Old Backup Tapes" in an IT storage room of a large corporation after discovery had closed. The tapes contained hundreds of thousands of e-mails, which had previously been believed to have been destroyed as part of the company's data retention program. As a result, the company faced significant sanctions.

A proper data preservation plan will call for those backup tapes to be set aside as part of the litigation hold or even an investigative hold. Many organizations now use other media besides tape for backup, including hard discs that can be accessed readily by applications that are managing those backups. In some cases, those backups and the applications that are managing the backups have the ability to search for data on an ad hoc basis. The purpose of early case assessment is to allow for an early look at data that is either active or at rest within an enterprise. In my estimation, early case assessment should also include the ability to access archival and backup data, as those data points will eventually become accessible to the various parties regardless.

There are a wide variety of backup tape systems, including digital linear tape (DLT), linear tape-open (LTO), 4-mm Dats, 8-mm tapes, Iomega tapes, super DLT (SDLT), Ultrium, advanced intelligence tape (AIT), and a wide variety of other outmoded systems. I have had many cases over the years where we have found that the backup tapes that are supplied to the investigation are residing on systems that are no longer supported by the current IT infrastructure, and as a result, there are challenges when it comes to the interaction with and review of the data contained on those tapes. Again, this harkens back to the importance of identifying vendors that can support the technology needs of an investigation in advance of the need taking place so that when you come across an old version of a backup tape during the collection of data, you have the ability to turn to a firm or an organization that will have the technical wherewithal to assist you in the extraction of the data.

By example, on one of my cases in the United States, a significant claim between two software companies hinged on our ability to restore backup tapes containing the original disputed source code, which had been found after years of laying dormant in a closet in a foreign country. The tapes were from the 1980s and were created on an old mainframe. Several forensic firms had attempted to restore the tapes without success. Fortunately for us, we were able to find a retired engineer and a museum-preserved mainframe of the right specifications that had been wrapped in protective plastic. Using the mainframe, the engineer was able to restore the source code from the original tapes. After years of wrangling, the opposing side settled almost immediately for $400 million.

There are also a wide variety of backup system software applications that give you varying degrees of flexibility in the extraction and analysis of that data. Three of the primary types of backups include full backups, incremental backups, and differential backups. Full backup would be a backup that contains all data on any number of systems over a period of time, whereas incremental backups will be the additional data that has been added to those systems after the last full backup.

Computer Crime Analysis and Reconstruction

Computer crime analysis almost always requires the forensic capture and preservation of electronic data. This is primarily collected at the scene of the crime. It is the computer, the network, the hard drive, and the many interconnected computers. It is the iPhone, the iPad, and the thumb drive. Preservation of the crime scene is fundamental to any investigation and therefore the standards and steps that are taken in cybercrime forensic investigations have to meet the highest standards to ensure that justice is served, that victims are compensated, that criminals pay their price, and that those wrongly accused are vindicated.

Computer evidence and electronic data in some ways are insidious and ubiquitous and nearly impossible to destroy, and in other ways, more subtle ways, are also highly volatile, dynamic, and subject to unintended modification or change. The simplest modification on an electronic file that seemed innocuous and irrelevant initially in an investigation could find itself as the linchpin of getting a conviction in the case.

I recall a matter involving a hacker who had created malware, and I examined line after line of code contained within a piece of malware. All of the code would appear to be computer gibberish, and even to a programmer much of it seemed unintelligible and without purpose. When I received the malware from the hacker, as an unintended consequence of that hacker co-opting thousands of computers on the Internet, which in turn sent variants of its malware to millions of other users, my first step was to preserve it forensically so that I would be able to analyze it without altering it and keep it in a preserved state. In this way, regardless of the outcome of my analysis, I could point back to a methodical, repeatable, and defensible approach that would withstand the scrutiny of opposing counsel.

During my examination, I found a string of code that was intelligible in the English language and had no relevance or meaning to any other code within the malware. By cross-referencing this small data set against publicly available information on the Internet, I was able to isolate a potential suspect that had used a name that was identical to the content that I found in the malware. As it turns out, the hacker had an ego and elected to sign his malware with his hacker moniker, thinking that no one would be able to isolate and preserve the content of the malware to the extent that they would recognize the data and draw the inference or relationship between the individual and the signature.

As a result of this finding and the continued investigation, which leveraged the computer crime squad of the FBI, we were successful in arresting and bringing to justice this hacker, who had caused tens of millions of dollars in damage through the co-opting of millions of machines throughout the world, using his clever piece of software. When I initially received the malware from the *wild*, which means via the Internet, I had no anticipation of solving the crime but understood that in the off chance I would get lucky and find a clue or two, I should be prepared. If I had not forensically preserved the evidence that I used, then it would stand to be challenged by the opposing side and a bad guy could go free. Therefore, I treated the malware and my own computer that received it as the crime scene and preserved the evidence according to protocol.

Computer crime analysis and reconstruction often requires the review and analysis of dynamic and volatile data. This is data that lives in the RAM (random access memory) of a machine or in highly transitory log files and other applications that are not designed to necessarily store data for long periods of time and that can be modified in the millisecond by other incoming or outgoing transactional data. This is particularly the case when the crime scene is a network of computers that are being leveraged by an enterprise for transactional data, such as an airline and its reservation system, a bank and its ATM system, a large factory and its production systems, or a hospital and its patient monitoring system. These are large, complex systems that are vulnerable to attack and that cannot be shut down for the simple task of running an investigation because the damage would be exacerbated by such an event and the victims would multiply.

So, harkening back to commentary earlier in the book, where I explained that it is necessary to have established a protocol and a team for the response to electronic data investigative requirements prior to the need arising, the same holds true for large organizations that are managing enormous, complex systems that must be investigated but cannot be shut down and are subject to maintaining highly volatile dynamic active data that could be relevant to the investigation.

An example would be an investigation I ran in which the victims were several large Fortune 500 companies whose stock was shorted with regularity just prior to their announcement of the corporate news via electronic press releases. Over time, regulators were able to observe patterns that would indicate that an individual or individuals may have had access to insider information prior to it being released to the public through the use of these electronic press releases. It was only through the examination of volatile data within the press release management system that was deployed by each of these Fortune 500 companies that we were able to determine that these organizations were the victim of a sophisticated software injection attack also known as an SQL injection attack. This attack would allow the bad guys to view the press release that was intended to be issued to the public from the actual companies' bona fide systems minutes, and in some cases days, prior to its actual release.

The SQL injection attack would fool the press release system into displaying a press release waiting in the queue to go public early, but the evidence of these attacks lived fleetingly in the log files of the web interface that the press release system used at each of these firms. If one were to turn off the machines and image the computers, the log files would have been flushed and the evidence would no longer be retrievable, so the investigation required a unique dynamic capture of this data while it was live on the systems. It is for this and many other reasons that I counsel victims of cybercrime to act not only quickly but also prudently when developing their course of action to respond to an event that is taking place. It is often the case that the first steps taken by the response team did not adequately prepare for all of the possibilities of attack, and in fact accidently destroy the evidence that they were seeking to preserve. Unfortunately, this would forever prevent these victims from solving the crime and seeking redress.

The *Who, What, Where, How* of Data

It is important to understand where data lives, who controls the data, how it flows, where it can move from and to, and so forth.

Mapping Logical and Physical Networks

An important component of good investigative practice as it relates to technology is to undertake a data mapping exercise at the beginning of an investigation, memorializing what you learn about the location and disposition of the data and its custodians so that that information is not lost and so that you can leverage the interactions and relationships between those parties properly. As the investigation evolves, the map continues to be updated. See Exhibit 5.3.

In the most practical sense, I like to use Visio, a product by Microsoft, for building these data maps. It allows you to drag-and-drop icons that represent custodians, computers, laptops, desktops, servers, routers, or cell phones on a screen and draw connections between them to indicate what the relationship is between those devices.

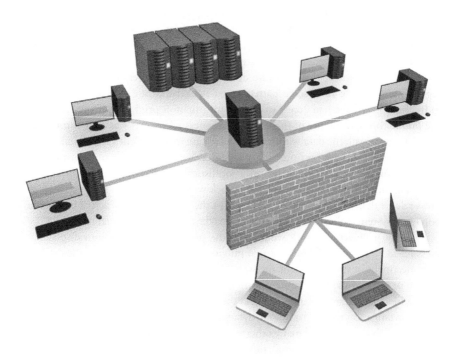

EXHIBIT 5.3   Illustration of a Simple Corporate Network

These maps of systems can provide graphical illustration and understanding to the various parties in an investigation, from the lawyers to the executives to even the computer forensic investigators. This illustration shows three outside salespeople who are laptop users and have the ability to access corporate resources through the firewall. The map also shows a network and e-mail server that allows for four internal employees to access the network and resources. Among these resources are four application servers that can be accessed through the company's intranet, which is also hosted by the machine in the center of the illustration. These data maps are vital in understanding the logical, physical, network, and human properties of any network and are required in most investigations and electronic discovery matters.

Visio also allows you to fill in fields related to the name of the device, the IP address of the device, the operating system and applications that are running, the user name of the custodian, the physical location of the custodian, and any other notes or information you may have about the custodian.

Issues of which you need to be aware include passwords, log-ins, and other relevant information. Over time, as the data map grows, you will have a graphical representation of the environment you are investigating that you can very easily have modified or manage within the context of your laboratory and investigation. This data map can also be used in the context of presenting the information to a client or a courtroom so they can better understand the environment and data relationship that you are examining or reporting on.

It is important on a data map to account for both the physical and logistical aspects that represent the actual geographic and physical location of a particular device, and perhaps the environment within which it lives, such as in a locked room, whether that room is within a locked building, whether that building is accessible by your elevator, at night, and so on. The logical disposition of the data map revolves around the electronic and digital aspects of that same system. You must determine if that computer is connected to the Internet through an Ethernet cable or if it is wireless. If it is connected by the Ethernet cable, then is it logged in all the time or does it require a log-on password? If it requires a log-on password, then what is that password? Does the machine itself require a password to log on? What applications are running on the machine? Who has access to the machine? And so on and so on.

Revealing Anonymous Identities

Because individuals are able to create identities online without using their true birth identity, it is easy for individuals to conduct fraud behind the cloak of anonymity, false identity, or secrecy, providing a whole new layer of challenges for the forensic investigator. Not only does the investigator have to solve the crime, understand how it happened, who the victim was, and the process of the activity, he or she also must also try to identify the culprit who is masked behind a veil of secrecy.

In many cases, the bad actor has set up an account using an invented identity on an e-mail system such as Yahoo, Gmail, AOL, or Hotmail, and as a result, when the investigation acquires electronic data as evidence related to the activity of that individual, investigators only find the evidence of the crime, but not the evidence of the real identity of the perpetrator. To find these perpetrators, one must remove that cloak of secrecy, but the Internet is designed for anonymity, and its rules and practices support this, so a forensic examiner is often left the challenge of having a victim, a scene of the crime, and a weapon, but only a phantom suspect.

Fortunately, through the power of due process, subpoenas, and other instruments of the court and government agencies, it is possible, from time to time, to acquire clues from these catalysts of anonymity, such as Gmail, Yahoo, or Hotmail, which will reveal the true identity of the perpetrator. This is often the case when an actual IP address can be gathered from the e-mail provider of the individual, who set up the account using the anonymous moniker. This is possible because when an individual goes to a site such as Yahoo.com and registers an account, even an account with a false name and false identifying features, the IP address of the inbound request to create the identity is recorded by Yahoo. If the fraudster is less sophisticated and has failed to mask that IP address, and there are certainly many ways to do that, then through the power of subpoena investigators can learn the IP address that the individual used during the account creation.

In some cases, this may be a static IP address of the individual at his home or at his office or it may be an IP address at a cybercafé. If it is the latter, one must then pursue the cybercafé for additional records, including determining the Mac address of the computer that made the request and then running a computer forensic analysis on its hard drive to determine if there is any further information that can be learned from the unallocated space or from its active files. This might include listed users who actually used the machine at the given date and time; or perhaps the cybercafé was paid by that individual with a credit card, in which case one can learn the identity. Perhaps the cybercafé has video monitoring, in which case you may be able to re-create a video picture of the individual who set up the Yahoo account to conduct the fraud. In either case, revealing anonymous identities is also a little like peeling an onion one layer at a time; you just don't know what you are going to get each time you peel back another layer.

Social Engineering

Many things can be done with computers and the analysis of electronic data can be highly revealing as to the original intent of an individual or group of individuals. Fundamentally, computers are dumb machines and they perform tasks at the direction of humans, either directly or indirectly. During the course of an investigation it may be required for an investigative computer forensic examiner to interact with humans in person, electronically, over the telephone, or by inference. One of the components of the computer forensic investigative world that is borrowed from hacker parlance is called *social engineering*. This has historically been a hacker-defined term for hacking one's way into a human network or past the human individual or causing an action or effect by a human that was not intended by that person.

An example would be when a white-hat hacker is tasked with the process of conducting a penetration test on behalf of an organization for the purposes of testing its defenses. One of the techniques used by hackers and penetration testers is to attempt to compromise a human component of that organization's defenses. Although the hackers or penetration testers may spend considerable time and effort looking for vulnerabilities and holes in the organization's computer networks and technology-based defenses, either directly or through third parties, it is not uncommon for those same penetration testers to seek to compromise some individual or individuals who can assist in the goal unwittingly, allowing the penetration tester or hacker access to systems.

For example, a hacker may call the help desk of an organization under the pretense of seeking to reset a password on his or her company-issued laptop while traveling in the field. During the exchange between the hacker and the help desk, the hacker may be able to convince the help desk to provide the hacker with credentials to log on to the network. This soft spot in the corporation's defenses, which relies entirely on the good judgment and training of the individuals who could potentially compromise that organization, is a favored target by hackers, penetration testers, and unfortunately, criminal cybergangs.

Just as insiders may use their powers of persuasion to gain access to a departmental share on a corporate network to which they ordinarily would not have access, a bad actor within the organization could use the same persuasion to steal confidential, proprietary information of the company. This act is still cybercrime or a technology fraud, even though the bad actor used traditional methods of human interaction to push his or her scheme forward.

Social engineering, as it is used in the hacker and penetration testing parlance, is easily transcribed into the world of the computer forensic investigator because of that individual's reliance on seeking facts from human beings as much as from computers. The fact-gathering may be taking place during the course of an internal investigation, in which the bad actors or trusted members of the organization's team are being duped by the investigators into believing a particular set of facts so that their behavior can be observed as they defraud the company. It is also not uncommon for forensic investigators to be charged with the task of interviewing IT professionals or stakeholders within an organization during an investigation, whether external or internal, for the purpose of fact-gathering for the broader legal team or investigative team.

I feel that it is important for forensic investigators to have some good measure of interviewing skills so that they may adeptly navigate the concerns, hostilities, or other challenges faced by the targets of those interviews and more effectively report their findings back to the stakeholders, senior investigators, or counsel. Ordinarily, these investigative forensic analysts or technicians will not supplant the traditional investigator's role but will augment it because they speak the language of technology, and as a result, may interpret responses and findings in a nuanced fashion that will help the overall investigation.

For complex investigations involving real-time surveillance, particularly in foreign nations, the notion of social engineering becomes even more relevant to the investigation. Having the ability to communicate effectively with persons from different socioeconomic, national, or geographic backgrounds can make the difference between finding the lucky break and finding no break at all in an investigation where technology can take you only so far and your team must rely on social interaction with other humans for fact-finding.

Encryption

Encryption is becoming ever-more popular in the corporate world as organizations seek to protect information that is in transit or work that is being used within the enterprise. Organizations are beginning to understand that housing and transmitting data without encrypting leaves them vulnerable to that data being compromised by its loss, theft, or internal espionage. However, encryption carries a number of risks with it, being that if your organization loses the encryption keys that are used to encrypt the data, then it may no longer be able to recover the data.

Encryption algorithms continue to evolve and have become stronger and more resilient over time and often in the course of our forensic investigations we are finding that the data that is recovered off hard drives can be in encrypted form. The investigative technicians must be able to deal with the encrypted data that they come across and often are left without the ability to recover that data. Many organizations deploying current encryption technology are using state-of-the-art systems to store the keys or at least backdoor keys to systems that are employed within the enterprise. In this manner, the individual who turns out to be a bad actor within an organization may have his or her computer seized. However, if the computer is encrypted and he refuses to turn over the keys, that act will not hold the organization hostage because the organization will have a backdoor into the system or will have a copy of the key, a master key if you will.

When a forensic investigation is taking place, among the many points that the examiner should review is whether encryption has been deployed on the systems that he or she is collecting; if it has been deployed, then the investigator should seek to secure the encryption keys as early as possible before facts on the ground change. I should also note that in many cases it is preferable for the forensic examiner to encrypt the data that is to be transferred from his or her forensic lab to a third party, such as a processing facility, a vendor or outside counsel, or in some cases, even the opposing side, so that, while in transit, should the data become compromised there will be little risk that the evidence will be exposed to unintended parties.

Cyberprofiling

In the evolving world of the information technology revolution, individuals and machines often develop identities other than their natural human identity or the intended identity of the machine or device in question. An example of this would be individuals who maintain a screen name other than their actual birth name, which does not reveal their true identity and which they use to communicate and populate chat rooms, user groups, website blogs, and other online vehicles. Millions upon millions of users of technology services maintain these alter egos for communicating in the ether, and as a result, one of the steps that a forensic investigator may be charged with is the profiling of that individual or individuals on the global networks.

This is an area of investigation that managers of an investigation should be aware of so they can include it in their checklist of possibilities when building an understanding of the subject matter of the investigation and the players or a specific suspect within the investigation. Over the course of hundreds of investigations, I have seen individuals who are party to a matter who maintain separate identities online. These identities may not be nefarious and may be used for legitimate purposes. However, without taking the time during interviews or examination of electronic media to determine whether these identities exist, one may not be uncovering the full scope of the activity of the user, and thus will not know the true pattern that the investigator is seeking to uncover.

Contracts Agreements, Third Parties, and Other Headaches

Every forensic investigator, at one point or another, has to deal with contracts, agreements, third-party individuals, and other issues that can quickly become a headache. Most common among the agreements that a forensic investigator will have to deal with are confidentiality statements, noncompete agreements, mutual and one-way nondisclosure agreements, protective orders, license agreements for software, renewal agreements, and letters of agreement or contracts with employers or clients that spell out the terms of an engagement, including pricing, billable rates, expenses, liability, payment, statements of work, and other exclusions or inclusions to the agreed-on services rendered by the technician or investigator.

I have found most computer forensic investigators to be competent, intelligent, and clearly able to understand the contents of such agreements. However, not to be underestimated, the new agreement that is poorly crafted can hurt your party down the road if it does not anticipate activities and issues that should be taken into account. I have often counseled forensic technicians to ensure that they are properly vetting their agreements with in-house counsel, with the companies they work for, or their own attorneys if they represent themselves, in order to protect their interests and those of their clients. Operating as an investigative computer forensic specialist, whether on behalf of an organization, an agency, corporation, or even for oneself, still requires a measure of common sense, business etiquette, legal analysis, and other standard business activity that cannot be discounted and requires sound judgment and clarity.

Ethics and Management

In recent years, much has been written and said about ethics and electronic discovery and the proper course of behavior for practitioners in that space. The same must hold true for investigative computer forensic professionals that they should strive to achieve the highest ethical ground possible during the course of their employment or deployment, before, during, and after an investigation. Investigative computer forensic professionals should be held to the same standard of practice and care to which any other diligent professionals should be held, whether they be a certified public accountant, an attorney, a traditional investigator, a physician, or a member of the judiciary.

I am not saying that investigative computer forensic professionals must behave as a member of the clergy, but I do strongly feel that investigators should practice what they preach in their personal and professional behavior and refrain from activities that can be viewed poorly, should their behavior be called into question in a court of law. For instance, computer forensic professionals who are investigating illegal activity should stay widely clear of fraudulent behavior in the pursuit of their fact-finding and should escalate issues of an unethical nature to their superiors or client in a professional, unambiguous, and matter-of-fact manner.

Investigative computer forensic professionals have an ethical obligation to search data and follow the fact pattern wherever it leads them and to refrain from inserting their own bias or predispositions as they relate to the subject matter or the parties involved in the process. There will be ample opportunity at the appropriate times for speculation, discussion, hypothesizing, and what-ifs, but these steps must be insulated from the pure objective and dispassionate fact-finding with which the computer forensic investigator is tasked.

I should note that I have seen many computer forensic investigators over the years misinterpret their findings. Even though their findings were accurate, the meaning given those findings in the context of the investigation and the relationship given to the behavior that those bits and bytes represented was different in reality from what the forensic investigator interpreted. It is for this reason that objectivity in the analysis of digital evidence is so vital, for it is often only through the tempered and nuanced interpretation of the facts that are gleaned from the computers by individuals who are qualified for that interpretation, whether it be an investigator, lawyer, or business executive, that the true meaning behind the findings may be understood.

There are times when the meaning behind an action on a computer is very clear, where it is black and white and without any vagaries at all, or so it seems. An example would be, in its simplest form, in an investigation where one must determine when a computer was stolen from a building. One of the tasks of the computer forensic examiner may be to try to determine when the computer was turned off, and the examiner may very well have the ability to find out, through the examination of the computer, the video surveillance cameras, network log files, and other electronic data points. The task of the forensic examiner may be entirely fulfilled by reporting that the computer was turned off at 1:05 P.M. Central Standard Time. It may be that the computer was turned off by a janitor, not by the culprit who stole the computer, and it may be that it is not within the scope of the forensic examiner to determine *who* turned off the computer, but rather *when* the computer was turned off.

Now, in discussion the examiner may be able to point to other facts that would lead the examiner to believe that the computer may have been turned off by the janitor, such as the review of the surveillance equipment, combined with an access log from a key card system that showed that the thief, the former employee who stole the computer, had actually left the building prior to 1:05 P.M. That certainly is fair game for discussion, but the charge for the forensic examiner is to answer the question: *When* was the computer turned off? That must be the first and foremost, paramount objective, to identify the exact time that the computer was turned off.

The ethics involved in computer forensic examinations require the diligent examination of the machines. Ethical behavior within the computer forensic space is critical to the integrity of the fact-finding process, and investigators, particularly computer forensic investigators, should not act as advocates for their party unless it is so stated. Instead, their charge should be fact-finding in the abstract and in the most objective of forms, reporting what they find so that conclusions may be drawn or additional fact-finding requested.

Also, underpinning the computer forensic process is the management of one's time and responsibilities, as well as those of the parties who are reporting to you or who are relying on you to report to them. The management of time is essential, so as to set expectations correctly with the various parties who are relying on the findings. The management of responsibilities and relationships with third-party vendors, fellow employees and clients, and other interested parties is also vital to the successful outcome of an investigation.

CHAPTER 6

Tactical Objectives and Challenges in Investigative Computer Forensics

The technical challenges the computer forensic examiner faces are broad and varied and with each case they differ. Therefore, it is important as an investigator not only to have a solid grounding in the fundamental mechanics of computer forensics, but also to understand the interplay and relationships between various potential interested parties. The consumer of computer forensic investigations, such as an attorney, or business executive, or others who order investigations to take place, are often well served to ensure that the computer forensic examiners who are collecting and analyzing the data are in fact aware of the broader mandate and circumstances that brought them to this place. Not seeing the forest for the trees, whether intentional or not, can lead to missed opportunities and clues being overlooked or overstated. See Exhibit 6.1.

Among the objectives and challenges that the investigative computer forensic professional faces are the many languages the different parties use. Whether they are technologists, lawyers, operations individuals, accountants, investigators, or even juries, each of them have their own vernacular, their own frame of mind, and their own point of view with which they will see the investigation. Additionally, forensic investigators may need to prepare in advance for an attack or an event by ensuring that they have taken steps within the enterprise and behind the firewall to establish methodologies for the proper collection of electronic data, particularly volatile or dynamic data that could evaporate moments after an event takes place.

Challenges also include developing proper pacing and timing and setting expectations for the investigative team, those to whom they are reporting, and the user, who will report to you, so as to ensure that you are harnessing your resources most effectively and getting the feedback that you need when you need it. Many new developments in technology add to the tactical challenges of today, including how one collects electronic data in the cloud or social media or even from newfangled tablets,

EXHIBIT 6.1 The Ubiquitous Computer

Computers come in a variety of forms, from desktop to tablet, handheld to embedded within other components such as an automobile. Regardless of the shape, size, speed, and capacity of the computers they work on, computer forensic investigators' process and procedures are uniformly applied to the identification, preservation, collection, processing, analysis, and presentation of the data that they contain, thereby assuring predictable reliance on the findings and conclusions drawn from the investigation.

which may not have the proper input/output connectors. These may present all sorts of new challenges to the investigative party, who may be on a tight deadline to find answers yesterday.

Preparing for the Attack

Organizations around the world have begun to take the threat of external attack much more seriously over the past 10 years. Standards of care and best practices have evolved in the information security world, which allow these organizations to deploy firewall systems and rules and manage internal data-handling practices in such a way that they can minimize the risks associated with external attack. However, the risk is always present and evolves with time. For every virus, worm, or piece of malware that is discovered and for which a workaround, a patch, or a signature has been developed, new variants or wholly new viruses, malware, and Trojan horses are developed with modified insidious behavior that allows for penetration into even the most fortified information security–protected data systems.

Computer forensic analysts, in preparation for the inevitability that their systems will be penetrated, are wise to work with information security systems professionals within the organization and from behind the firewall, in conjunction with internal security compliance folks and other interested parties, to develop methods and procedures for responding to an attack and for the preservation of electronic data that will be central to determining that the attack occurred and who is responsible for it. Without a plan in place for this rapid response, the organization is setting itself up for adding insult to injury. If an organization has not established protocols for responding to an attack and properly preserving the electronic data associated with it, then the organization will further compound liability and exposure that it may have by losing precious moments during and after an attack. These are crucial moments for the collection of vital data that may still be present on systems within their control or close at hand.

Information security is not only a technical challenge, it is also a human challenge, a process challenge, and an enterprise challenge to the mind-sets of the individuals who work within an organization, from the CEO to the data entry clerk. Each component of a network, including suppliers, contractors, and customers, is a possible failure point for that network and a potential vulnerability that can be exploited by a cunning hacker.

Early Case Assessment

The term *early case assessment* has developed over the past several years to explain a process whereby corporations or other institutions have the ability to collect and analyze data behind the firewall and within the enterprise, prior to its being extracted and collected for either a full-blown investigation or traditional electronic discovery requirements. A number of tools have been developed to assist in this process, the leader for a number of years being Clearwell, now owned by Symantec.

Today, however, there are many tools that are efficient in the early case assessment space, including Nuix from Australia, EnCase Discovery, FTK, X1 Rapid Discovery, Autonomy, and Zylab. These tools are all designed to remain resident within the IT infrastructure of the host company and are either software-based, hardware-based, or a combination thereof. These tools allow investigators within the company to quickly isolate specific data types that are of interest, such as e-mail, transactional data, and office documents from shared, personal, or corporate computers. They also provide a work flow to allow that data to be duplicated, processed, and presented in such a way that either in-house counsel or internal investigators can work through those data sets to determine if there is a rationale for a more robust investigation; if certain claims or allegations are true or false; and to determine the scope, cost, and size of the potential response to an e-discovery request in the pursuit of determining whether the company should settle with its adversary.

These early case assessment tools provide yet another important step in the electronic discovery life cycle and in the broader information governance world to give companies insight into the true meaning and proper nuances of the data that they are hosting and that has been created by employees, partners, vendors, customers, or any other combination of relevant parties.

Investigative Pacing, Timing, and Setting Expectations

From the perspective of the forensic examiner, it is particularly important to set expectations correctly for those that are poor at managing individuals or for clients to whom those managers report. Computer forensic examinations are often not well understood or appreciated and are often viewed by the purchasing party as a simple exercise in connecting a hard drive to a computer and pressing the big red button. However, nothing could be further from the truth. There are a host of challenges pitfalls and tasks that need to be undertaken, all of which take time to properly manage and that without undertaking would subject the investigation to unnecessary risk.

The buyers of these services, the clients, managers, and so forth, need to be informed upfront by the forensic examiners or their managers as to the true expectations that the forensic examiners have for the time frame required to undertake and achieve the goals that have been set. On many occasions, I have witnessed computer forensic examiners or companies underestimate the time required to conduct certain tasks with the result that the client is frustrated, results are not provided to the court or to a client on time, and tensions rise. This is easily avoidable if the computer forensic examiner is clear upfront and does not wither under an attorney's demands that they finish it quicker than is reasonably expected.

The timing and pacing of computer forensic work is somewhat predictable, particularly in the collection phase. Of course, there are always issues and anomalies, such as hard drives that fail, encryption that is encountered, logistical problems in arriving on the scene in time, uncooperative employees at the destination, and every other possible roadblock of which one can think. However, the fundamental work involved in collecting electronic data is well understood and a number of efficiencies can be gained through imaging multiple machines at the same time and having appropriate staffing levels to handle the paperwork in detail, paperwork that is required to accompany these forensic images.

Where pacing and timing is more challenging is in the analysis of the electronic data. Should the analysis only require the extraction of traditional reports, such as a file and directory listings or deleted but recoverable files, this is quite predictable from a timing and pacing perspective. However, when forensic examiners are required to undelete deleted fragments of files, reconstruct events on a computer or computer usage itself, examine registry settings and other operating system artifacts, or compile records from log files and network-based equipment, the time required to conduct these efforts can vary wildly.

For example, I have had cases where the collection of forensic evidence has been completed within a few short hours and the indexing of the machine was completed within a day, thereby allowing the forensic examiner to generate reports to satisfy the initial curiosity of the field investigators and outside counsel. However, as soon as requests for further analysis on the reconstruction of electronic data on these computers came in, it quickly became evident that manpower would be required to analyze these systems in a manual fashion, and the net result was that the computer required three weeks of analysis in order to understand the chain of events that was central to the claim in the litigation. Because of the uncertainty of the time required for analysis, computer forensic professionals need to be clear and up front with their handlers or managers, so as to set expectations correctly and not overpromise and underperform.

Working with Multinational Teams

Many of today's investigations require individual forensic investigators to work with multinational teams of investigators, employers, victims, or other stakeholders, with whom they may have had little prior interaction. During the investigative process, senior management of the investigation should take steps to set expectations and requirements in a clear and predictable fashion, or at least as much as possible. There are cases where the cultural differences are so severe that fact-finding may not only be challenging, it may also be impossible due to obstructions or barriers that are presented by individuals in the process. See Exhibit 6.2.

One of the tools that is useful to employees in these types of investigations is to ensure that there is a predefined process for escalating issues in a confidential manner so they can be discussed and acted on. For instance, I have had a number of cases in Japan where the senior management has demanded that certain forensic acquisitions take place but local on-the-ground management have not fully understood the implications, and, as a result, have either tried to delete data prior to its being collected, or to move data, or simply refused to allow access to the data. In some cases, even after they had supposedly allowed access to the data, barriers and instructions were presented that made it more difficult to understand where that data actually existed. Then the question would invariably arise, "Was this intentional and obstructionist or simply a cultural misunderstanding or barrier?"

Through cooperative communication and through working to understand the concerns and personal or professional challenges that the individuals on the ground may have had over time, most of these objections were overcome and eventually the electronic data that was required to be preserved was in our hands. I have also witnessed more heavy-handed approaches where forensic investigators, at the behest of their managers,

EXHIBIT 6.2 Internal Hard Drive Removed from a Suspect's Computer

This IDE-style hard drive has 100 GB of available space and contained the recovered deleted e-mail, which implicated the CEO of a Chinese manufacturing company in an industrial espionage case.

have made unreasonable demands in host countries of the individuals who are potentially subject to the investigation or are charged with assisting the investigation, and as a result all cooperation failed and the objectives of the investigation were thwarted.

Collections of Electronic Data in the Cloud and in Social Media

Collections of electronic data in the cloud and within social media present unique challenges to the computer forensic examiner. This is in part because the computer forensic examiner does not, in most instances, have direct access to the devices on which the data lives. In most cases, the computer forensic examiner is required to access cloud data, application data, or social media data in its native application as viewed by the user. When electronic data is captured in this fashion, often the metadata is not captured or preserved and the functionality and interactivity that the original data points may contain could be modified or lost.

New tools, such as X1 Discovery, are now allowing for a computer forensic examiner to access social media websites, such as Facebook, LinkedIn, YouTube, or Twitter, and preserve in a predictable manner any electronic data that is identified to be of interest on those sites. This new tool allows an examiner to achieve an investigative work flow in much the same way that EnCase has provided a platform for forensic examiners to manage data in a predictable manner.

Among the unique attributes of this product is that it allows for the forensic preservation of and the assigning of hash values to every artifact that is found on each page. For example, for a forensic image that is retrieved from a Facebook page, each artifact on that Facebook page is preserved as it is at that moment in time with its own hash value, including photographs, banners, graphics, embedded applications, and all other artifacts on that page. Because the tool was built using the SDK (software development kit) for each one of these social media sites, the tool has also been constructed so that the use of the tool on the site itself does not impact the data or leave a footprint.

For example, on the LinkedIn website, when one visits a LinkedIn page, LinkedIn automatically records that visitor as having visited the page and provides statistics related to that visit on the right-hand side of the user's LinkedIn page. The X1 Discovery tool does not leave a footprint, and it is not registered as a LinkedIn visit when it is deployed against a page to which it has access. The X1 Rapid Discovery tool, by extension, allows for the predictable and defensible electronic collection of data in the cloud by deploying virtual servers within the cloud environment. These virtual servers can be remotely managed and can collect data for the purpose of an early case assessment for electronic discovery or for investigative and litigation purposes, and will capture data resident within a cloud environment using forensic methodology and proper hashing so that the forensic analyst can certify to the court that the data has not been altered or modified during the collection process.

As users continue to migrate to the cloud and applications continue to evolve in that space, there will be a greater need for predictable collection of this type of data. Presently, among the challenges that are faced are jurisdictional and contractual challenges. Jurisdictional challenges arise because different jurisdictions where the data might exist may have different privacy and regulatory requirements as to how that data will be managed. One might be collecting data from a screen in front of him or her for an investigation that is taking place in the United States, but it may be that the data actually is physically resident in Canada, the European Union, or elsewhere. Therefore, forensic investigators not only need to be aware of the data privacy laws within the jurisdiction in which the collection is taking place but also have sufficient tools with which to manage the collection without running afoul of those regulations.

On a contractual basis, forensic investigators frequently run into complications when collecting data from the cloud because cloud providers are not likely to provide access to systems within the colocation environment or other large enterprise environments. I recommend to users of cloud services, particularly corporate users who have the ability to negotiate such contracts, to develop a contract prior to using cloud services that provides them with certain rights for both the preservation of and access to the data that may be housed and/or managed by a third party. This may include having the ability to run tests, drills, or even audits of that data on an annual basis to ensure that there are proper policies, procedures, and systems in place for the collection of electronic data when needed.

Investigating Internet Service Provider Records

An important component of investigative computer forensics, particularly when one is investigating an individual's use of the Internet or e-mail, is trying to determine the origin of a particular entity that has access to your systems, particularly anonymous individuals. Perhaps this person has posted a note on your website or blog, or perhaps he or she has sent an anonymous e-mail and you are trying to determine the identity of the original author of the e-mail or posting. The process is to work with Internet service providers to find records relating to the true identity of the individual. Internet service providers are loath to give up this information, unless compelled by subpoena, so here are some initial steps you can take to try to learn this information on your own.

The computer forensic examiner or cybercrime investigator has the ability to run certain commands from his or her desktop to try to reverse-trace the origin of a particular Internet protocol (IP) address to learn its physical location and/or the owner of the IP address. For instance, using the *ping* command, a computer forensic examiner has the ability to ping a particular website and learn the IP addresses of that website.

If you ping the website www.yahoo.com, you might receive a response on your computer that is a reply from 69.147.125.65. This numeric value is an IP address, and it represents the physical Ocean City, Maryland, numeric location of the website and a transliteration of the website's alphanumeric name, yahoo.com. That IP address has been either sold or leased to Yahoo.com by a provider of IP addresses, and through a lookup on a variety of systems that provide what is known as a *Who is* command, the cybercrime investigator may have the ability to determine who is the owner of the IP address that is registered to Yahoo.com.

There are a variety of tools that allow you to do this type of work in a more automated fashion, including a tool known as www.domaintools.com. If the cybercrime investigator is able to determine that the anonymous e-mail came from Yahoo.com, then you will be able to produce a subpoena that will list that IP address, and you can send the subpoena to Yahoo.com to request the identity of the owner of the e-mail account.

If the owner complies, it well may be that you will receive information related to the user of the account, which could in fact be the name of the contact and e-mail address and other data points. For example, the account may also have a Mac address, which is a set of physical numbers that are associated with the computer that actually set up the account. However, in many cases, the Internet service provider, whether Yahoo or another provider from which you are requesting this information, may challenge your request, even if it is a subpoena.

Bridging the Actual World with the Cyberworld

Folks who speak tech are different from those who speak law and are also different from those who speak business. These different worlds often collide during the course of an investigation and can result in missed cues, clues, opportunities, and connection points. Each of the stakeholders in an investigation that involves technology has a responsibility to try to understand the vocabulary, inference, and frame of reference of each of the other parties.

The cyber-technician, aka the *computer forensic analyst*, is often required to think in a linear fashion, seeking out causes of action and reaction, as a result of their being steeped in programmatic concepts from the software world, whereas attorneys can often draw conclusions or inferences that are not necessarily closely linked. Investigators can often shadow attorneys in depositions or during investigative and strategy meetings to assist them in interpreting and understanding the facts as they are being exposed and providing context as to why those facts may or may not be relevant in a given investigation.

In many of my investigations, I have seen where important facts have been neglected or ignored by parties because the relevance of a seemingly innocuous data point was not fully appreciated. A good computer forensic examiner has the ability to highlight these issues as they arise for his or her client. Similarly, forensic examiners may not fully appreciate or comprehend the relevance of particular actions that were taken by a subject, a suspect, or an individual as it relates to the investigation and need to be guided by counsel or senior management during the analysis phase.

My conclusion from all of this is that there are both efficiencies and genuine benefits to be gained by maintaining a cooperative and collaborative investigative environment between the business stakeholders, counsel, and the forensic technicians, and at times victims or even general IT stakeholders within an organization. This collaboration should be fostered wherever possible.

Packaging the Findings

Packaging the findings is an often-overlooked area of forensic analysis. It is how that data will be properly packaged and delivered. I use the term *package* from the perspective of how you will prepare the data that was collected in such a way that it is understandable and informative and meets the requirements of the investigation.

Most of the time your readers or your audience for the collected electronic data will be nontechnical individuals. The audience might be a judge, law enforcement, attorneys, or corporate executives. Regardless, forensic examiners are well-served by understanding effective report-writing techniques, which are straightforward, concise, and to the point.

Reports should not only include the memorialization of the tasks that were requested but also the steps that were taken to achieve the results. These steps may include the names of the custodians and devices that were accessed, the times and places in which they were accessed, the tools and systems that were used for the analysis, and a timeline of the various events undertaken by the forensic examiner.

Most reports will also have appendices that will be attached to the report in either paper or electronic form. These appendices may include, for example, copies of the e-mail, spreadsheets, and Word documents or transactional data, and copies of reports from databases or snippets of data from the unallocated space, illustrating the times and dates a particular web page had been seen by a user. The possibilities are endless, but the report writer has an obligation to develop and construct a report that is easily understandable and digestible by the reader and should refrain from providing unnecessary narrative or inference. It should also, to the extent possible, stick to the facts and to the clear conclusions that are drawn.

CHAPTER 7

The Cyber-Firefighters

Computer forensic investigators often work hand in hand with network security professionals, law enforcement, or traditional investigators and are required to respond to events as they take place in real time, from both the monitoring perspective as well as the data collection perspective. Sometimes, data has been created seconds ago, and in other cases, the data may have been created a decade ago. In either case, the forensic examiner has the tools to deal with these scenarios. See Exhibit 7.1.

The cyber-firefighters are almost exclusively relegated to the world of reactive or reactionary tasks. A company is hacked, the data is breached, a system fails, the hackers extort the denial of service, attack begins and shuts down the systems, the botnet acts on its own and redirects your users, your clients are victimized by Internet fraud, or a foreign government has sponsored a hacking group to bring down your power grid. These are all real-world events to which cyber-firefighters need to be prepared to respond.

Many of these matters do not get reported in the mainstream press, and others are never reported at all, due to their confidentiality or extreme sensitivity. Rest assured that nearly every nation and most major corporations have teams prepared and ready to respond to these and other types of events. Each organization has its own risk profile, and as a result, the cyber-firefighters are shaped and molded for the task most prevalent to the potential victim. This could be the theft of trade secrets from within an organization, the misuse of corporate systems for personal profit, or the risk of attack by Russian underground criminal groups. In each case, the cyber-firefighter stands at the ready to cooperate with the investigating party, outside counsel, executives, teams, management, and a host of other parties.

Incident Response Fundamentals

Incident response is a subject that should not be taken lightly by the stakeholders in an investigation. From the moment the anomalous event is discovered to the examination of network logs that occurs when a party becomes aware of fraudulent or anomalous

167

EXHIBIT 7.1   Corporate Server Cluster

This cluster is in four standard racks containing file servers, e-mail servers, web servers, application serv-ers, firewalls, archival and backup systems, antispam, antivirus, and intrusion detection systems, voice mail systems, smartphone servers, transactional servers for e-commerce, time and billing applications, logistics applications, video surveillance systems, thin-client services, and a large transactional database. This overwhelming and highly concentrated environment is where advanced computer investigators often find themselves tasked with preserving or monitoring data without adversely impacting day-to-day or second-to-second operations of the company.

behavior that would require investigation, an investigative response should be met with a predictable and well-orchestrated response. In many cases, the first responder may be security personnel or management within an organization, people who had access to the computers or devices that are being held by the potential suspects. An example of this would be when a senior executive is terminated from his or her position. One of the first steps that should be taken is to secure the electronic devices to which that individual had access and which are company property. In addition, that individual's access to network-based systems or cloud-based systems should be quickly brought under the investigation or organization's control and perhaps decommissioned.

I have seen a number of cases over the years where executives who were terminated on a Friday night after the office was closed and whose computer was seized by corporate security quickly get on the telephone and call their assistant or a co-conspirator within the organization and request that certain documents and files be spirited out through this third party. Prior to taking action, such as relieving employees of their responsibilities, the investigative team or the security team, in conjunction with in-house or outside counsel, should avail themselves of as much information as possible about the systems, tools, and technologies to which the individual had access and the people who worked within his or her sphere of influence so that those individuals may be monitored and investigators can be aware of potential leaks or holes that the individual could exploit.

Responding to a data breach is sometimes the most important part of data response activities because there are so many customers who may be adversely impacted by the activity and there are numerous investigative streams that need to be addressed. Maintaining a clear and defensible chain of custody of all material that has been seized or taken control of is vital to the early response. However, among the concurrent streams of activity it is necessary for companies to engage their public relations, media relations, or in some cases even crisis management teams, to ensure that the correct message is being prepared for the public, customers, and employees. This message should address the activities that have taken place and the steps that the company is taking to remedy any potential exposure of its customers and partners.

Equally important, the company should instruct its employees in what can and cannot be said as it relates to the event in question. Most companies will give clear instructions that any and all comments must be routed through a central individual or team, such as a crisis management group, and that comment to the press, industry coworkers, or even family is completely prohibited. In the early days of the crisis or investigation, information management is key to both ensuring the success of the investigation itself and maintaining on-point messaging for the company or individuals who have been victimized.

Rapid response from a technical standpoint is vital and should be conducted wherever possible under the auspices of individuals who have a mandate for this type of work. There have been investigations in years past where solo actors within an organization would take it on themselves to investigate activity without escalating it to the appropriate individuals within the organization. In some cases, these individuals do not have a broad enough perspective of all the facts and issues to understand the implications of their ad hoc investigative actions, and this type of unsupervised activity can further damage the interests of the company. Therefore, all organizations should have clear-cut rules of engagement for kicking off an investigation, for escalating issues that warrant an investigation, and for an analysis of whether an investigation should take place at all.

When responding to an event, the appropriate tools, systems, applications, and procedures should already be in place so that the forensic investigators who arrive on the scene are not inventing the process as they go along. When forensic investigators are forced to create processes ad hoc, there is a greater chance that errors may be made or shortcuts taken. This is easily avoidable by taking the time to develop an incident response plan in advance. Having a well-thought-out incident response plan, which also takes into consideration outside vendors and third-party applications and systems that may become compromised, can pay dividends should an event actually take place.

I'm a big advocate of maintaining fire drills with some level of regularity, whether annual or semi-annual, particularly as it relates to responding to events in the cloud, where the electronic data is out of your control and would require third-party intervention to secure. For organizations that have far-flung operations in different time zones, in different geographies, or, worse yet, on different continents, the importance of maintaining a well-defined incident response plan cannot be overstated. The basic construct of an incident response plan should take into account the primary stakeholders of the environment within which the response is contemplated.

For example, if the response plan is designed for a retail operation that maintains a distribution center and 100 retail locations across a particular region in the United States and that also maintains the executive office, a design center, a manufacturing operation, and the field sales force, all of these primary stakeholders should be taken into consideration when constructing the plan. A representative from each one of these constituencies should be consulted in the development of the plan so as to account for all of the various systems, procedures, and real-life activity of the individuals who are part of that user group or constituency.

Also, as part of the incident response plan a liaison and predefined connections should be developed with outside counsel, as well as inside counsel and certain senior executives with whom the line of communication is clear when the event takes place. Also, the technical investigators coupled with traditional security and potentially even relationships with outside law enforcement should be contemplated and thought through in advance. This, as it relates to technical investigators or forensic investigators, should include billing rates, forms, availability and response time, technical competency, and a host of other factors that will play a role in the success or failure of the investigation during the early moments or days in which the response is required.

Data Breaches

Data breaches are among the most fundamental of all cyber-attacks on organizations. Data is the currency of the day. Whereas Spanish galleons carried treasure and gold or spices across the oceans of yesteryear, today those same oceans have buried deep beneath their water fiber-optic cables carrying electronic communications and data around the globe at the speed of light, allowing for instantaneous communication between hundreds of millions of people simultaneously. Managing that data and holding secure and critical data close at hand has become a central component to any organization's information security profile.

Similarly, criminal hacking groups and bad characters around the globe have placed data access and the ability to breach systems for the purpose of gaining access to data as job number one and are continually tweaking their arsenals and sharpening their spears to find holes in systems that will allow them to extricate data in a clandestine manner. The data breach may be as simple as an employee who is convinced that he or she is dealing with a bona fide supplier and provides access to a particular database in order for that supplier to gain routine access to systems that the individual expects the supplier to use. Unknown to the employee, the supplier is actually a fake or a front that provided an electronic trapdoor through which the unsuspecting employee has just fallen. Often, these ploys are managed by using what is known as social engineering. A data breach may also be the result of an organization placing code on a website, allowing for what is known as an *SQL injection attack*, tricking a website's back-end SQL database server into spitting out hundreds of thousands of records in an automated fashion over the course of minutes or hours.

Often, these hacks and exploits go undetected until long after the criminals have had a chance to cover their tracks and closed the doors behind them, well on their way to selling their loot. Data breaches account for hundreds of millions of dollars in losses annually around the world by corporations and individuals, academic institutions, government agencies, and every other type of organization. Hackers routinely exploit systems that are not patched or properly maintained by their network administrators or security administrators and extract large volumes of data that may be in the form of customer lists, credit cards, account numbers, personal identifiable information of every known type, and all manner of other sensitive data that would have a value to some interested party and that can be sold on the black market.

The Internet is littered with websites known as "Carder" websites, or other forums on which hackers can engage in the business of buying and selling the stolen data. Computer forensic examiners are called to the scene of the crime moments, days, weeks, or even months after the fact, to try to reconstruct the events that took place that led to the data breach. I have had a number of cases where the data breach has in fact been the result of lax standards inside the enterprise and behind the firewall. These are cases in which a trusted individual has been given access to systems and has used that access for personal gain, effectively walking out the front door with some drives full of electronic data that can be used on the outside for personal gain.

I have also had a number of cases over the years in which external hackers have managed to find some technical glitch within a website, a database, or a system, which would allow them to exploit that vulnerability in order to dig deep into the database at hand and remotely extract the electronic data. In some cases, that data would then be transferred across the globe a number of times to hide the origin of the hack and the destination of the material that had been stolen.

Because of these risks and vulnerabilities, computer forensic examiners are well served to understand the mechanics of network controls and systems beyond the simple desktop or laptop. Often the data that has been stolen has left through the front door on a vulnerable website that has been breached, and forensic examiners, if they do not have the requisite skill set to understand these web-based technologies, should collaborate with other specialists who can help guide the investigation.

Theft and Fraud

The growth area within the business of the bad guys is theft and fraud. Companies and individuals are victimized and targeted ad nauseam from every possible perspective. Clever fraudsters and thieves, hardened criminals, and opportunists who are entrenched within an organization are all looking for vulnerabilities to exploit within the technical, physical, human, or distributed networks of companies large and small. As we discussed elsewhere in this volume, the commodity of the day is data, which translates into dollars. Information is data. Communications equals data. Operational applications and information created on those systems take the form of electronic data; e-mail, transcriptions, Excel spreadsheets, Microsoft Word documents, database output spreadsheets, tax information, web traffic stats, and photographs from red-light cameras all translate into electronic data.

This data must live somewhere. In many cases, it lives in duplicate, triplicate, and quadruplicate in multiple locations as a result of forwards, copies, BCCs, archives, e-mail backups, and a host of other technologies that have the ability to quickly replicate electronic data in the blink of an eye. Every time the data is replicated and stored in new location, it is subject to new vulnerabilities and the potential of it being stolen increases. The thieves know this. For example, when one of the largest credit card transaction processing firms in the United States was compromised a few years ago, it was not through the front door. Instead, the bad guys who stole millions of credit card records went through a side door, a marketing department within that organization that had temporary custody of every copy of credit card data so that it could run analytics on the data to determine how to more effectively market services to its credit card users.

This is an example of data at rest that has been copied from the active data and that has been moved from its primary location and is no longer under the control of operational procedures that are put in place to protect that data. Once this happens, it lives in the hands of a different department with a different set of operational controls and awareness over data security, which may be compromised. The net result was that the organization was breached, millions of users' data was released to the bad guys, and the organization lost its contract with that credit card firm, so that it no longer processes data on its behalf; a big blow to the organization's management and shareholders but even more so to the sanctity of the data and the individuals whom the data represents.

Systems Failures

I listed systems failures as an area of overview in this volume because often computer forensic examiners are called on to review electronic data as it relates to the failure of a particular system. However, when I refer to systems failures, I'm referring to either software-, hardware-, or enterprise-related technologies that either have failed to per-form as advertised or have simply failed. See Exhibit 7.2.

In actuality, systems failures happen regularly, whether the website that was de-signed to accommodate a certain number of transactions per minute fails to live up to the expectations of the owners of the website, or a medical billing system is unable to properly manage electronic records as they are being entered into the system. Other systems failures can include hardware failures that are the result of failed backups or failed hard discs. Computer forensic examiners can be called in to examine the commu-nications between individuals charged with building, maintaining, or designing these electronic systems, hardware, and software, or can be called in to examine the method-ologies that were deployed for the development of the systems and why they may have failed to meet the mandate set forth to detect things such as defective products.

Internal Investigations

Internal investigations take place all the time across corporate America. They can be as simple as a human resources department conducting a background check on a new

EXHIBIT 7.2   Damaged Backup Tape

The damaged backup tape was essential to the electronic discovery response of a Fortune 500 company to a U.S. regulator during a financial malfeasance investigation. Through forensic reconstruction of the tape, data was preserved.

employee or as complex as a special committee acting on behalf of its directors to investigate potential malfeasance by corporate executives in response to a Securities and Exchange Commission inquiry. Regardless of the size of the investigation, each of them should be handled with professional procedures and diligence. The results of an internal investigation often impact the lives of those who are investigated. In some cases, people lose their jobs, their reputations are tarnished, companies are thrown into upheaval, and careers and lives lose their balance.

Investigative computer forensic professionals, who are part of an internal investigation, which is increasingly the case today, bear as much responsibility as the lead investigators or auditors. It is their responsibility to ensure that their systems and applications, protocols, and procedures are of the highest ethical caliber. They must also ensure that shortcuts are not taken and that when confronted by an investigator, a manager, or a lawyer who demands results that require shortcuts or unethical behavior to be taken. The investigation must take its course and must be prosecuted with independence and clarity and without outside interference.

Internal investigations today often rely on electronically stored information and its rapid access so that an early determination can be deduced as to the veracity of the allegations that are being made. In some cases, investigators have the luxury of time to observe behavior and to set traps, honeypots, or listening devices, such as keystroke loggers, to understand what is taking place within the enterprise. In other cases, the investigators must rely on quickly securing digital information, sometimes in the middle of the night while the operators of the devices that are being forensically imaged are asleep at home.

In these cases, where forensic investigators are required to capture digital evidence in a clandestine manner at the direction of an authority within the organization, they must exercise caution and care, both in the process of collecting the evidence and in maintaining a digital record of the product, of the techniques that were deployed, and the manner in which they found the physical systems. The point that I'm trying to make is: When investigators are required to collect the information from computers that are not being used, perhaps in the dead of night in a corporate facility, it is important for them to document how those systems were first encountered. This is usually done through the use of digital cameras so that once the exercise is complete, the forensic investigators can then reassemble the computers and return them to their original location and their original placement so that the user of the computer is not aware that the investigation took place.

Internal investigations are a common area of work for computer forensic investigators. These investigators are often called in to examine electronic data and communications between individuals within a corporation or among outside vendors and subcontractors, clients, or other parties that are suspected of some internal malfeasance, wrongdoing, or fraud. These internal investigations are generally going to be directed by a department or an executive within the organization, an audit committee of directors, the security department, in-house counsel, or, in some cases, outside counsel. These internal investigations can relate to issues as far ranging as Foreign Corrupt Practices Act allegations, where a corporation has been accused or suspected of essentially bribing foreign officials for some purpose, such as winning contracts and foreign markets. Or, as was the case a number of years ago, these investigations can focus on issues of stock option manipulation and backdating for bid rigging or any number of fraudulent activities that a corporation or its agents could have undertaken.

Sometimes corporations will initiate an internal investigation to review the activity or behavior of a particular department. Perhaps it could be a sales team that has over-inflated numbers for the purpose of an increase in their compensation, or it could be a CEO or CFO who has made improper payments to subcontractors or third parties in exchange for kickbacks. Perhaps it could be allegations of fraud as a result of contracts with the federal government. There are innumerable reasons why the corporation would undertake an internal investigation. However, one thing is consistent and that is that, by and large, computer forensic analysis of electronic data is available and is often at the forefront of the objectives of the investigators and often requires that the computer forensic examiners assist in the effort of collecting, managing, preserving, and, finally, analyzing electronic data in accordance with the goals of the investigation.

The Real-Time Predicament

One of the challenges faced by computer forensic examiners and investigators in today's ultra-connected world is that events happen so quickly that it is sometimes nearly impossible to collect the electronic data representing those events in time and before it has been overwritten or modified. Crime today takes place in seconds, as opposed to yesteryear when a guy would walk into a bank and rob it, and police would have the opportunity to give chase, an alarm system would go off, eyewitnesses would be at the scene, and even some photographs or video surveillance of the heist would be taken. In today's world, the criminals are operating with great anonymity and over extraordinary distances, and, most important, at the speed of light.

Organizations that are taking steps to preserve electronic data as it is being created stand a better chance of capturing relevant forensic information for the purpose of an investigation than those who are simply reacting to an event that is taking place, often an event for which they are ill-prepared. Forensic practitioners are often called *cyber-firefighters* because they are the ones who are called in at midnight to respond to an event that took place earlier, thousands of miles away, and that has impacted their client. It is up to them to get into gear and organize a plan to preserve electronic evidence that will be required to conduct the eventual investigation into the events that took place. For this reason, computer forensic laboratories and practitioners should be designed with this real-time predicament in mind.

Building a Global Resource Network

For computer forensic investigators who are supporting operations of a large corporate environment it will be important for them to develop a network of service vendors and resources that they can turn to at a moment's notice for assistance with projects. This may mean that you have established relationships with scanning and coding vendors for the purpose of scanning physical documents and coding them into document review platforms. You may have these vendors and resources in a variety of locations where your organization has operations or it may mean you have contracted out the work to third-party computer forensic professionals in various locations, who can collect electronic data in the field on your behalf.

Although many organizations maintain the capacity internally for all of the various aspects of computer forensics and electronic discovery, most organizations cannot afford this luxury and are required to outsource many of the tasks that are part of the computer forensic work. It is highly advisable for those organizations to make the effort to identify resources and vendors that they can rely on in the locations of the anticipated litigation or investigative work and they should do so in advance of the need for these resources and vendors. This will reduce the requirement to scramble at the last minute and to potentially end up with subpar service vendors who are not prepared to meet your actual requirements. As a commonsense risk management exercise, building this network in advance will pay dividends down the road.

I have always found that if I have solid resources in locations in which my team cannot directly provide services, then when the phone rings late at night and a client is demanding forensic collection in a far-off nation, whether it be in Pakistan, India, or Nigeria, or even closer to home, I should have preidentified individuals or companies that can assist with this type of work, and more often than not, they are all too pleased to receive a phone call from me directing them to go out and collect the data that is required in the investigation. On the other hand, if that legwork had not been undertaken in advance, then I could find myself scrambling at the last minute, looking for resources and taking any warm body that picks up the phone. This will lead to missed opportunities, time delays, and a potentially subpar work product for my client.

If this is your client or your organization, then taking these preemptive steps to build these networks can be quite useful. Typical areas are networks of individuals familiar with requirements that include scanning and encoding, as previously mentioned; computer forensic acquisition teams; local on-the-ground investigators, researchers, and project managers who have the ability to speak and operate within the local language; and technology vendors who are prepared to process electronic data that is harvested in short order and in a manner that is already understood and expected by both in-house and outside counsel.

Honeypots and Other Attractive Intel-Gathering Targets

A *honeypot* is an electronic location on the network developed for the purpose of collecting data about patterns of attack, processes of fraud, and other vulnerabilities, or for misdirecting attackers to benign, but seemingly important, sources of data for them to attack or occupy their time, activity, and resources while real business continues. Honeypots can take the form of a file or a database on a network, a specific server or group of servers, routers, a specific desktop, or even an application that is designed to attract the attackers and either capture details and data about them, for the purpose of reengineering where the attack came from, or act as a decoy to keep them busy doing what they are doing.

In some cases, honeypots can be developed into honeypot networks, where multiple machines or even dozens or hundreds of virtual machines are placed in various locations, either within an organization or across a geography. In one of my matters many years ago, the honeypot network was placed around the globe. In this particular case, we developed dozens of servers designed with certain vulnerabilities embedded within them so as to attract certain types of attacks. The servers were placed in Russia, China, Japan, Western Europe, and throughout the United States, with the design that once those attacks took place and the servers were compromised, additional software that had been placed on the servers would record that activity and allow us to burn DVDs locally and have the content and the signatures of those attacks delivered to our laboratories for analysis.

In one such scenario, the servers that had been set up on behalf of our client—a significant multinational corporation that would sustain regular and frequent cyber-attacks—were compromised within minutes of being placed online, such was the ubiquity and prevalence of the cyber-attacks that were taking place on the Internet at the time. Through our analysis of the resulting data sets from these honeypots within the honeypot network, and the analysis made by our client, countermeasures were designed to both fend off future attacks and identify the origin of some of the attackers.

This particularly useful data was collected and managed by computer forensic investigators, who leveraged network technology in line with software development skills and combined with web application knowledge and a general understanding of how the global networks function to provide results. It was historic in nature and very useful for the client to protect itself and its clients or customers in the future. Although this complex honeypot network is certainly not the norm in the corporate world, it is clear that many countries have set up honeypot networks in the hopes of warding off espionage and attacks by adverse governments.

Honeypots could be established on your own personal home computer by simply giving predominance to a particular directory. Perhaps you would call it "my personal finances and important information." This directory would be loaded up with meaningless Excel spreadsheets and backups of a sample user from Quicken. You would also maintain a directory elsewhere on your computer, with innocuous names, such as 6342, which would in fact contain sensitive data you are looking to protect. You would do this in the hopes that a casual hacker taking a quick inventory of your system would identify what appears to be an important directory and carry off only that.

sterical of reasoning

Databases and Structured Data

Although the great majority of data that is analyzed during electronic discovery or computer forensic examinations is what is known as *unstructured data*, such as e-mail and office documents or residual data related to web transactions, browsing, instant messaging, or images, there is still a need, in many matters, to understand and manage what is known as *structured data*. Structured data is commonly in the form of a database. A database is a container that holds data in a predefined format and manages relationships between those data points for the purpose of computations, analysis, processing, and presentation. Databases include Microsoft Access, Microsoft SQL, and other variants of SQL, as well as Oracle, but this is not an exhaustive list. There are thousands of proprietary databases, applications, and designs for specific industries or purposes, such as Quicken and QuickBooks, which contain data in a structured format for accounting and financial purposes.

Most industries have some number of structured data applications that may contain data that would be relevant to an investigation, whether they are related to inventory control, logistics management, human resource management, medical billing, or a multitude of other industries. In analyzing structured data in databases, from a forensic perspective, there are a number of challenges that can be present, the biggest of which is not having access to the original application that managed the data set.

Because databases are often a collection of tables that contain data in predefined orders and with predefined relationships to one another, if the forensic examiner does not have access to the original application that managed that data set, then he or she will be faced with the daunting, and sometimes an impossible, task of reconstructing relationships in a meaningful way. Certainly, with some databases it is possible to export the raw data from the tables, but without understanding how those data points and tables interacted with one another the data may be useless. In some circumstances, when databases are incomplete or it is not possible to reinstall and run the applications that managed those databases, it may be preferable to print out reports and tables or export those same reports and tables to a common format, if the opportunity allows.

Organized Crime in the Cyber-Underworld

As the Internet has graduated from the academic backwaters to the mainstream world, nearly all social structures, organizations, and human interaction has been affected. These structures have either begun to fade away or adapt to the new medium and find their footing. Organized crime is one of the great success stories of the Internet age. In nearly every nation and in nearly every city, fraudsters have leveraged the Internet and its power to reach deep into the personal lives of its potential victims in order to further their criminal activity. It seems as though criminal activity on the Internet is as old as e-mail, for if you study the hacker movement and the lives of many of the early criminal or renegade hackers in the 1960s, 1970s, 1980s, and early 1990s, then you can see that technology could always be leveraged for purposes not intended by the designers.

What may at one time have been playful hacking or tinkering with technology, including hardware, software, and interconnectivity, quickly morphed into criminal activity as the dark side of that human endeavor soon recognized the power of leveraging technology for malintent. Criminal organizations that once thrived on street-side prostitution and drug operations soon discovered that by leveraging the Internet they could reach a much broader audience, while reducing their own personal risk, and in some cases, using less effort in achieving the same or even greater financial goals.

Today, it seems quite astounding that an individual would have the gumption to walk into a bank with a gun and demand money, when if that same individual is given the appropriate computer skills he or she can rob 10 banks at the click of a button and remove much of the risk to his or her own personal safety, while increasing hundredfold the potential return on investment. Criminal gangs have formed around the notion that if they leverage computing technology, then they can develop scams and threats in criminal activity that will operate 24/7 and around the world.

Much of what we see in today's headlines focuses on the theft of personally identifiable information, otherwise known as *identity theft*. This has had, at its heart, organized criminal activity, which spurs on this type of activity and provides the catalyst for solo hackers or gangs of cyber-thugs to break into systems in the hopes of collecting personally identifiable information that can subsequently be sold on the black market for the purpose of financial gain.

The Cyber-Underworld in Various Regions

The cyber-underworld in the United States has a long and glorified past, much of which has been media hype and some of which has been truly nefarious and dastardly activity at the hands of diligent cybercriminals. The cyber-underworld has its roots going back decades and was initially firmly rooted in the hacker community. I use the term *hacker* not as a pejorative but as a descriptor of a type of mentality and behavior of a group of individuals who are challenged by tinkering with the status quo and looking for vulnerabilities, unintended manifestations, and quirky side benefits or failures of any particular given system, whether it be technological or not. However, the reality is that as cybercrime and its lure expanded, the cybercriminal world quickly eclipsed the hacking community, which is still very much alive and well today and has developed an ethos of its own, with a pecking order that in some cases is quite rigid.

Hacking conferences attract the cyber-curious, conferences that once attracted bona fide hackers almost exclusively and that today have turned into true security meet-ups from which numerous cyber-underground organizations have taken root. Today, there are thousands of chat rooms on the Internet dedicated to various cyber-underground topics, from hacking credit cards to cell phones, set-top boxes to automobile onboard computer systems. With proper credentials, and an anonymous hacker ID, which is accepted by the users or hosts of the group, one can access these systems and join in the fun. Most of the real bad guys are on tightly controlled online forums in which any member has been vetted carefully.

However, the reality is that these are also breeding grounds for the criminally minded and those who harbor malcontent to their fellow citizens. U.S. criminal hacking groups abound and are often closely related to those overseas, such as hacking groups in the ex–Soviet Union and its satellite states. Ukraine and Russia, as well as many of the Eastern European nations, have evolved into hotbeds of criminal digital activity.

The strength of the Eastern European nations and ex–Soviet Union as a breeding ground for cybercriminal activity is in part due to the participation of individuals with structured computer science, math, and engineering backgrounds, along with a general pervasive lawlessness that reigned in some of these regions throughout the 1990s and into the first few years of the new millennium. This coupled with an institutional disdain for authoritative power gave birth to a criminal social stratum of cybercriminals who initially often worked alone, but as they became more sophisticated began to work in packs. These gangs eventually became embedded within or co-opted by the traditional criminal institutions of the region. Many Eastern European nations have been reluctant to crack down on cybercriminals, particularly in Ukraine, where cybercrime is big business and the criminals themselves are sometimes big stars in the social circles of those countries.

The criminal gangs in Ukraine and Russia have often focused on the theft of personally identifiable information for the purpose of running credit card scams and other financial shenanigans. This contrasts with the bulk of cybercrime activity emanating from East Asia, and particularly China, which finds its roots in the theft of intellectual property for the purpose of economic or nationalistic opportunity and ordinarily at the expense of the United States and Western European nations and their business enterprises. Criminal gangs in China have manifested themselves in many cities and have focused on traditional hacking to gain access in the form of back doors into U.S. corporate juggernauts and small businesses alike.

Many of these gangs are co-opted by Chinese government agencies for their own purposes and help to augment the great Chinese firewall, as well as what is known as operation Golden Shield, which is, in essence, the Chinese federal government's effort to sustain information control within their country for both inbound and outbound activity, but which often finds itself at odds with the West due to its offensive information-gathering tasks and successes.

South America and Africa have not been immune to the world of cybercrime and have had to endure their own tortuous evolution of street thugs morphing into online criminal enterprises that control numerous rackets. They have given birth to unique specialties, which today continue to confound business owners and individuals alike. For example, in Nigeria the decades-old 419 scam, which previously would bring in victims through mail and then by fax and now by e-mail, continues the promise of riches to its intended victims over the cyber-airwaves, but in fact, only leads to the theft of thousands of dollars, further enriching criminal Nigerian cyber-gangs and supporting further activity. In the case of South America, particular emphasis has been placed by the sophisticated hacking gangs on cyber-extortion, where denial-of-service attacks have been threatened against unsuspecting business owners and online entities that are attacked by these techniques if they fail to pay as ordered.

Throughout the world there are pockets of cyber-expertise that have given rise to criminal activity and that are being fought on the local and national level. However, it seems that the criminals are often a few steps ahead, being that they can so often operate with anonymity and impunity, victimizing legitimate users of information networks in the pursuit of their day-to-day lives.

State-Sponsored Cybercrime

One of the most insidious types of cybercrime is the type that is sponsored by the state, and unfortunately, I have to report that virtually no state is without complicity. Whether it is China, the United States, Israel, Germany, Japan, France, England, Russia, or dozens and dozens of other states, each has its own cyber-policies, either stated or not, which involve espionage, counterespionage, and various levels of surveillance and countersurveillance techniques of both internal and external parties. This is a fact of life, just as spying on one's neighbor is a fact of life in the traditional international sense.

The United States has gone so far as to stand up its own cyber-command, thereby giving legitimacy to the approach and escalating the importance of cyber-warfare and intelligence-gathering within the command structure of the U.S military, which is more transparent than other states such as China, Russia, India, Pakistan, or Iran. However, each of them has developed protocols and systems, including offensive and defensive contingency plans, for dealing with cyber-threats they face as nations. With the advent of the STUXNET worm or malware, the world witnessed a very real wake-up call to the power and promise of cyber-war.

In the case of STUXNET, Iranian nuclear enrichment facilities were targeted by a very sophisticated and well-designed piece of malware that disguised itself as a Microsoft Windows update, but in fact infected the Siemens-based SCADA (supervisory control and data acquisition) systems within the Iranian nuclear facilities, which resulted in an attack on the centrifuge machines designed to enrich uranium. The attack instructed the centrifuges to spin wildly out of control, which resulted in their physical destruction. The complexity of such a project ensures that, at present, it can only be undertaken by nations or organizations with significant resources. However, by no means does that leave us any more secure.

In fact, this illustrates that, just as with an atomic bomb or any other destructive device, given enough time and resources any group or organization can build one. In the case of cyber-weaponry, there is plenty of value in concentrating one's efforts on building a cyber-weapon against a very targeted and specific victim, for the purpose of accomplishing either a political goal or a financial goal.

Identity Theft

Computer forensic examiners are often tasked with reviewing electronic evidence related to some of the most interesting and contemporary criminal challenges. Among these are the new and emerging threats of identity theft. In recent years, identity theft has become a multimillion-dollar business, in which organized criminal gangs have designed clever systems and programs and have identified vulnerabilities that allow them to steal information relating to the identity of tens of millions of individuals. These criminal gangs subsequently use this data to impersonate individuals in a variety of ways, including online shopping, banking, and even the sale and distribution of counterfeit credit cards, which are used to steal millions of dollars in goods and services from unsuspecting merchant victims.

Identity theft is made easier through a lapse of user habits, such as maintaining passwords that are easy to crack; failing to regularly change passwords; and providing easy access to confidential personal documents, such as bank statements, credit card statements, and other mail that can be easily pilfered from a mailbox, trash can, Dumpster, or even the top of the desk of an unsuspecting employee. Unfortunately, due to a significant strain on resources and the inability for law enforcement to respond to every claim of identity theft, countless victims are unable to find redress and catch the culprits who have stolen their personal information. More often, law enforcement will focus on cases in which tens of thousands, hundreds of thousands, or even millions of consumers' identities have been stolen. Fortunately, credit card companies, for the most part, assume the risks associated with identity theft. However, the ultimate costs are undoubtedly passed on to consumers in the form of higher fees, tighter credit, and other hidden costs.

Computer forensic investigators have the ability to review electronic data stored on a wide variety of devices that can provide insight into the origin and source of the theft of personal information. Among the first steps that are taken by investigators, once it has become evident that identity theft has taken place, is to secure the electronic communications devices that managed and carried the electronic communications of the victim or victims. This can include desktops and laptops. However, it can also include file servers, e-mail servers, and other devices that are connected to the network that is used by the victim.

In examining these devices, a forensic examiner has the ability, in many cases, to determine if unauthorized access took place on the network, including content management systems and content-filtering systems. They also have the ability to provide further clues from firewalls and other network appliances that help manage network activity. Understanding what anomalous network behavior looks like is key to being able to interpret these important sources of information. Investigators can learn an IP address or other relevant data from the examination of these logs.

A forensic investigation, particularly as it relates to network activity, is often an exercise in piecing together multiple clues. Many of these clues may seem innocuous or unrelated, but when examined in their entirety, provide insight into the intentions of the hacker. Computer forensic professionals who are charged with responding to identity theft matters understand that time is of the essence and the speed at which they collect the electronic data can mean the difference between solving the case or failing to identify the culprits. Electronic data that lives in systems such as routers, firewall logs, and other transient data often has a short shelf life and can be overwritten in the course of weeks, days, or even minutes, depending on the volume of data that is flowing across the network and the steps that have been taken to proactively preserve data in a conscientious manner.

Identity theft will continue to challenge ordinary individuals, as well as forensic investigators, because the rewards of collecting this data, reselling it, and/or using it for one's own criminal behavior far outweigh the risks. Let's face it. Why would you walk into a bank with a gun and demanded money, when, for far less personal risk and from the comfort of your living room, you can hire a team of hackers out of Romania or some other country to break into 20 banks and deliver the goods to you?

Intellectual Property and Trade Secret Theft

Intellectual property theft is one of the most challenging areas facing businesses throughout the world today. Significant new threats to the sanctity of business data seem to emerge daily. Theft of trade secrets has emerged as one of the easier crimes for disgruntled, unethical, or unscrupulous and opportunistic employees to commit. These employees may wish to harm their employer or wish to achieve some personal gain by selling or trading the trade secrets that they are able to obtain through the course of their trusted access to company systems. These thefts are most often committed by individuals who are looking for alternative employment or who are looking to start their own company, all on the backs of the good work of their current and soon-to-be-former employer. These thefts can be devastating to companies, damaging their reputation, morale, value, and standing in the business community, not to mention their competitive advantage.

In numerous cases in which I have been engaged to investigate the theft of trade secrets or intellectual property from companies, we have found the computer forensic analysis of the hard drives of computers used by the individuals who had trusted access is the most important first step in acquiring evidence of wrongdoing. These computers will often illustrate the types of files that were stolen and how they were stolen. A savvy computer forensic examiner can review the metadata of the files, including time stamps of when the files are created, when they were last modified, when they were accessed, and/or when they were deleted in order to draw conclusions and inferences as to how those files were used by the individual who had access to the computer.

Files that are maintained on the Windows operating system, for example, are marked with these file attributes, and every time an individual touches one of these files to open it, move and copy it, edit and delete it, that action is recorded in the metadata of the file. The computer forensic examiner has the ability to collect this data and examine and identify the specific behavior that led to the theft of files. This might include moving those files to a thumb drive or an external hard drive through a USB port on the computer or transferring them over a network or over the Internet to a place such as Dropbox or some other repository of computer data. Many times, computer files are simply printed out, in which case there may also be a record on the computer of that activity. In some cases printers can even be examined to determine what documents were received over a network and printed.

Theft of trade secrets includes every conceivable type of data point from customer lists to secret formulas to financials and spreadsheets to marketing and strategic plans to CAD/CAM drawings and diagrams and every other type of document or file known to the business world. When investigating the theft of trade secrets in the computer forensic environment, technicians, lawyers, and investigators should work close at hand and quickly to secure all of the various devices that could have contained data relevant to the matter, including desktops, laptops, router logs, file servers, e-mail servers, wireless router logs, wireless access logs, third-party application data and access information, and a wide variety of other network data.

Analyzing this data can help investigators better understand whether trade secrets were stolen, and if so, by whom and when and how. In many cases, the detailed analysis of unallocated space and the residual information that may be contained there is possible, and if so, then you can also extract fragments of communications, which in many cases can lead to understanding where the data that was stolen was sent and whether there continues to be bad actors within the environment.

Botnets, Malware, Trojans, and Phishing

Computer forensic examiners often are faced with trying to acquire electronic evidence related to botnets, malware, Trojan horses, and phishing. All of these terms relate to malicious activity conducted on the Internet or other networks that is ordinarily initiated by hackers and script kiddies or other bad seeds on the Internet who have the ability to wreak havoc. A botnet is a network of computers that can essentially be hijacked by software code that is distributed by computer hackers. This software code leverages resources on these computers without direct input or knowledge of the computer owner or user and causes these computers to communicate with one another and provides additional horsepower for the purpose of either a distributed denial-of-service attack or other Internet-based shenanigans.

Malware refers to the combination of malintent and software and is ordinarily a piece of code that has some malicious behavior programmed within it, which will allow a hacker or some other individual to conduct malicious behavior on a computer or a network. I use the word *computer* rather loosely because, frankly, malware can be targeted against cell phones or any device that communicates over a network.

The Trojan or a Trojan horse is a type of malware. It is software that has been designed to appear as genuine or innocuous code in the form perhaps of an e-mail, a graphic, a movie, or a web page, but its ultimate purpose is to install a backdoor or some type of software onto your computer or device that will give the hacker or malicious computer user control over or access to your computer to gather information without your knowledge or participation.

Phishing, spelled with a *ph*, is a technique that is used by hackers and other malicious actors on the Internet for the purpose of trying to acquire access to systems that you control, such as your e-mail, by posing as a legitimate computer user offering an authentic service and requesting information or input from you that would in some way allow you to compromise your security.

A case in point includes when you receive an e-mail from your bank requesting that your password be updated. Often, these types of e-mail are bogus and are what we would call a phishing attempt to get you to respond in the affirmative with your password information by typing it into an online form or by responding to the e-mail, thereby providing the hacker or the malicious computer group information about your personal log-on name, address, telephone number, and other particulars that will assist them in potentially accessing your systems for the purpose of collecting personally identifiable information about you. This will in turn allow them to compromise your identity. Computer forensic technicians and investigators are often charged with collecting, reviewing, and analyzing electronic evidence that would illustrate how these types of activities have taken place.

Data Breach Vulnerabilities

These days, companies, corporations, and institutions of all sizes and shapes are vulnerable to data breach activity. Data breaches occur when an external attack successfully breaches an organization's data infrastructure for the purpose of capturing information about that organization. Often, that information will include personally identifiable information about users of that organization's services, such as patient records, employee records, and customer records. These records often include credit card numbers and other actionable information that hackers and organized criminals can leverage for profit.

Consistent with identification theft and the other types of malicious behavior on which I comment in this section, data breaches can often be documented on the user's computer by using a forensic analysis of the available evidentiary record. That evidentiary record will include routers, firewall logs, server data, wireless information, and other data points that, at some point, will provide clues as to how the data breach took place.

There have been numerous data breaches that have occurred because of lax standards and procedures within a company, such as failing to secure desktops and laptops while in transit or failing to manage passwords effectively. These easy-to-remedy issues that companies often face are what the hackers and malicious computer users are counting on when it comes to corporate computer behavior, thus allowing them to leverage this soft underside of a corporation's organization in order to acquire electronic data and, hence, proceed with a successful data breach.

Hackers and Their Environment

Hackers come from every walk of society and are not necessarily going to be your traditional 18-year-old male computer whiz-kid with blue-black hair, tattoos, and nose piercings. They could just as easily be a sophisticated computer engineer, an author with an eye toward technology, an encryption researcher, a professor, a businessperson, a military professional, or even a stay-at-home mom. In my various investigations, I have come across hackers of all of these descriptions.

By and large, hackers hold to a hacker ethos, which prizes the ability to overcome obstacles, particularly obstacles of an institutional nature. These institutions can be as diverse as a governmental organization or simply a piece of software that a hacker will challenge in order to find its vulnerabilities or to overcome some perceived barrier that it presents. These barriers can be anything from functionality to access to licenses and beyond.

Hackers often congregate at hacker conventions in the real world. These conventions include the world-famous DEFCON convention, held in Las Vegas in July every year, as well as countless other conventions and meetings small and large in dozens and dozens of nations, where hackers convene to trade war stories, learn of new exploits, socialize, and, from time to time, brag of recent conquests. Computer forensic professionals should understand the hacking mentality and the hacking culture. They should understand how hackers communicate with one another on Internet relay chat channels and other clandestine online vehicles. Computer forensic professionals should understand how hackers find their targets because it is not only for profit for which a hacker will work, but for the thrill of overcoming a significant challenge. This is much like when mountaineer George Mallory was asked in 1922 why he kept attempting to climb Mount Everest and his answer was "because it is there." He was killed on his next attempt in 1924.

Many of the younger hackers are actually moving through a rite of passage as a test of their skills and compete among their peers to determine who is the cleverest of them all. Often, these hackers graduate into full-time employment with some of the largest and most respected technology firms and governments around the world. It is not unusual for me to review a résumé of a computer forensic engineer who cut his teeth in the hacking community, disassembling and assembling computers, analyzing the hardware for deficiencies and issues, searching the code base of software vulnerabilities, and, from time to time, exploiting these vulnerabilities to verify their hypothesis.

The hacking community serves an important balance in the technological world, forever keeping software and hardware manufacturers and providers on their toes, ensuring that they are working to develop systems of a higher standard that cannot be compromised for fear of both the reputational and genuine damage that may take place. The benevolent hacker has challenged software companies over the years by using the swords, lances, and spears of his or her age—the keyboard and mouse—to elicit deficiencies in products on which ordinary citizens are meant to rely.

I've had the pleasure of working with a number of software companies over the years that genuinely respect and appreciate the benevolent work conducted by some computer hackers. However, the unfortunate reality is that not only are some hackers unethical and not only do they sometimes leverage their knowledge over vulnerabilities in systems to extort companies, but some of these hackers go much further and deploy their services on behalf of organized criminal gangs, governments, and other sinister players to defeat the systems that we rely on for communications and commerce. Forensic technicians are often found in the challenging position of having to retroactively reverse-engineer the activities and exploits of a seasoned hacker whose goal it is to cover his or her trail from the beginning. These challenging cases can truly test the mettle of even the best forensic specialists.

CHAPTER 8

E-Discovery Responsibilities

Because electronic discovery has taken on an increasingly important role in the litigation process over the course of the past 15 years, it is vital for any investigator or executive managing an investigation to understand the basic concepts of this area of the law. This section discusses some of the primary components of the electronic discovery process and the impact that the intersection of forensic investigations may have on it.

Lawyers, investigators, and practitioners within the electronic discovery space have wrestled for years with the challenge of producing a model or framework that can best describe the electronic discovery and information management life cycle. As a result, the model that has gained most universal acceptance is what is known as the *EDRM* or *electronic discovery reference model*. This very basic high-level model of the electronic discovery life cycle provides some universal concepts and vocabulary to an industry process that many view as fractured, inconsistent, and challenging to understand and manage.

The electronic discovery reference model's primary proposition is that it allows an individual with almost no prior experience to quickly understand the basic roles, responsibilities, and processes of the electronic discovery life cycle. It begins with the premise that the goal of the electronic discovery process is to reduce a large data set to a smaller data set while simultaneously increasing the relevance of that same data. It starts with the premise that one has little understanding of the specifics of the particular corpus of data that is being worked with and that through a process of intelligently managing the data one will arrive at a point in time when one has a complete comprehension of a very small data set, derived from what was previously a large, amorphous collection of unidentified electronic data.

Data Identification

To accomplish this, the electronic discovery reference model begins its life in the world of information governance and information management. And as the participants in the model move from left to right, new processes are introduced, starting with identification. The purpose of the identification phase is to memorialize the process of identifying data that lives within the corpus of available data. The first of the primary steps within the identification phase is to develop an identification and strategy plan. This is an important first step as it allows the e-discovery team members to marshal their resources and to prepare a first draft of the discovery plan. The second step is to establish an identification team. This team would have the mandate of identifying all the locations and distinguishing criteria of the relevant data. The final step in the identification process is to certify potentially relevant sources of electronically stored information. Throughout this process, best practices require that status and progress reporting is maintained and that appropriate documentation of the process is kept for a defensible audit trail. As in all of the steps articulated in the electronic discovery reference model, it is also important to develop a quality control and validation procedure to ensure accuracy and process and work product.

Among the most important tools that can be leveraged during this identification phase is what is known as a *data map*. A data map will outline in concrete terms the locations and interconnections between all the various data sources. My preference has always been to see a graphical data map that illustrates the physical locations of the data sets and articulates characteristics of each one of them, including the type of hardware and software that is used to maintain the data, names, and points of contact with persons who control the data set and any other information that may be learned about how that data set may be communicating with other data and if any particular parties can impact that data with or without appropriate controls. This graphical data map should be backed up by a detailed spreadsheet that can be shared among key members of the information management or discovery team and often provides important foundational insight for the forensics investigative teams that will need to rely on the same data sets.

Managing the identification phase effectively can pay off handsomely downstream for all parties; however, should this area be addressed in a lighthearted fashion it is quite possible that the electronic discovery and forensic investigation work can be easily derailed. Additional important tasks during the identification phase include identifying key witnesses and custodians, determining the key time frames of events, developing key word lists for searching of data, identifying potentially relevant documents and data types, and identifying file storage systems, e-mail systems, backup media, and decommissioned hardware systems.

The identification process can often expand far beyond the generic file server and client desktop environment and can include legacy systems (generally older technologies that maintain data prior to its migration to current system), cloud computing systems, or even third-party systems controlled by organizations not party to the litigation.

Electronic Discovery Reference Model

The electronic discovery reference model was developed by George Socha, Jr. and Tom Gelbmann for the purpose of trying to quantify the various stages of the electronic discovery process and how those stages interact with one another against the backdrop of the overarching goal of producing large volumes of data, increasing the relevance of the final data that is output. It begins by moving from left to right in nine principal stages. However, the stages are often iterative and data can move between the stages numerous times as it slowly makes its way from left to right. The left-hand side of the model represents the world of electronic data and information, within the context of an organization, with or without the luxury of an information management protocol. The electronic discovery reference model may be found at www.edrm.net.

Ordinarily, at this stage in the electronic discovery life cycle, the volume of data that may be identified as having potential relevance to the case will be larger than the eventual output that will be the result of the discovery life cycle, so as one moves from left to right in the model, the relevance of data increases while the volume of data decreases. The first step in the model is information management. This is where you get your electronic house in order and mitigate risk and expenses, should discovery become an issue from the initial creation of electronically stored information through its final disposition. Many organizations don't have a strong information management protocol in place, but more and more are starting to adopt information management as they understand the cost savings and benefits of having strong information management protocols securely in place. When it comes to electronic discovery, eventually nearly all corporations will have to face the issue of information management.

The next stage in the electronic discovery reference model is identification, which involves the locating of potential sources of electronically stored information and determining its scope, breadth, and depth. The next stage in the model is preservation. This is the stage at which you ensure that electronically stored information is protected against inappropriate alteration or destruction. The next two steps are coupled. They are collection, which is the gathering of electronically stored information for further use in electronic discovery process, such as review and processing, and the series of processes that reduce the volume of electronically stored information and convert it, if necessary, to forms more suitable for review and analysis.

The next three steps are also joined and entered together. They are review, analysis, and production. The review stage is the evaluation of electronically stored information for relevance and privilege and is often one of the most expensive components of the discovery life cycle. The next is analysis, which is the evaluation of electronically stored information for content or context, including patterns, topics, people, and discussions. This analysis often feeds into the review process. Next comes production, which is the delivery of this electronically stored information in appropriate formats and with the appropriate mechanism to others, such as counsel, management, or opposing counsel.

The final component of the electronic discovery reference model is presentation, which is the process of displaying electronically stored information in front of audiences, such as in depositions, hearings, and trials, in native and near-native or image formats, in order to elicit further information, validate existing facts or patterns, or persuade an audience.

This model, as simplistic as it is, has truly assisted the electronic discovery and computer forensic space in helping to define the primary steps in the average case. This has the benefit of building common language and vernacular throughout the industry so that attorneys, technicians, investigators, and others are all speaking from the same playbook.

E-Discovery Stages

In the e-discovery model, there are numerous stages with corresponding responsibilities that flow through the forensic life cycle both early in litigation and investigation and right through to trial testimony

Data Collection

Electronic data collection is often a task that takes place at the hands of both the counsel investigator's internal IT teams and others within an organization who are conducting either interviews or early case assessment work to establish where the electronic data lives. Often, this leads to the development of what is known as a *data map*. The data map will provide a graphical representation of the physical and logical locations of data throughout the organization and, hopefully, will also include key information, such as passwords, user names, and other criteria, that will assist in the eventual collection of electronic data. See Exhibit 8.1.

Electronic data itself, once it has been identified, generally needs to be collected, and this is where the computer forensic investigators and computer forensic professionals play a vital role. The process of identifying electronic data and the collection of electronic data go hand in hand. However, the collection process is far more rigid and structured than the identification process, being that the identification of electronic data can be as simple as conducting an interview with key stakeholders and jotting down the results of those interviews, whereas the task of the forensic collection of electronic data should be completed under procedures and policies that are consistent with industry best practices.

Among these best practices is the notion of maintaining a chain of custody for electronic data and evidence, which are collected and preserved so that one can determine at any given point in the future how and when an individual piece of evidence was handled and by whom; who had access to it; and where it lived during its life cycle. There are a number of reasons for maintaining chain of custody. Among them is to ensure the integrity of the data itself and the process that is used to collect the data.

Data collection responsibilities are often a team effort, employing counsel and internal resources to handle the organization, the forensic analyst to physically perform the collection of data by using computer forensic techniques, and other interested parties who will help shape and formulate the strategy of the investigation, the regulatory response, or the litigation itself.

EXHIBIT 8.1   Network Attached Storage Device

A network attached storage (NAS) device, which once would normally exist only within the corporate IT infrastructure, has now become very affordable and can be used and maintained by individuals at home or in the office. These devices allow for large volumes of data to be accessed by a stand-alone computer or a network, either over a wired or even a wireless network. This unit, which contained four 1-TB drives, was an unauthorized personal NAS and was attached to an employee's work computer under his desk. Because the employee was a high-value custodian of data in an electronic discovery matter, it was necessary to preserve and process the data contained on these drives, which resulted in significantly higher costs for the producing party. Better IT inventorying and data mapping within the company may have identified this risk prior to litigation.

The collection of the electronic data is one of the vital initial components of the investigation and computer forensic professionals are often charged with assisting to develop a game plan to collect that electronic evidence. Whether this evidence is in the context of a single laptop or desktop at an individual's home or it involves hundreds of computers distributed across multiple entities in multiple jurisdictions, both foreign and domestic, there are significant challenges with each.

One should not take for granted or assume that simply because a computer forensic acquisition relates to one device in one physical location it does not have the same risk profile as the data that is collected across multiple jurisdictions and dozens of locations.

Each piece of evidence needs to be treated with an equal level of care, with the handling of that evidence vital to the positive outcome of the exercise.

Data Processing, Analysis, and Analytics

The next logical step after data collection has taken place is the process of analyzing the data that has been collected. This often means that the forensic images that have been collected in the field will be duplicated into what are called *working copies*. These working copies will subsequently be integrated into some processing procedure that will allow for the analysis of the electronic data and the exclusion of irrelevant data. The processes that are available include simply running the EnCase or FTK software against the forensic images that are collected and extracting extraneous documents or temporary files, such as program documents and other known documents that would not be relevant to any case because they are machine-created or are part of known programs, applications, and operating systems. On the other hand, the size and volume of the data that has been collected may necessitate farming the processing out to an electronic data processing firm that specializes in managing data volumes in the millions of records.

Once the data has been initially culled and the extraneous documents removed, the resulting subset may include various document types, such as Excel documents, Microsoft Word documents, PDFs, instant messages, e-mail, and other forms of user-created documents. Other data types that may exist could include temporary files that relate to user activity on the computer, such as files that illustrate the usage of USB ports or show the usage of the Internet while the computer is connected to a corporate network, a wireless network, or other applications that record data and the activity of the user of the computer. This could range from the manner in which CD-ROMs were burned to the documents that were printed from the computer to the number of times the computer has been logged onto a specific website.

All of this information is potentially reportable by the computer, and should it be relevant to the case, the data analysis or processing phase is where this data should be segregated from other data sets. In many cases, the computer forensic investigator will need to work hand in hand with an e-discovery vendor who operates a suite of tools or systems that are designed for the fast and robust processing of electronic data for the purpose of segregating relevant documents and subsequently moving those documents to a document review tool.

Systems such as LEXIS-NEXIS Law, Trident by Wave Systems, Nuix, Access Data's FTK, the EnCase eDiscovery processing platform, and others have the ability to process the initial document population and segregate out documents and date ranges or keywords, or pick a file extension and a wide variety of other specific differentiating characteristics. The resulting data set will then be prepared as what is known as a *load file*, which is to be loaded into a document review platform, or will be prepared to be scanned for text so that it may be reproduced in printed format.

Hosting and Review

The next phase in the electronic discovery process is data hosting and review. Once the data has been collected, analyzed, processed, and harmonized into what is known as a *load file*, that document file can be uploaded to a document review platform such as Summation, Concordance, Case Logistix, Relativity, S-File, File Control, Autonomy, Zylab, Xerox, Recommind, Kroll OnTrack, iConnect, Catalyst, or many of the other systems that allow for the online review of documents that have been set aside in the repository.

These document repositories will then be accessed by attorneys or other interested parties associated with the case, primarily and initially for issues of privilege but also for issues that are fact-finding in nature and for segregating out documents that are responsive or specific to a particular issue that is relevant to the investigation or to the litigation. As discussed in earlier sections of this volume, there are a wide variety of individuals who may be required to review these documents, including review attorneys, who will be brought in, sometimes en masse, to review large volumes of documents for very specific issues.

It is not inconceivable that in a large case where millions of documents have been produced you will deploy at least 100 review attorneys for the purpose of reviewing documents that contain a particular word or particular phrase in the hopes of selecting or segregating out documents that are of high value to litigation. These might be documents that indicate you mention a particular issue or don't mention a particular issue, often in a highly truncated time frame.

This process of data hosting and review is often found to be the most expensive component of the electronic discovery process. It is also during this process that certain documents may be kicked back to a computer forensic investigator for further analysis and review, once they are identified in the linear review, which is taking place under the direction of counsel. It should be noted that, as of this writing, there has been tremendous progress made in the development of what are called *machine-assisted review platforms*. These are software programs that have been developed to include appropriate logic based on certain criteria in order to supplant human judgment calls on the relevancy of certain documents.

This machine-assisted review has been shown in many cases to be equal to, if not superior to, the human review in terms of errors and consistency, and in some cases will actually save on cost. It is my prediction that, as computing power continues to evolve and software engineers continue to develop new methodologies for integrating artificial intelligence and neural networks into their code, the role of the review attorney will continue to be diminished as machines take on more of the hard labor, particularly that of the first part of the review of electronic documents.

Presentation

Presentation is the final component of the electronic discovery process. This is the phase in which documents that have been selected during the electronic review and are deemed to be of relevance, are not privileged, and have met all the various criteria for production by the opposing side or regulator or simply by internal investigators are finally produced. This procedure generally involves selecting a group of documents out of the electronic data review platform that have met those criteria, marking them for production, and going through a series of processes where these documents are *BATES-stamped* with a numeric value and endorsed with various components, which may be something such as a "For attorney's eyes only" or "Confidential" or other endorsements that can be applied through the computing process.

These productions, in some cases electronic and in other cases paper-form productions, are made available to the opposing side. Over the past 10 years there has been a significant debate over the issue of reviewing and producing documents in native format versus image format, and for the most part I believe this has been settled and the native format argument has won the day. The native format document is a document that is preserved and viewable in its original environment. For instance, a Microsoft Word document would be viewed in either Microsoft Word or in a viewer that is compatible with Microsoft Word and would allow the viewer to see all the functionality that exists within the document as it was created by the original user. This includes the track changes notes and other aspects of the document such as the full metadata analysis.

The concept of an image or document is that one has literally taken a photograph of the document and provides that photograph in one format or another. It could be a printed format or could be as an image file, such as what is known as a TIFF. These types of files lack the interactivity and flexibility of native documents, but in some cases they are easier to manage during the review process and the production process. A case in point is when one needs to produce Excel documents. The reprinting of Excel documents can be rather cumbersome, particularly large documents with the significant volumes of data and formulas that will not show up during the printing process. However, if one were to produce Excel documents in a native format, where one can view the various formulas behind each of the cells, this would potentially be relevant electronic data, the production of which would be required and relevant to both parties.

Common E-Discovery and Foreign Data Challenges

The electronic discovery life cycle has numerous significant challenges embedded deep within each one of the tasks that are represented by the electronic discovery reference model. Within the world of responding to electronic discovery in foreign jurisdictions, there are significant challenges that are slightly more definable. They include preparing yourself to manage local data and protection laws, and acquiring the necessary consent from the custodians of the data that you intend to collect.

The European Union data and privacy directive has strict protocols regarding the collection and export of electronic data. In China, due to the opaque and Byzantine application of the Chinese state secrets act, you can never be too sure that the data that you are collecting is not actually going to be classified as a state secret after the fact, which clearly has the potential to put you and your client in jeopardy. When collecting data overseas, among the most important items to manage are your visa and entry document requirements and making certain that you don't run afoul of them when transporting electronic equipment, computers, data, and so on across a country's borders.

Another challenge is resource identification and scheduling. Understanding whom you have "in country" to rely on for translations, logistics, and planning may be vital. Without putting forethought into how you operate within any particular nation you may find yourself in some rather challenging positions. Good computer forensic examiners or lab managers will generally have preestablished relationships in key countries where they expect to collect evidence so that when the time comes, it's simply a matter of a few e-mails or a telephone call to activate those resources.

When managing an overseas collection, the safety of your team in the field must be your paramount concern. The collection of the data and the sanctity and safety of the data is key, but your team and your personnel must come first, and you must alert your team members so that they understand how to escalate issues that develop on the ground that could potentially put them in harm's way.

Another challenge for cross-border collections and data management, which is shared with domestic work, is budgeting. Because of the fluctuations of currency overseas and different pricing models, at times it is difficult to maintain a one-for-one relationship between the forensic teams that you will deploy in foreign nations versus those you will maintain in the United States.

The identification of data sources and custodians can be another challenge when operating in foreign jurisdictions. Working with local IT staff and local resources presents its own unique hurdles, certainly when you integrate language and cultural barriers. I have had many cases that involve foreign collections in which the IT director's initial understanding of the scope of the engagement was very different from my own or that of the party who authorized the collection to begin with, which was often the U.S. counsel. In many cases, the local IT staff underestimated the scope of the number of machines that would be subject to data collection, and only when you are on the ground and visually inspecting the premises do you learn of the true extent of the forensic collection work that needs to take place.

Among the problems that teams face while working with on-the-ground computer forensic technicians is determining which collection method will be used to preserve the data. In most cases, standard tools such as EnCase, FTK, Logicube, and Tableau can be used, but often you will be faced with outlying technologies that require special handling or techniques, particularly when it relates to servers, cloud computing devices, and handheld devices. Many practitioners in foreign jurisdictions will maintain practices that are quite different from what many U.S. teams are used to. For this reason, frank and open dialogue with subcontractors and other third parties prior to deploying overseas is useful.

Problems can also arise regarding the manner in which the data will be handled, including how it will be taken out of the country. Encryption issues should be covered in advance, as well as whether the data being collected is already encrypted and/or whether there will be challenges from local officials in exporting encrypted data. If you have to manage encryption prior to transport, the appropriate resources and time should be blocked off for that process as the encryption of forensic images can dramatically increase the amount of time that is necessary to spend on the ground.

Another challenge that is found in foreign collections or applications and systems is that they are constructed or developed by providers in the local market. Some of these applications may not be known to the technicians arriving from the United States, and it is important to have members on your team who are able to adapt under such circumstances. Once the data has returned to the United States, you face additional challenges in the processing world, including how to handle data that has been created and collected and is often in a foreign language. This can be even more complex.

The risks and challenges associated with electronic discovery carry special weight because of the possibility that those failures will result in sanctions in the U.S. court for monetary damages or adverse inference, all of which can be devastating to a client's position. Among the most critical of the discovery failures are those associated with the misrepresentation of the composition or universe of data that can be collected or has been collected for review: the failure to make truthful representations to the court, all around misrepresenting the status of the discovery process, failure to accurately disclose electronically stored information, failure to accurately report in general to the court, and failure to base objections to electronic discovery on substantiated facts.

During the e-discovery process, it is ordinary practice for a discovery plan to be put into place through the agreement of both parties or a discovery order to be issued by a judge, magistrate, or a special master or neutral. There are a number of failures that can take place within that realm, including the interference in forensic review, which is potentially the result of a denial of access to certain systems, machines, or files, or a general refusal to provide appropriate technical support to the team that is collecting and analyzing the data.

Other big missteps that can take place with respect to executing the discovery plan would be a failure to retain forensic experts at the appropriate time, resulting in mismanaging the process and potentially missing deadlines. When engaging in the early discovery process, even prelitigation, there are additional potholes into which one can fall, including the failure to communicate electronically stored information preservation instructions—in other words, a failure to manage the legal hold process or the failure to investigate all the potential custodians, including both internal parties as well as third-party custodians.

Additional potholes include the failure to understand the client's document retention policies and data architecture, a failure to further investigate missing or destroyed electronically stored information reports, and a failure to consult with information technology teams when needed to develop the discovery plan. These and other risks make for treacherous waters in the electronic discovery process and buttress the argument that strong project management, clear vision, and quality personnel are critical to executing plans effectively in the discovery world.

Tools, Services, and Technologies

The electronic discovery space is littered with failed attempts by technologists of every shape and size to harness computing power and to address the issue of mountains upon mountains of data that are kicked off by contemporary electronic discovery engagements. Over the course of the past 15 years, many companies have come and gone. However, there are still dozens of quality companies offering excellent technologies and services to assist in the management, review, processing, production, and presentation of electronic data in the electronic discovery life cycle. These tools, services, and systems run the gamut from computer forensic shops that are focused exclusively on the identification, preservation, and collection of electronic data to more sophisticated shops that also offer forensic analysis and testimony to technology houses that have built significant platforms for the hosting, review, and analysis of electronic, discovery-based documents in the cloud, allowing teams of attorneys to review these documents for privilege and for issues. See Exhibit 8.2.

The electronic discovery services and tools space includes companies that are focused exclusively on providing those very attorneys to do the review. There are companies that specialize in preparing paper productions out of the review tools. There are companies that specialize in preparing PowerPoint presentations that will be presented in court. There are companies that can address virtually every other aspect of electronic discovery. I have highlighted a few companies here in this volume and have shared the value proposition that they offer, but by no means is this an exhaustive list, nor is it a preferential list. It is simply a very small sampling.

Nuix

Nuix is an Australian company that produces a suite of tools designed for processing data in the electronic discovery space, as well as solutions for information governance, investigation defensible deletion archives, and other enterprise-related server solutions. The primary Nuix tool that captured the attention of the electronic discovery market was its "Nuix workstation," which allowed companies to rapidly find critical evidence, people of interest, and documents on which the case will turn. The Nuix workstation processes virtually all forms of unstructured information in all languages. It can process complex proprietary formats, such as Lotus Notes, Microsoft Exchange, Microsoft SharePoint, and Forensic Images.

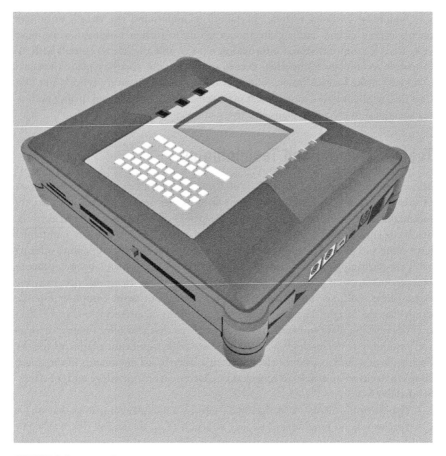

EXHIBIT 8.2   Logicube Dossier

The Logicube Dossier allows for the capture of two suspect drives at the same time, or the creation of both master copy and working copy drives, simultaneously. An important cost saver, particularly on larger matters, this device can capture data at more than 5 GB per minute.

Its data extraction algorithm identifies and makes searchable information many other software products routinely skip. For this reason, and for its portability and cost-effective design, Nuix is rapidly becoming a preferred choice for processing forensic images in preparation for data to be loaded into review tools for discovery or for early case assessment, which is done to gain a quicker understanding of the key players, events, and evidence in a matter that is developing within the corporation and behind the firewall. The exported data that Nuix produces can be sent to a wide variety of applications, including Relativity and Concordance.

Another product developed by Nuix is called Nuix Investigator. According to Nuix, its advanced electronic investigation technology is engineered to process, analyze, and bring to the surface critical evidence, including entire data sets, regardless of its geographical location, repository, file type, or size. In addition, Nuix can identify key intelligence items, such as e-mail addresses and phone numbers and Social Security and credit card numbers. The Nuix solution is often able to save significant time and effort and may be of major benefit for overwhelmed technicians and investigators or agencies that are on tight budgets. The output of the Nuix platform can supplement a forensic investigation, or in some cases perform the necessary tasks for the investigation to run its course.

LEXIS-NEXIS Law

LEXIS-NEXIS, which is a division of Reed Elsevier, has a wide variety of legal products and services. Among them is a product known as Law V.5.0 PreDiscovery software. This software allows for the early processing and management of electronic data in preparation for that data to be reviewed. This is commonly known as *processing*. LEXIS-NEXIS begins its projects by creating a case, whereby the case name and a description of the case is applied to the database. Second, the user will go through a process of document acquisition, loading the electronic discovery documents or extracting text and metadata from the documents, processing various mail stores, electronic documents, and file lists in Outlook folders, and performing MD5 hash deduplication on the data as well as creating file-type filters.

In the next stage, an early electronic discovery review or management process will take place in which groups are broken out into subsets of electronic documents. Documents are filed and filtered and full-text searches are run. The tool has the ability to then batch-process producible documents by adding headers and footers, Bates numbers, and OCR in the documents, endorsing them, printing them to paper, or converting them to TIFF files. The tool also has the ability to export these files into what we call *load files*, which allows the electronic document file that may have been text-searched, deduplicated, or received to be exported to Concordance, Summation, Relativity, or other products for further review.

Relativity

Relativity is an online review platform that allows attorneys to review, tag, and produce electronic documents in a manner that is sufficient to meet the needs of electronic discovery obligations in a U.S. court. The tool, like many online repositories that are available on the market today, has a rich feature set. Relativity provides image and native file review, diverse coding options, flexible work flow capabilities, integrated productions, foreign language support, text analytics, and visual data and analysis.

Among Relativity's features is computer-assisted review, whereby it combines processes with technology, allowing reviewers to train Relativity to recognize what qualifies a document as responsive or nonresponsive. Structured data analytics allows Relativity to analyze key data to reveal trends and patterns in a case. The interactive results can be displayed visually through charts, allowing you to drill in and take action.

Among the more unique aspects of Relativity is the Relativity ecosystem. The ecosystem allows litigation support professionals, independent consultants, and third-party software providers to design and build applications that extend the functionality of Relativity, providing new solutions or integration with Relativity via application programming interfaces. This model has allowed Relativity to gain a deep foothold in the electronic discovery processing and review space because the company itself does not compete with the third-party companies that would use this platform to assist law firms, corporations, and government agencies. This open environment is a dynamic advantage.

Additional Tools

The legal technology landscape is littered with amazing success stories and stunning failures. Each year there are nearly a dozen relevant entrants, closures, or mergers between companies in this dynamic space. Among the tools and services that I can cite, which any practitioner should be familiar with, I would include Summation and Concordance, which are the two granddaddies of electronic document review. There are numerous other relevant tools, such as Case Logistix, S-File, Recommind, and Zylab, that all produce qualified e-discovery review platforms that address particular aspects of the marketplace. For example, S-File has positioned itself as an affordable option to some of the more complex and top-heavy applications, whereas Zylab, which was originally made in Holland, introduced extraordinary search capabilities, foreign-language processing, and other unique complements to the review space.

The various features and aspects of e-discovery technology companies and their tools should be evaluated when determining the system in which to invest for your case. These decisions should not be taken lightly as choosing a system that does not provide the performance, scale, cost, technical features, and/or support that your case requires can have a severely negative impact on your ability to meet any e-discovery obligations, and consequently, your ability to prevail in the investigation may be jeopardized. There are so many more systems and tools to mention, from Kroll Ontrak to Symantec's Clearwell, that several chapters could be dedicated to this one area alone.

Emerging E-Discovery Realities

There are a number of new themes in the e-discovery world that are impacting the space, including the use of special masters and neutrals for the purpose of streamlining the process of electronic discovery, reducing costs, and bringing some sanity back to litigation. There is also the adoption or development of machine-assisted review, whereby computers are learning from the patterns and programmed routines integrated into the e-discovery software so as to reduce the reliance on human review of documents. These and other issues are touched on in the following section.

Machine-Assisted Review

Among the more interesting new areas of focus in the electronic discovery space is machine-assisted review, also known as *technology-assisted review, computer-assisted review, predictive coding, concept searching,* and *meaning-based computing.* The promise of machine-assisted review is that it offers software programs with the appropriate logic built in so they can achieve equal, if not better, results in the review process for specific types of data analysis, such as review for a very specific issue or set of issues, the review of documents that contain certain keywords that could relate to a particular issue, or documents that could be considered privileged or not privileged.

At present, the technology works in much the same fashion that a spam filter would work, in so far as the software analyzes each document for specific information; correlates that information against its own index, which may have been built specifically for the matter; and then ranks the documents based on the thresholds that are set prior to beginning the review. In tests that have been conducted, there has been every indication that machine-assisted review can compete head-to-head, within the right parameters, with human review. Although at present, machine-assisted review is not sophisticated enough to take on complex issues where highly nuanced wordsmithing is used or for documents that contain complex definitions or issues that are not easily transcribed; it is expected, however, that these machines eventually will have this capability.

There are a number of companies leading the way in this space, including Zylab out of Holland, with operations in the United States, and Recommind and Equivio, both also here in the United States. What is driving machine-assisted review is the cost associated with applying attorneys to a manual, linear review of documents. This is particularly the case when those document populations are in the tens of thousands, hundreds of thousands, or even millions of individual documents.

If the machine-assisted review can get through the initial phase-one review of privileged documents, this alone can result in significant cost savings. If the machine-assisted review can then further cull documents based on certain key issues in conjunction with other filters, such as date ranges and key words and phrases, then again, this can reduce the overall discovery costs. However, at some point in the present world, humans do need to get in on the action. Not only do they need to review the eventual documents that are kicked out, but it is also incumbent on humans to run validation tests to ensure that the assumptions and programming applied to the predictive coding application are in fact holding up.

Special Masters and E-Discovery Neutrals

Among the new tools available to both federal and state courts is the use of special masters and neutrals for managing electronic data and computer forensic-related tasks. The use of these specialists has been increasing with regularity in recent years. Special masters offer the court the ability to offload some of the laborious and complicated technical issues associated with these tasks to specialists who are able to work at the direction of the court and report to the court on their findings.

Often, a special master's orders carry the full weight of the court, and the defendants and plaintiffs will have to abide by the special master's judgment calls. Special masters have the ability to hold hearings and conduct enquiries into a wide variety of issues, as dictated by the judge or magistrate who is managing the case on behalf of the court. Special masters are often retired judges, attorneys, arbitrators, or, in some instances, specialists in a particular field.

The specialties of the special masters can include anything from forensic accounting to computer forensics and electronic discovery, and they will often be able to provide the services that are required by the court. This is to the benefit of both the plaintiff and the defendant because the special master is able to harmonize issues such as costs, procedures, processes, technologies to be used, and other problems that may come up and that are often the source of dispute during litigation.

Courts also have the ability to appoint e-discovery neutrals, who will also work at the direction of the court. In the case of using a special master and/or an e-discovery neutral, these individuals often have the ability to appoint or direct computer forensic investigators, who will work at the direction of the plaintiff, the defendant, or the court as a whole. In all of these cases, the special master or the e-discovery neutral looks to streamline the process and provide a sense of balance between the competing needs and desires of both plaintiff and defendant, while at the same time meeting the mandate of the court of bringing forth justice and helping to keep the court calendar free for new cases to be resolved.

A good source for locating and identifying special masters is the Academy of Court-Appointed Masters, available at www.courtappointedmasters.org. There is also a good source for the identification of certified e-discovery neutrals for federal and state court matters at the American College of e-Neutrals, available at www .acesin.com.

Computer forensic investigators and specialists would be well served to avail themselves of the general rules governing the appointment of special masters, as well as e-neutrals, and how they may either work with them or in fact be appointed as one themselves. This is a unique area of case work that can greatly assist both plaintiffs and defendants to swiftly bring their claims to the forefront of the court without getting bogged down in overly protracted and expensive e-discovery.

The Sedona Conference

There are many organizations that have set out to define and establish standards of care in the electronic discovery space. These initiatives have all had an effect on the role of the computer forensic examiner, for it is at that stage in the e-discovery life cycle, where the computer forensic examiner collects and analyzes evidence and prepares it for production, review, or the handing off to an electronic discovery vendor, that key decisions are made in the handling management of that data. These decisions are impacted by case precedent, by the rulings and opinions of the judiciary, by the realities of technology, and by the musings of industry experts, both bona fide and self-appointed.

This work is also impacted by the more serious implications of organizations, like the Sedona Conference, that have taken on meaningful, thoughtful, and deliberate analysis of the e-discovery challenges of the day. The work of the Sedona Conference is publicly available on its website, www.theSedonaconference.org. The organization hosts forums and conclaves where key experts come together to discuss specific issues in the electronic discovery process. Working groups within the Sedona Conference, which are made up primarily of volunteers, then work to develop commentary on these issues, taking into consideration the opinions of a broad spectrum of the industry.

Two of the primary working groups within the Sedona Conference that focus on electronic discovery and, by default, computer forensics are working group 1, titled Electronic Document Retention and Production, and working group 6, titled International Electronic Information Management Discovery and Disclosure. Although the size of this volume will not permit a discussion on all of the many groups that address e-discovery and computer forensics from a theoretical and practical perspective, I chose to comment on at least one that deserves mention and your attention for review—the Sedona Conference.

European and Asian Observations

Electronic discovery as we know it is a U.S. invention and a creature of the U.S. litigation scene. There are judges, lawyers, barristers, magistrates, and litigants of every shape and size in nations around the world shaking their head in disbelief at the significant machinations, barriers, and complexities that we cast on ourselves in pursuing justice in the American way.

Having managed many forensic collections and investigations in numerous European and Asian nations over the years, I for one would rather argue against the restrictive codes of many nations and their interpretation of debasing the value and sanctity of pristine evidence, preserved and presented in defense of an action or in favor of a position taken by a plaintiff. The complex set of rules and procedures that have been established in the United States to afford individuals the right to defend themselves with evidence that holds equal weight to the evidence that has been offered against them is a notion that I find challenging but supremely fair.

Slowly, but certainly, entities in the European Union and in East Asia and elsewhere around the world are being drawn into U.S. litigation, where they are a party to some action, and, as a consequence, they are learning of the complications of electronic discovery. Yet they may also be learning that there is benevolence in providing a framework whereby both sides are entitled to request documents from the opposing side and are compelled by legal precedent and the power of the court to comply, laying everything bare for the judge and all to see.

There are courts around this great earth of ours that do not hold evidence of a physical nature or electronic nature in the same exalted status, and instead rely on a notion that you are guilty until proven innocent and other constructs that we should have no time for.

The work of the computer forensic examiner, in the pursuit of meeting electronic discovery obligations, is a noble one, and it is one of the foundations of our free society, which tries to balance the responsibilities of power equally and justly among all constituencies. To that end, I have seen the bewilderment in the eyes of European, Chinese, Japanese, Taiwanese, Korean, Singaporean, Australian, Middle Eastern, and Indian clients alike when it is explained to them what their e-discovery obligations are if they choose to prevail in a U.S. court of law.

There are those in the United States who say we have gone too far, and that the result of modern e-discovery is that justice is all too often averted, that the merits of the case are not heard, and that the financial burden of the process forces litigants into unwanted and unwarranted settlements. Perhaps some of this is true. However, it is also true that our technology may very well catch up with the requirements of the court and our ethical obligations, and that through the marvel of artificial intelligence (which, if done right, may not be artificial at all) our computers will learn and are learning to cope with the scale and complexity of the documents and digital artifacts thrown at them.

In fact, if Moore's law and the promise of cognitive computing (the intersection of neuroscience, supercomputing, and nanotechnology) hold up, then in the not-too-distant future it is not inconceivable that searches for relevant documents will encompass all data on all known sources, as opposed to solely targeted custodians. This is possible because the computing systems themselves will have evolved to a state that surpasses human capabilities and scalability. At that point, perhaps foreign legal systems may be required to take note that the obligation of the trier of fact is to consider all of the available evidence and that the barrier to observing electronic data is no longer cumbersome but rather a great equalizer in the pursuit of equality and justice.

Until then, U.S. computer forensic examiners should make themselves knowledgeable on the data preservation, privacy, and evidentiary handling regulations and rules in the primary nations in which they expect to have to work. It is not acceptable, in my opinion, for a forensic examiner working for a U.S. company with operations in Italy not to understand what his or her obligations are in the Italian court, just as the general manager of the Italian branch must be familiar with his or her obligations under the U.S. system for the protection and management of evidence in the context of e-discovery.

All too often cases are lost because of sanctions for spoliation. These are cases that should see the light of day in a courtroom and be heard on their merits. In many cases, a U.S. foreign counterpart "didn't get the memo" and the hard drives were destroyed, the paper was shredded, or the preservation did not take place. Business from every reach of the globe should have some fundamental understanding of the evidentiary obligations of the jurisdictions in which they operate. This holds true for the forensic examiners who are supporting or working on behalf of those organizations.

Digital Evidence in the Courtroom

By the time a case makes its way to a courtroom, the electronic evidence that will be used is often highly distilled and laser-focused. Sometimes the document that will be produced in the case will be one e-mail, complete with its metadata, and that e-mail will be blown up on the screen and projected on the wall for all to see. In other cases, spreadsheets containing hundreds of thousands of lines may be produced, in which case summaries of those spreadsheets will have to be entered for the court to understand their implication. In many cases, graphics and images need to be reproduced in some fashion to be entered as evidence.

Digital evidence can be produced in paper form, in electronic form, or both. In some courtrooms, computer monitors have been installed for jurors, as well as courtroom staff and the judge, so that data can be reviewed with these in a close-up fashion. When these exhibits are produced in electronic form, attorneys will often work with the original computer forensic technicians who completed the analysis in order to ensure that what they are representing to the courtroom is accurate, and discussions will often focus on what is the most effective approach to taking a complex technical issue and distilling it down to a simple concept that can be grasped by all. Maintaining a laser-sharp focus with productions and exhibits in the courtroom is important so that a testifying expert witness will not stumble over the data that has been produced.

CHAPTER 9

The Future

Investigative computer forensics has a bright future, in so far as, in many cases, computer forensic practitioners are the last line of defense and the final arbiters of truth, privacy, and fact as it relates to digital evidence, which is often nowadays at the center of most human disputes. As the global networks continue to coalesce and expand and while new technologies continue to develop in order to harness electronic communications and data, the need for investigative computer forensics will continue to grow. New technologies, tools, systems, and processes will evolve as there is ample opportunity for innovation and development in the field, and professionals within the space will continue to assist in its maturing as a professional vocation. See Exhibit 9.1.

The future is fraught with numerous risks related to evolving technologies, but age-old risks will continue to apply and most fundamental among them will be those that relate to interpersonal communication between relevant parties. As we move farther away from our historical roots of interacting with one another face-to-face, greater effort will need to be placed on bridging the interpersonal divide that is created when one relies on electronic indicators and signals for all interaction.

Practitioners of law and criminal justice will continue to require the specialized services of technologists and investigators who have a computer forensic skill set, and there will be a broadening of the practice of computer forensics to allow for greater subject matter expertise in specific subdomains, such as network forensics, hardware forensics, data collection, data analysis, data review and analytics, nano-forensics, cloud-based forensics, and volatile forensics. Not every case requires these sophisticated subdomains and so, in the coming years, we will see the stratification of expertise within the computer forensics profession to allow for a more efficient marketplace and more effective use of available resources.

Privacy and the Data Ecosystem

As mentioned earlier in this volume, privacy is dead, or for some it is dying and soon to be declared DOA. However, privacy will continue to be an important pillar in the data

EXHIBIT 9.1   Moore's Law in Action

An illustration of a computer hard drive from the 1980s that had a capacity of 10 MB, a hard drive from the 1990s with a capacity of 500 MB, and a thumb drive from the 2000s with a capacity of 64 GB. In the future we may wear our data storage as a thin-film adhesive painted onto our clothing or our body.

ecosystem, for some level of privacy, however temporary or limited, is still required for the establishment of trust, which we know is foundational to the success of the promise of the Information Age, which, when you break it down, is *equal access to all informa- tion by all people at all times*. Privacy will be for sale, and those who can afford it or must afford it will have it, albeit in limited doses and within defined parameters.

For example, businesses are able to define privacy within the construct of their enterprise for the employees and customers who use its systems. However, ultimately that privacy can be compromised by regulators under the auspices of their jurisdic- tional powers. While those powers may never be enforced in any given industry or setting, the fact that the data exists and that it can be accessed and mined implicitly implies that privacy is dead because the reality that the activities of the employees and customers have been recorded is in fact a removal of anonymity and privacy and a memorialization of that behavior.

We all know that although a regulator or management may never actually view the memorialized data, it is also possible that data will be compromised by an internal, trusted bad actor or by an external source seeking to penetrate the enterprise's systems. At present, individuals can force some level of privacy through encryption, which one would expect can continue into the future. Although the encryption algorithms of today may be cracked by the greater processing power of tomorrow, tomorrow's encryption algorithms will also be more robust and should stay a step ahead of the processor's capacity to crack the code.

In this respect, there is some limited privacy that can be afforded to individuals or organizations that choose to leverage encryption, but by no means am I suggesting that one can encrypt his or her entire digital DNA, for the reality is that even highly encrypted individuals will still have to interact electronically as they go about their day and will be recorded by surveillance systems, monitored by household and business systems, and recorded in every activity that they take, from purchasing orange juice at the market, to being admitted to the hospital, to checking out a book from the library. In its aggregate, as a species, we have given up privacy in exchange for the benefits of access to information.

Access Controls and the Evolution of Trust

In the future, trust will be fostered in participants in the networked world by the introduction of complex access controls that rely on a variety of vectors so that a cross-collateralized framework or web of trust may be achieved. Today's world has seen the breakdown of the key elements of trust on the global networks. From the cracking of the RSA tokens to the collisions of the MD5 hash algorithm and from the perpetual kernel-based hacking of key systems and spoofing of identities to the juvenile phishing techniques of criminals around the globe, it is incumbent on future technologists, sociologists, government officials, corporate executives, and wild-thinking futurists to extract out of their imagination an evolved infrastructure for trust that can be integrated into our daily lives in a seamless manner and that may be relied on wholly. As I discussed in the beginning of this book, trust is one of the foundational elements of the success of any society and certainly vital to the success of the global networks and those who participate in them, which today is nearly everyone.

Global Communications Systems in the Cloud

When speaking of the tangential and rather amorphous future, which is partially on our doorstep, but has yet to fully arrive, it is easy to speculate how trust, privacy, and the global networks will impact the average citizen, and it is quite possible to paint a picture that is benevolent and benign or one that is dark and sickly. However, one thing is for certain, and that is that the global communications systems on which we rely today, including the concept of the cloud, are among the important building blocks to transform the human communication experience from one that is centered on oneself and the first-person experience to one that is fully interconnected with all other beings and machines.

For the information revolution to fulfill its promise of equal access to all information by all people at all times, it is required that all people be interconnected. This interconnectedness will be harnessed and made possible by the global networks and what we now call the *cloud* because it will be the backbone that will allow the connection of all the independent nodes on the network. In other words, individual humans will be able to upload and download their data. What will we upload? Our thoughts? Will it be our shopping lists? Will it be our plans for tomorrow night? Or will it be a notification that we have arrived at a coffee shop? Much of this already exists with Facebook and Twitter, yet the integration with the human being is not fully complete. It is still rudimentary and raw; it is in its formative stages. What will we download? Will it be our agenda for the day, our child's homework for the night, our map to the park for bicycle route, our bank statement, our archived historical record of an e-mail sent three years ago, a photo of our great-great-grandmother? What would you like to share? These data points are the focus and the bread and butter of the computer forensic investigator whose job it is to string all of this information together into a meaningful evidentiary record.

Nanotechnology and Cognitive Computing

The information technology revolution's promise will require the integration of technology with the human being. This will be accomplished through nanotechnology and cognitive computing, the building blocks of the future, which will allow for the miniaturization of computing components to the extent that they can be integrated into and onto the human body coupled with processing and applications that will allow for cognitive computing, whereby computers will think and will assist humans. Perhaps this will happen by simply absorbing cycles or perhaps by empowering our ability to recall information and communicate in real time with all people, any time, albeit with the appropriate restrictions, controls, and privacy safeguards that will allow for trust to flourish.

The promise of these extraordinary technologies coupled with the massive advances that we will continue to make in information management will provide continued relevance for the fact-finder who will remain a vital component of any effort at securing the truth and the evidentiary record to support it.

Digital Demographics and the Emerging Global Citizen

The self-imposed boundaries that have defined the human experience for tens of thousands of years, which include the boundaries of nations and states, are no longer as clearly defined as they were in the past. Today's individuals cross national boundaries, intentionally or unintentionally, on a whim. Space, distance, and geography have less relevance in the monopoly of challenges that businesses and individuals currently face. Society has conquered the challenge presented to us by mountains and rivers, lakes and oceans, and vast distances, initially by using roads, ships, and airplanes, and now by the global electronic networks that have allowed for the fundamental evolution of the human communication experience to take place before our eyes.

As individuals gain access to the *information superhighway*, as it was quaintly called in the 1990s, their world is forever changed. The Bush tribesman in Tanzania, who 10 years ago only carried a spear and walked barefoot for miles through the Bush tracking animals with his compatriots, now carries a cell phone connected to the global networks that allows him, if he chooses, to access the website of the Smithsonian Institution in Washington, DC. This cross-pollination of ideas and people is equaled only by the great migrations of millennia past, or perhaps by the European settlement of the New World and the impact experienced by the native peoples of the Americas, most of whom died from disease introduced by the Europeans.

Although most do not expect the dire outcome of the experience of the American Indians to be cast on global populations by the information revolution, there are still other risks that percolate below the surface. Among these risks I cannot help but highlight are the risks of information control, specifically global information control by the darker forces of dictatorship and societies that are not committed to freedom and equality for all. Nonetheless, whether you are an African tribesman or a Manhattan businessperson, you are now connected by more than simply membership in the human race and strands of DNA that serve as markers to your ancient ancestors (available for viewing in such groundbreaking websites as www.23andme.com). You are now connected to the same network and, given some time and energy, can reach out and communicate with one another with relative ease.

This is a remarkable development with such wide-ranging implications that one really does not know where to start in determining what our "New World" will look like. However, one thing is certain. As a result of these currents comes the emergence of global citizens whose identity is more closely associated with their network of friends and colleagues and the choices that they have made as a result of access to information, than with any nation-state. Nation-states are not going to go away anytime soon and certainly not without a fight, but as the social constructs with which we have grown up continue to be shattered or melted away by the game-changing technologies we are now deploying, it is only a matter of time until new definitions of citizenry and social participation begin to emerge. These new definitions, no less than those of today, will still rely on trust and, to some degree, privacy in order to succeed and will require the efforts of investigative forensic examiners to settle disputes, establish the facts, and serve as a vital checkpoint for the converging data traversing the multiple information flows that will govern and record the activity of human events.

Extra-National Investigative Networks and the Information Union

As a result of this consolidation of information management, the closing of the ranks of available information sources into the global networks, and a blurring of the transnational and social borders to which we have been accustomed, societies will require extra-national investigative networks to take root for the purpose of identifying and solving crime and fraud. In the not-too-distant future, it will no longer be acceptable or sustainable for old-world jurisdictional barriers to prevent investigative parties from seeking the factual evidence in a matter, regardless of its origin.

Things are simply moving too quickly and people are more informed. The fluidity of information will serve as a model for other structures, including law enforcement, rights management, and the preservation and expansion of the rule of law, which will need to expand way beyond the developed world. This movement will be demanded by the generations to come. We have seen tastes of it in the Arab Spring, the proliferation of the micro blogosphere in China and the resulting information exchange, and the explosive outpouring shared across India in late 2012 in support of women's rights as a result of the rape of a 23-year-old New Delhi medical student.

Certainly the world can turn another way and retrench to greater compartmentalization, which will be at odds with the promise of the information revolution. However, should we continue along the path on which we find ourselves today, a robust United Nations–style investigative or security council will be required to manage the information-based investigative needs of nations, organizations, and individuals around the globe. It is quite possible that this will also give rise to citizen cooperative agreements, where individuals, groups of individuals, or even entire industries enter into cooperative agreements so as to allow the proper preservation and capture of electronic data in the course of litigation, fraud analysis, self-policing, or criminal investigation.

These cooperative networks, which I liken on some level to the unions of yesteryear that were designed to protect the collective rights of workers, would in fact be "information unions" and would be designed to ensure that the limited privacy required for an individual, organization, and/or industry is protected. In addition, these extra-national investigative networks would help to ensure that the trust required between these parties is preserved so that the individual, organization, or industry can thrive.

Zero Day Forensics

Computer forensics faces increasing logistical challenges as a result of the enormous volume of data that must be reviewed during investigations. This is coupled with the expansive nature of the usage of electronic data throughout every individual's life, every organization's structure, and in every possible capacity whether intentional or in a passive manner. The pursuit of the goals and objectives of investigations has historically had some reasonable amount of time within which to conduct analysis and reach conclusions; however, increasingly the answers that are required must be found immediately.

As a result, forensic examiners and the investigator's administrators, business owners, lawyers, and government officials who are directing their activities are under significant pressure to find the right answers quicker and within ever-increasing volumes of data. The computer forensic examiner is required to leverage ever-more sophisticated equipment and tools with greater power and resources to crunch through unbelievably large volumes of data to find the salient points and facts that are being sought out.

By example, the U.S. military increasingly finds itself in real-time battlefield tactical operations where an intercept has taken place on a communication and a physical geographic fix must be completed in order for a response, attack, or defensive action to be implemented. This is a scenario that will transcend to the business world in short order for both actual operations and defensive work against bad actors that exist within and outside its operating environments.

Policing agencies as well are required more often these days to respond in real time to surveillance and observational data, which is being acquired as a result of physical surveillance or electronic monitoring in which computer forensic analysts must dissect the data as it is being fed in real time to the investigators and provide answers that are meaningful and relevant.

What is presently the realm of law enforcement and military will soon be a commonplace aspect of corporate investigations where an organization is looking to protect its digital assets in real time and will leverage forensics to pinpoint with accuracy data breaches as they are happening so that a rapid response can take place. The corporate world will learn how to leverage these real-time forensic tools to more effectively mine dynamic volatile and active data off of systems and networks for usage patterns, behavioral patterns, and other anomalous behavior that needs to be responded to in order to more effectively calculate and perhaps predict the behavior of a specific market segment in real time.

In the future, this notion of zero day forensics will lead to the real-time forensic analysis of electronic data as it is being created for actionable intelligence in both the commercial and investigative world.

Concluding Thoughts

While this book was primarily designed to give an overview of the world of investigative computer forensics to a buyer or user of those services, such as an attorney, a business owner or executive, an accountant, a regulator, or a government official, I have infused the writing with various commentaries that are designed to contemplate computer forensics and the role that it plays in the broader information revolution contextually so as to allow the computer forensic practitioner to view the relevancy of his or her work through an alternative lens.

As a result, I have concluded this volume with some forward-thinking ideas in this last chapter. These may be futuristic thoughts on some level, but they are still ideas that are grounded in the possibilities of technology as society continues to learn how to deal with the many new constructs that impact the way people, organizations, and machines communicate. From the simple task of making a deposit at a bank to assisting a child with homework—nothing is as it was a mere 25 years ago, and in 25 years, nothing will be as it is today.

This is certainly true in the world of investigations and law. Technology has been the driving catalyst for change in these two industries. At the forefront of that change for the last two decades has been the practice of computer forensics, which has forever changed the way the people look at communications, documents, and the record of behavior, activities, communications, and intent.

We have killed off privacy, we have changed the constructs of trust, and we have brought ideas, thoughts, and communications back from the dead. Deleted is no longer deleted.

The depth and density of the available data, which can now be harnessed for defensive, offensive, or simply operational purposes, is extraordinary, and for the first time in the history of humankind, access to data can serve as the great equalizer between all people. It provides more than a conduit to greater learning; it provides an actual personal channel for every individual to communicate, be heard, and observe from.

This fulfillment of science-fiction fantasy from the age of Jules Verne and beyond will continue to fuel investment in computer forensic science for the purpose of meeting the needs of the Information Age, and in the process the practitioners of investigative computer forensics will have quite a ride.

About the Author

Erik Laykin, CHFI, CEDS, is a Managing Director of Duff & Phelps, LLC, Disputes Practice in Los Angeles and was a founding Co-Chair of its Global Electronic Discovery and Investigations Practice. Focused on large-scale international corporate investigations and high-stakes litigation issues in which computer forensics and electronic discovery play a major role, Mr. Laykin is often appointed as an expert witness, e-discovery neutral, or special master in state and federal courts.

In the 1990s, Mr. Laykin was the cofounder of Online Security, Inc., one of the world's first computer forensic consulting firms, and helped establish the first commercial computer forensic labs in Los Angeles, Chicago, and Hong Kong. Later, as the chair of Navigant Consulting's Information Technology Investigations practice, Mr. Laykin assisted in the expansion of that firm's global computer forensic and electronic discovery footprint in Asia, Europe, and the Americas while assisting clients with discovery, technology, and cybercrime challenges in the United States and abroad.

Mr. Laykin is a frequent contributor on the converging space of law, technology, and fraud for the media and industry conferences. He has worked on numerous groundbreaking Internet-based investigations and examinations of corporate fraud. He has been featured in a number of periodicals, publications, and media, including CNN, FOX, CNBC, ABC, the Investigative Discovery channel, and the Smithsonian channel. He is active with several industry organizations, including the American Bar Association, Forensic Expert Witness Association, Academy of Court Appointed Masters, High Tech Crime Investigators Association, Electronic Commerce Council, and the FBI's Infragard program where he is a past president and Pacific Rim director.

Index

Printed and bound by CPI Group (UK) Ltd, Croydon, CR0 4YY

23/04/2025

14660919-0001